A Defense of Intellectual Property Rights

Richard A. Spinello

Boston College, USA

and

Maria Bottis

Ionian University, Greece

With a Foreword by Professor Dionysia Kallinikou, Athens Law School, Greece

Edward Elgar

Cheltenham, UK • Northampton, MA, USA

Published by
Edward Elgar Publishing Limited
The Lypiatts
15 Lansdown Road
Cheltenham
Glos GL50 2JA
UK

Edward Elgar Publishing, Inc.
William Pratt House
9 Dewey Court
Northampton
Massachusetts 01060
USA

A catalogue record for this book is available from the British Library

Library of Congress Control Number: 2009928597

ISBN 978 1 84720 395 3

Typeset by Manton Typesetters, Louth, Lincolnshire, UK
Printed and bound by MPG Books Group, UK

Contents

1. Introduction: intellectual property on the line

In a provocative speech at Harvard University's Berkman Center in Cambridge Eben Moglen likened the fight for free software to the civil rights movement. The Columbia University professor wants to liberate software and other forms of information from the clutches of companies like Microsoft, the Hollywood 'culture vultures', and the greedy 'telecom oligopolists'. He proposes 'anarchism' as a better mode of software production. Moglen is equally concerned about the general lockdown on 'creative, communal resources'. In his eyes, there is something 'morally repugnant' about intellectual property rights.[1] Thus, for Moglen and many others, the stakes in emancipating content from the thralldom of property protection couldn't be higher – nothing less than the 'perfectibility of humankind'.[2]

While Moglen's philosophy may sound extreme even to some of those who support the Free Software movement, it typifies the anti-property rhetoric that has escalated dramatically over the last two decades. Headlines such as 'Creativity in Chains' and 'The Tyranny of Copyright' are now commonplace even in the popular media. Scholarly articles attack intellectual property rights as unjust monopolies or even as 'restriction[s] on the liberty of everyone' (Palmer 1990, p. 831). Conferences with intimidating names like 'Knowledge Held Captive' have become fairly commonplace in academia. Books such as *Free Culture* by Lessig (2004), *Copyrights and Copywrongs: The Rise of Intellectual Property and How it Threatens Creativity* by Vaidhyanathan (2001), *Owning the Future* by Shulman (1999), or *Steal This Idea: Intellectual Property Rights and the Corporate Confiscation of Creativity* by Perelman (2002) develop sharp indictments of the current intellectual property regime. Consider Perelman's (2002) dire warning that this regime 'represents a serious threat to both scientific and technological progress'. Or Shulman's (1999) concern about a coming 'meltdown' in the software industry due to the omnipresence of software patents (p. 70).

The motto adopted by some of those who believe that intellectual property should no longer be an entitlement is simple and unambiguous: 'information should be free'. For Barlow (1994), who has propagated this message relentlessly, information is akin to a self-replicating life form that should not be constrained. Since legal protection for intellectual property is inconsistent with this normative claim, such protection is illegitimate.

It is not surprising, therefore, that 'intellectual property' has become a term of opprobrium among some in the academy, especially at major law schools, since it evokes the specter of unjust enrichment for greedy corporations and the suppression of free speech by large media oligopolies. This groundless enclosure of intellectual objects is now a great *cause célèbre* among many scholars, who talk frequently about the perils of 'patent thickets', the tragedy of the 'anti-commons', the 'demonization of piracy', and the dominance of the 'property' paradigm in the public psyche. There is a sense of urgency about this epic battle to save our culture. We are told that the copyright 'wars', including the music industry's recent efforts to protect its content, are the equivalent of the new 'Homeric tragedies' (Lessig 2002).

In light of this enclosure movement, some scholars call for a radical revision of the law in order to narrow the scope of intellectual property rights. Others go further and attempt to undermine the assumptions underlying those rights by deconstructing the conventional idea of authorship along with correlative notions such as genius and originality. With these traditional notions out of the way exclusive property rights, at least in their current form, will simply collapse. Property implies a reified, stable text, but, according to deconstructionists, every text can be liquidated into its shadow along with its creator.

To be sure, certain excesses have worked their way into intellectual property law and everyone in this field has his or her favorite 'copyright horror story'. One of the reasons behind this anti-property rhetoric is the unnecessary expansion of rights, thanks in part to the ability of those 'culture vultures' to capture an impressionable Congress. The breadth and duration of copyright entitlements have been extended for questionable purposes and the case for certain reforms is compelling. More and more objects are eligible for a patent, which is awarded too easily. Trademark rights have also broadened in scope. But is intellectual property itself really an anachronism? Has the copyright, which dates back to the Statute of Anne in early eighteenth century England, outlived its usefulness in this dynamic digital era? Has this right become merely another potent weapon in the arsenal of avaricious corporations? Or are such rights still necessary for the purpose of stimulating innovation? And are they consistent with the norms of justice?

Our primary purpose in this book is to answer the last two questions in the affirmative. We admit, however, that intellectual property law has overreached in recent years. Some legislation such as the Copyright Term Extension Act (CTEA), which extended copyright protection for an additional 20 years, has gone too far. The scope of patent protection is too broad, and as a result many dubious patents have been approved to the detriment of real innovation. Is it really necessary to have patents for trivial innovations such as the 'Buy it now feature' used by eBay?[3] In addition, there must be a broader interpretation of compulsory licensing so that a patent can be suspended if it prevents life-saving medication from reaching those in developing countries. Finally, while some commercialized cultural objects deserve stability of meaning, there has been an unwarranted expansion of trademark dilution doctrine. This has made it more difficult for individuals to offer critical or parodic commentary about a brand or trademark. For example, anti-cybersquatting legislation known as the Anti-cybersquatting Consumer Protection Act (ACPA) clearly broadens the application of trademark infringement. This new law equips trademark owners with the ability to pursue claims against domain names that are similar to or dilutive of their trademarks, including domain names that offer a critique of a particular trademark (such as 'wal-martsucks.com').[4]

There is also concern about policies such as the Digital Millennium Copyright Act (DMCA, 1998) that presumably undermine the balance in intellectual property law between content creators and consumers. Digital technology makes it much easier to reproduce, distribute, and publish information. But thanks to code in the form of digital rights architectures, it is also possible to control or enclose digital information to a degree never before possible. When buttressed by laws such as the DMCA that forbid circumvention of these protection systems, the digital content becomes tightly sealed. Rights management systems give content providers the ability to define what rights users will have to use, copy, or edit a work which they have purchased.[5] Code becomes the new enforcer of property rights and that code need not honor copyright's internal safety valves such as fair use or first sale.

But the answer to these problems is not to dismantle or radically overhaul the whole system. Nor is it to jettison traditional concepts of authorship and originality in a post-modern conceptual frenzy. Rather, it is to concentrate on finding the right balance, to re-calibrate the requisite measure of legal protection so that authors and creators are justly rewarded and future innovation stimulated, without impediments to the vitality of the intellectual commons or the free flow of knowledge and information. Boundaries need to be reconfigured without making copyright so thin that authors cannot control the meaning of their works nor appropriate their economic value.

Thus, our main objective in this book is simply to reinforce the center and to demonstrate the need for balanced intellectual property rights as a matter of economic pragmatism, but primarily as a requirement of natural law and justice. Our focus is far more theoretical than practical. We believe that reinforcement of traditional theory is necessary, however, given the growing movement against copyright along with the prevalence of anti-property rhetoric, idealistic talk about collective ownership, and renewed demands for the dilution of author's rights. But while this rhetoric is sometimes hyperbolic, it is not all hype. There has been an unhealthy trend to expand intellectual property rights without an adequate normative justification, and so the need for balance and reform must not be understated.

In this introductory chapter we provide a cursory overview of the main axis of discussion in this book. Before we can defend intellectual property rights we must review their long history along with the current legal regime in the Western world. That history shows a consistent sensitivity to natural justice issues and the need to safeguard creative works from free riders. An understanding of history is particularly important. Contrary to recent claims, copyright has been understood as property for over 200 years.

Our narrative then concentrates attention on the principal reasons behind the sustained assault against intellectual property rights. As we will see, some of these reasons are valid, but many represent exaggerated contentions about the dangers of exclusive property rights in this post-modern world that questions the very notion of 'individual' rights. Once we perceive the spuriousness of most post-modern arguments against the traditional notions of property, authorship, and originality, and re-focus on the author's legitimate interests, we can defend an author-based entitlement that is fair and measured.

1. RESCUING AUTHORS AND THEIR PROPERTY RIGHTS

The term 'intellectual property' refers to patents, copyrights, trademarks, and trade secrets. According to Lemley (1997, p. 895), 'patent and copyright law have been around in the United States since its origin, but only recently has the term "intellectual property" come into vogue'.[6] Similarly, Vaidhyanathan (2001, p. 11) refers to the term intellectual property as 'fairly young'. However, this historical account is inaccurate. Hughes (2006) thoroughly documents how courts and legislatures regularly characterized copyright as works of property. He cites the use of the term 'intellectual property' in *Davoll v. Brown*[7] in 1845 and *Mitchell v. Tilghman*[8] in 1873. In the former case the Court refers to intellectual property as 'the labors of the mind', which are 'as much a man's own … as what he cultivates, or the flocks he rears' (p. 199). Hughes also cites other sources such as Van Dyke's 1888 treatise calling for the extension of copyright to foreign authors where the term 'intellectual property' was used without 'initial discussion or definition' because it was taken for granted that the readers were familiar with this phrase (Hughes 2006, p. 1006). As we will see in the next chapter, the antecedents in European jurisprudence for the use of this term are also quite extensive.

Thus, intellectual property was not a foreign concept until several decades ago. For 200 years copyright has been described as 'artistic property', 'literary property', and now as intellectual property (Hughes 2006, p. 1083).[9] The purpose of intellectual property law has always been to safeguard the integrity of intellectual objects, which are quite different from physical objects because they are not subject to scarcity. There are practical limitations to the number of physical objects one can own or reproduce, but the same can usually not be said about intangible forms of property. Laws that establish and protect intellectual property rights create artificial scarcity, and hence they require some justification from both an ethical and economic viewpoint (Cornish 2004). The focus of this treatise is to provide a fresh look at the former justification for creating such a scarcity.

The assault on intellectual property rights has come from several different directions. Critics of the current intellectual property regime often point to the damage done to the intellectual commons by privatization. According to Opderbeck (2004, p. 201), the 'commons' metaphor has achieved the status of a 'meta-narrative for all debates about proprietary rights'. This intellectual commons includes ideas, concepts, theories, scientific or research methods, scientific principles, mathematical algorithms, laws of nature, words, names, symbols, and so on. It also includes works of literature, music, or art, whose copyright protection has expired. In normative terms, this domain is commonly regarded as a space that should be open to everyone, given its importance for free speech rights. Of course, open access to this domain is also important to ensure future innovation and the evolution of technology. Hence the problem with enclosing or individuating the commons, and thereby depriving others of the raw material they need for their own creative endeavors.

A second problem for exclusive property rights is the general trend against supporting individual rights. Our attachment to individual property rights is interpreted as symptomatic of the individualism at the core of Western society that needs reappraisal and deconstruction.[10] On the other hand, collectivist approaches to free speech, property, and privacy rights are now quite commonplace. Often this type of collectivist theory is predicated on a rejection of the idea that people are really autonomous. When this premise is denied, legal regimes dedicated to preserving autonomy are destabilized. In this context, classical notions of 'private' property and free speech rights become difficult to validate. Tushnet (2004), for example, claims that the current model of free speech in the US is far too individualistic and so courts are too fixated 'on the individual on his soapbox' (p. 567). Advocates of collectivist theory often seek to improve democratic speech by stifling or restricting the speech of those with disproportionate power such as media conglomerates.[11] The control of culture, they contend, is too concentrated in the hands of big media companies who exercise excessive control over 'meaning-making processes' (Elkin-Koren 1994, p. 399).

Along these same lines, some legal scholars want to subordinate an individual's interests in his or her intellectual property to the needs of the 'collective', such as the public good represented by the intellectual commons. Intellectual property rights are pejoratively categorized as a form of 'possessive individualism' which has given rise to many of the worst abuses of capitalism.[12]

We are encouraged to regard property, privacy, or speech as 'social values' rather than support the idea that they are individual entitlements or natural rights. Proponents of this thesis argue that 'normative individualism' is simply an outmoded way to understand property rights issues. They contend that the narrow conception of an individual property right provides an insufficient framework for formulating sound public policy that promotes the social good. Since Locke's philosophy is 'a celebration of the individual, the unencumbered and autonomous human being', it is no surprise that his arguments on behalf of exclusive property rights have been so discredited (Borgmann 1992, p. 25). According to this school of criticism, Lockean individualism, along with the system of individual natural rights which it undergirds, needs to be reconceptualized in light of new economic and social realities.

The justification of intellectual property rights has also been undermined by many intellectual forces, but in particular by recent post-modern scholarship, which has expressed doubts about the source and originality of intellectual objects. There are clear echoes of Marx in the writings of some post-modernists who describe a crisis of human subjectivity and who see the structures of social and economic domination inscribed in that human subject. The assumption had always been that the correlate of the creative work (such as the novel or poem) was the creative subject, who was responsible for his or her work. But critics argue that it is arbitrary to assume that this isolated, Lockean subject is the ultimate responsible source of the work. Why not revert to something more primordial such as social or communal sources, which have so heavily influenced the authorial subject?

The most radical alternative to intellectual property rights is to establish a regime where all intellectual products remain unowned, by either individuals or organizations. Language, for example, can be freely used by anyone, and the results of most scientific research is public knowledge. Proponents of this view, which we might label 'information socialism', argue that the elimination or radical curtailment of intellectual property rights will lead to the expansion of the intellectual commons and the fostering of creativity. It will also engender 'greater political and economic equality' (Martin 1998, p. 311). Along these same lines, Rifkin (2000) describes this new millennium as an 'age of access' where access to information and digital networks takes precedence over individual property rights. Those who oppose patents for the results of scientific research claim that the norm for such research should be 'communism' so that scientific advances are the product of the community.[13] Other critics of intellectual property rights resist such solutions. Rather, they simply believe that intellectual property rights have become too strong and broad, and therefore need significant adjustment.

There are several reasons for being hesitant about overthrowing the traditional intellectual property rights regime. First, a strong property right is justified for social welfare reasons – it is still necessary to induce innovation and to expedite the most productive organization of economic activity. Even Thomas Jefferson, who is often lionized for his anti-intellectual property convictions, admitted that 'an exclusive right' to the returns from one's invention will most likely be 'an encouragement to men to pursue ideas which may produce utility' (Hughes 2006, p. 1030). The courts have often underscored this economic orientation of intellectual property rights in their decisions about copyright or patent protection. There is evidence that property rights have a dynamic incentive effect and are necessary to promote progress, especially in discrete industries such as pharmaceuticals, chemicals, and medical equipment.[14] Alternatives to patents such as government-awarded prizes seem unworkable. As Jaffe and Lerner (2004) point out, if the government tried to reward innovation with prizes it would often fail to set the right amount, whereas patents by their nature are 'proportional to the size of the discovery' (p. 39).

Even if we grant the need for patents in certain industries such as pharmaceuticals, what about the necessity of patent protection for products like software? Patents for software applications (excluding their underlying algorithms) were validated in several landmark court cases such as *Diamond v. Diehr*.[15] They have been rebuked in recent years, however, especially by the advocates of open source code. Moglen (2003, p. 112) has argued with some insistence that programmers do not need incentives to write software. The idea of 'incentives', he contends, is a 'pretty crummy' metaphor for describing human creative activity. In his view, if we can adapt technology and change our social structures it will be possible to bring creative people together who will produce software without the need of exclusive property rights. We will address this question in later chapters, but let it suffice to say that it's certainly questionable whether or not the 'gift culture' envisioned by those in the open source movement is a viable substitute for market-based incentives.

Western societies, of course, have provided an ample level of intellectual property protection in order to promote future innovation and creativity. They have tended to presume that without such protection creators would not always be able to recover their initial investment, and thus would refrain from creative activity. If society wants big-budget epic movies and expensive technological innovation, it will have to protect those items from free riders. Precisely how that level of protection is calibrated in order to maximize productivity, however, is a matter of interminable debate. But it is difficult to argue with the results. Software companies in the United States typically spend billions of dollars each year on research and development, thanks in part to the fact that they can count on some sort of intellectual property protection for their inventions. The US pharmaceutical industry invests about $40 billion a year to develop new drugs thanks to the stimulus provided by a patent.[16]

There are many commentators who grudgingly admit the need for intellectual property rights for these pragmatic, economic reasons. These rights, they acknowledge, are a 'necessary evil', because they restrict the free flow of information, but they are required to encourage investment in innovation.[17] This rationale, however, hardly provides a strong enough foundation for a 'right'. Nor has this rationale been the driving force behind the evolution of intellectual property rights (see Chapter 2). When rights are contingent solely on maximizing the social good, those rights tend to be thin and tentative, with limited scope. They are also more apt to be subject to arbitrary restrictions based on some utilitarian calculus.[18] Moreover, as Yen (1990, p. 558) points out, 'economics alone cannot serve as copyright's normative touchstone' because of the problems involved in defining and measuring society's welfare.

Our primary line of reasoning is that an exclusive intellectual property right is not just a necessary evil, required and tolerated as a stimulus for productive innovation. Rather, this right is also deserved as a matter of justice – creators have a moral entitlement to capture substantial value from their creative, original work, so long as there is no exhaustion of common resources and no trampling upon the right of others to do the same. Authors also have a right to control the integrity of their works, at least for a limited amount of time.

In order to make a morally persuasive case, it is essential that we retrieve a sensible notion of authorship and clarify the meaning of concepts such as originality and creativity which have been called into question. We must directly impugn the deconstructionist vision of the author as a participant in a process rather than as the source of a creative work. Otherwise it becomes unintelligible to talk in terms of an author-based entitlement. As Goldstein (1991) observed, 'Copyright, in a word, is about authorship' (p. 110). Hence we will try to demonstrate that many of the arguments undermining individual authorship or redefining the author as a 'participant' are illogical and rest on questionable assumptions about human nature.

Once we clear the obstacles we turn to the task of constructing a coherent theory of property rights. By orchestrating the texts of Fichte, Locke, and Hegel we can defend the case for an author's moral right to appropriate the value of his or her creative expression. An exclusive intellectual property right, ultimately grounded in each person's self-dominion, is a just entitlement as long as it rewards the creator without causing direct harm to the intellectual commons. Locke's theory is especially helpful in reconciling strong intellectual property rights with a commons composed of intangible goods.

Hence our analysis will rely most heavily on Locke, whose classical discourse on property rights still resonates several centuries after the composition of the *Two Treatises of Government*. Key Lockean arguments will be invoked to present a convincing case for a natural intellectual property right under certain conditions. We also turn to Hegel's theory for support because of its emphasis on how property rights enhance an author's personhood interests in her work.

This moral or non-economic argument for intellectual property rights begins with a reaffirmation of Locke's insight that the creator or author has the foundation of a property right within herself in the form of the personal labor that she performs. If labor is mine it is logical to assume that what I make with that labor is also mine. Locke's primitive articulation of these ideas is not lost on many later thinkers from diverse sources who have reflected about the need for individual property rights. Even those who reject Locke's anthropological premise of atomistic individualism recognize the cogency of the labor theory of ownership. In his encyclical *Centesimus Annus*, the 'philosopher-pope', John Paul II, enthusiastically embraced that theory.

Traditional readings of Locke emphasize his claim that a property right is engendered by 'mixing' this valuable labor and skill with something that is held in common. While the mixing metaphor has been confusing, Locke is simply saying that purposeful labor is appropriative so long as certain conditions are met and the granting of the property right causes no harm. These conditions are captured in Locke's famous proviso. Creators too deserve a property right in their original works. An author or inventor who invests his or her time, energy, skill, and personality in a creative, original project surely has an abiding and 'morally significant' interest in the end result (Himma 2007).[19] This entitlement is a simple matter of fairness. If we accept the argument that the creator has a morally significant interest in his or her work, it should logically follow that the creator has a presumptive claim to its appropriation, so long as no one else is injured by the recognition of this claim.

This argument presumes that any appropriation of abstract ideas or the intellectual 'raw materials' used to construct a creative project is not legitimate. In the case of intellectual or ideal objects meeting this condition is usually not as problematic as it is when material goods are at stake. Thus, Locke's theory actually fits better with intellectual property. Developing creative expression that borrows from ideas in the 'intellectual commons' does not deplete the commons, since consumption or use of those ideas is non-rivalrous. Rather, it conserves those ideas as valuable inputs for others to use. The virtual appropriation of newly created intellectual objects does not harm the other commoners, so they have no reason to complain. In Locke's language intellectual property rights (which he does not explicitly consider) do not 'entrench upon the right of another' (1988, II: § 36). On the contrary, with abstract ideas protected, and the new work disclosed for all to see and utilize in a limited way, society actually benefits from this enlargement of the commons.

With Locke's theory in mind we will argue that *information socialism*, where all intellectual objects are commonly owned, is an impractical and unworkable alternative to the current system. But we also contend that rigid *information capitalism*, which denigrates the value of the intellectual commons and promotes 'hyper-thick' protections such as a perpetual copyright, is also misguided. The information capitalist (as we conceive the term) favors absolute property rights and rejects the principle of just distribution embodied in Locke's proviso.

Instead, what's necessary is a prudent level of protection that approximates the ideal of the Aristotelian mean. Accordingly, property rights must be measured and proportionate to an author's need both to appropriate a fair portion of the value of his work and to protect that work's integrity within a limited time frame. Those legal rights should also be structured to help induce future creative effort. Property rights, properly configured, should mediate two polarities. One polarity overemphasizes the exclusive, private ownership of intellectual objects, while the other polarity is represented by the radical viewpoint that all intellectual objects should be collectively or jointly owned.

As we examine some of the myths about the supposed evils of intellectual property rights, we will see that the fixation on 'control' and 'enclosure' is exaggerated, since perfect control of information is impossible. Positive externalities from published works abound whether authors like it or not. At the same time, flawed legislation such as the DMCA and particularly the CTEA reminds us that policy makers are subject to capture. This has led to the unwarranted expansion of intellectual property rights that is not in the public interest. In their zeal to thwart piracy and to protect fragile digital content there is also a threat that content providers will insist on greater control than the intellectual property system has tolerated in the past. Policy makers must find that elusive middle way that balances legitimate concerns about protecting intellectual objects with the need to preserve a rich substrate of common information resources.

We admit that discerning and legislating the 'right' or proportionate amount of intellectual property protection is a difficult process. But we will offer and defend some recommendations in the course of this analysis: shorter duration for copyright protection, more limited scope of patent coverage, thick patent protection only for genuine inventions that are costly to commercialize, responsible deployment of architectural constraints protecting digital content, and so forth.

Balanced intellectual property rights are one of the key foundations for a just and free society, as Abraham Lincoln and other leaders have clearly appreciated. In Lincoln's words, they add 'the fuel of interest to the fire of genius', and thereby encourage investment in the production of intellectual objects and expressive works.[20] Also they help to preserve the logical connection between a work and its author or inventor. If we subvert the traditional notion of authorship, it becomes increasingly difficult to allocate accountability or to fix responsibility for intellectual objects. And if we impose on the author the burden of responsibility for his or her creative work, it is only fair that the author should be able to reap its rewards as well.

Finally, these rights are critically important for autonomy. Hegel underscored the link between property and freedom, and that theme will thread its way through this book. An author should have the right to exercise some control over his or her creative expression, especially since that expression is an extension of the author's personality. An exclusive property right represents a decentralized incentive system, which gives authors and inventors the ability to control how their works will be utilized and distributed. In our estimation, it is preferable to alternatives such as a centralized subsidy system managed by the state. Moreover, a regime of information socialism or collective ownership would be unfair to creators and inventors, who would lose the ability to control the integrity of their work. As Hughes (1999) convincingly demonstrates, listeners and passive non-owners also have an interest in the stability of meaning of cultural objects enabled by durable intellectual property rights.

There is an old medieval adage which captures the spirit of this book written in general support of intellectual property rights theory: *abusus non tollit usum* or 'abuse does not abolish rightful use'. There are abuses in intellectual property law and those abuses should be swiftly corrected. But the presence of abuse should not interfere with the preservation of reasonable intellectual property rights that fairly reward authors and protect their ability to safeguard the integrity of their works.

NOTES

1. This claim appears in Moglen's (2002) essay called 'Anarchism Triumphant' (p. 123).
2. See Moglen (2003) for additional commentary on these views.
3. This business method patent case has gone all the way to the US Supreme Court. See *eBay v. MercExchange,* L.L.C. 547 U.S. 388 (2006).
4. In November, 1999 Congress passed the Anti-Cybersquatting Consumer Protection Act (ACPA) as an amendment to the Lanham Act or Federal Trademark Dilution Act (Section 1125(d)). The ACPA expressly prohibits 'cybersquatting' or other forms of domain name speculation. The paradigmatic cybersquatter seeks to register domain names in bad faith in order to extort a trademark owner. In other cases, however, while there is no extortionate behavior, there appears to be some form of abuse. These abuses can include the engendering of pre-sales confusion which can occur if users are misled about the origin of goods sold at a particular web site (often called 'initial interest confusion'). Thanks to the ACPA, trademark holders can file suit against domain name registrants who have allegedly misappropriated their trade name or a name that is 'confusingly similar' to their mark. See also *Bally Total Fitness Holding Corp v. Faber,* 29 F. Supp. 2d (1998) [C.D. Cal].
5. See Ku (2002).
6. Cornish (2004) points out that the use of this term became common in the 1960s once the United Nations created the World Intellectual Property Organization or WIPO (see pp. 2–3). References to intellectual property appeared prior to the establishment of WIPO, but according to Lemley (1997), these previous uses 'do not seem to have reflected a unified property-based approach to the separate doctrines of patent, trademark, and copyright …' (p. 896). It is indisputable, however, that copyrights and patents were understood as 'property' well before this time.
7. 7 F. Cas. 197 (C.C.D.Mass.).

8. In *Mitchell v. Tilghman* 86 U.S. (19 Wall.) 287 (1873) the US Supreme Court referred to intellectual property for the first time in its opinions.
9. See, for example, *Wheaton v. Peters,* 33 U.S. (8 Pet.) 591 (1834) where the Court held that 'law reports, like other books, are objects of literary property' (p. 612) and *Brady v. Daly,* 175 U.S. 148 (1899), where the court refers to the protection of 'dramatic literary property' (p. 157).
10. According to Chon (1996, p. 274), 'even in intensely collaborative environments, individual feelings of ownership (or perhaps possessiveness) emerge'.
11. For the most part, however, US courts have not yet been amenable to this radical re-interpretation of the First Amendment. See *Buckley v. Valeo,* 424 U.S. 1 (1976) where the Supreme Court rejected the idea that 'government may restrict the speech of some elements of society in order to enhance the relative voice of others' as incompatible with the First Amendment (p. 49). On the other hand, see *Austin v. Michigan Chamber of Commerce,* 494 U.S. 652 (1990).
12. See Ryan's (1984) discussion on this topic in *Political Theory of Property* (pp. 163–4). See also Rasmussen's (2001) article called 'Why Individual Rights'.
13. For a discussion of this position see Kieff (2001), especially pp. 691–7. This article is a reaction to an article by Rai (1999) highlighting the negative impact of patents on the prescriptive norms of scientific research.
14. The story is a bit different, however, in complex industries such as semiconductors and computers. See a summary of recent studies in 'Patently Absurd' (2001).
15. 450 U.S. 175 (1981).
16. For example, Pfizer's annual research budget is $7 billion, the highest in the industry. See Martinez and Goldstein (2007).
17. The idea that intellectual property rights are a 'necessary evil' has a long and distinguished pedigree. Lord Macaulay (1906) described copyright in the same bleak terms: 'For the sake of the good we must submit to the evil. But the evil ought not to last a day longer than is necessary for the purpose of securing the good' (pp. 203–204).
18. Skeptical supporters of intellectual property rights on utilitarian grounds argue that those rights should be quite constricted: 'copyright holders should receive only such incentives as are necessary to impel them to create and disseminate new works' (Litman 1996, pp. 31–2).
19. As we will see, the Lockean paradigm has had a notable influence on copyright jurisprudence. See, for example, *Emerson v. Davies,* 8 F. Cas. 615 [C.C.D.Mass.] (1845) which argues that a person 'has a right to the copyright of a map of a state or country, which he has surveyed or caused to be compiled from existing materials, at his own expense, or skill, or labor …' (p. 619). Other critical cases will be cited in the chapters ahead.
20. Quoted in Novak (1997), p. 58. Lincoln said these words in a speech praising the US patent system.

REFERENCES

Anticybersquatting Consumer Protection Act (1999), 15 U.S.C. § 1125 (d).

Barlow, John P. (1994), 'The Economy of Ideas', *Wired,* March, 84–6; available at: http://www.wired.com/wired /archive/2.03/economy.ideas.html.

Borgmann, Albert (1992), *Crossing the Postmodern Divide,* Chicago: University of Chicago Press.

Chon, Margaret (1996), 'New Wine Bursting from Old Bottles: Collaborative Internet Art, Joint Works, and Entrepreneurship', 75 *Oregon Law Review* 257.

Cornish, William (2004), *Intellectual Property: Omnipresent, Distracting, Irrelevant?,* Oxford: Oxford University Press.

The Digital Millennium Copyright Act (DMCA), (1998) U.S.C., § 103, Title 17, § 1201.

Elkin-Koren, Niva (1995), 'Copyright Law and Social Dialogue on the Information Superhighway: The Case Against Copyright Liability of Bulletin Board Operators', 13 *Cardozo Arts & Entertainment Law Journal* 345.

Federal Trademark Dilution Act (1996), Pub. L. No. 104–98. Codified as amended at 15 U.S.C. § 1127 (2001).

Goldstein, Paul (1991), 'Copyright', *Journal of the Copyright Society of the U.S.A.* 38 (1), 109–22.

Himma, Ken (2007), 'Justifying Property Protection: Why the Interests of Content Creators Usually Win over Everyone Else's', in Emily Rooksby and J. Weckert (eds.), *Information Technology and Social Justice*, Hershey, PA: Idea Group, pp. 47–68.

Hughes, Justin (1999), 'Recoding Intellectual Property and Overlooked Audience Interests', 77 *Texas Law Review* 923.

Hughes, Justin (2006), 'Copyright and Incomplete Historiographies: Of Piracy, Propertization, and Thomas Jefferson', 79 *Southern California Law Review* 993.

Jaffe, Adam and Josh Lerner (2004), *Innovation and its Discontents,* Princeton: Princeton University Press.

Kieff, F. Scott (2001), 'Facilitating Scientific Research: Intellectual Property Rights and the Norms of Science', 95 *Northwestern University Law Review* 691.

Ku, Raymond (2002), 'The Creative Destruction of Copyright', 69 *University of Chicago Law Review* 28.

Lemley, Mark (1997), 'Romantic Authorship and the Rhetoric of Property', 75 *Texas Law Review* 873.

Lessig, Larry (2002), 'Free Culture: Keynote Address to Open Source Convention', published on *The O'Reilly Network* (http://www.oreillynet.com/pub/a/policy/2002/08/15/lessig.html).

Lessig, Larry (2004), *Free Culture*, New York: Penguin Press.

Litman, Jessica (1996), 'Revising Copyright Law for the Information Age', 75 *Oregon Law Review* 19.

Locke, John (1988), *Two Treatises of Government*, edited by Peter Laslett, Cambridge, UK: Cambridge University Press. Original work published 1698.

Macaulay, Lord Thomas (1906), 'Speech Before the House of Commons', February 5, 1841 in Lady Trevelyan (ed.), *The Works of Lord Macaulay*, London: Longman's Green & Co.

Martin, Brian (1998), *Information Liberation,* London: Freedom Press.

Martinez, Barbara and J. Goldstein (2007), 'Big Pharma Faces Grim Prognosis', *The Wall Street Journal*, December 6, A1, A14.

Moglen, Eben (2002), 'Anarchism Triumphant: Free Software and the Death of Copyright', in Niva Elkin-Koren and Neil Netanel (eds.), *The Commodification of Information*, The Hague: Kluwer Law International, pp. 107–32.

Moglen, Eben (2003). 'Freeing the Mind: Free Software and the Death of Proprietary Culture', Keynote address delivered at University of Maine Law School (June 29); available at: http://moglen.law.columbia.edu.

Novak, Michael (1997), *The Fire of Invention*, Lanham, MD: Rowman & Littlefield.

Opderbeck, D. (2004), 'The Penguin's Genome, or Coase and Open Source Biotechnology', 18 *Harvard Journal of Law & Technology* 168.

Palmer, Tom (1990), 'Are Patents and Copyrights Morally Justified? The Philosophy of Property Rights and Ideal Objects', 13 *Harvard Journal of Law and Public Policy* 817.

'Patently Absurd' (2001), *The Economist*, June 23, pp. 39–42.

Perelman, Michael (2002), *Steal This Idea (Intellectual Property Rights and the Corporate Confiscation of Creativity)*, New York: Palgrave.

Rai, Arti (1999), 'Regulating Scientific Research: Intellectual Property Rights and the Norms of Science', 94 *Northwestern University Law Review* 77.

Rasmussen, Douglas (2001), 'Why Individual Rights?' in T.R. Machan (ed.), *Individual Rights Reconsidered*, Stanford, CA: Hoover Institution, pp. 113–35.

Rifkin, Jeremy (2000), *The Age of Access*, New York: Putnam.

Ryan, Alan (1984), *The Political Theory of Property*, Oxford: Blackwell.

Shulman, Seth (1999), *Owning the Future*, Boston, MA: Houghton Mifflin Company.

Tushnet, Rebecca (2004), 'Copy this Essay: How Fair Use Doctrine Harms Free Speech and Copying Serves It', 114 *Yale Law Journal* 535.

Vaidhyanathan, Siva (2001), *Copyrights and Copywrongs: The Rise of Intellectual Property and How it Threatens Creativity*, New York: New York University Press.

Yen, Alfred (1990), 'Restoring the Natural Law: Copyright as Labor and Possession', 51 *Ohio State Law Journal* 517.

2. An intellectual and political history of intellectual property rights

Intellectual property rights traditionally include copyrights, patents, and trademarks. An abstract concept of property does tie them together, but the endeavor to carve clear lines amongst them is destined to fail. They are, largely, amorphous legal creatures, which still belong to what has been called 'the metaphysics of the law'.[1] The right to print a book, for example, has fallen, in the past, in the domain of both copyright and patent, and all kinds of intellectual rights may, in particular cases, protect different features of the same intellectual object. Hidden behind copyrights, sometimes obviously and sometimes subtly, has been the somehow odd pair of commerce and censorship.[2]

Patents are exclusive rights of inventors to their inventions. They have been in existence for a long time, in both civil and common law countries, and they serve perhaps more obviously than copyrights the public interest in securing a fair number of inventions. Trademarks have been tied to commerce more than copyrights and patents. A trademark is primarily a way to ensure that the public will not confuse a certain product with another. It is difficult to overstate the commercial value of some trademarks, such as, for example, Coca-cola.

The history of intellectual property rights starts at different times,[3] depending on different authors. In this book, we will use the most commonly accepted, in the literature, starting point of relevant legal rules.

1. EARLY COPYRIGHT IN ENGLAND

Copyright presents quite a topic for the legal historian, for it grew in the different legal orders as the same flower in essence, but in many different kinds and colors. The timing also of the flourishing of copyright in different countries varies. The interpretation of older copyright rules depends upon the moment in time one attempts to examine them, through the glass of events before, during, or after the rule was enacted. The historical purposes of copyright laws embraced such diverse concepts as, for example, serving the public interest, protecting the authors' natural rights to their creations and securing a fair profit from publishing so as to safeguard the market.

Copyright does not need to exist without a real possibility of multiple copying. Its birth coincided with the invention of what was then, in the fifteenth century, modern copying technology: the printing press, an invention by Gutenberg in Germany, introduced in England by Caxton. Before this, the copying of a book by hand was a formidable investment of time and effort, in which usually monks in monasteries were engaged, as a routine part of their religious life.[4] That copying technology, in this case the printing press, necessitates legal rules, in this case copyright rules, is true and oft-stated. It is equally true, though, that technological developments firstly modify economic, cultural and social relationships and then, law.[5]

The torturing question whether *common law* afforded authors a post-publication perpetual right to the copies of their work or not, after the enactment of a particular law (the Statute of Anne), was finally answered by the House of Lords, in 1774, in the negative (*Donaldson v. Beckett*[6]). A vote of six to five of the Lords signals the extreme difficulty in the resolution of the matter and also, logically, its strong political as well as commercial nature. What remained was the statutory right born in 1709,[7] with the first copyright statute in England, the famous Statute of Anne. Both the Statute of Anne and *Donaldson v. Beckett* constitute turning points in the history of copyright, with an influence felt outside the common law world and far beyond the years of their appearance, therefore defying both place and time.

a. Copyright before the Statute of Anne

The Crown was always keenly interested in controlling the press and regulating the trade of books. To serve these purposes, royal proclamations such as Mary's in 1555 were issued. Henry VIII was very productive with this sort of proclamation; he issued a series of these in 1529, 1530, 1536, 1544, 1545, and 1546. Edward VI also issued his own proclamation in 1551. The content in these rules was, as expected, similar: to suppress, mainly, 'heretical' (other terms also used: 'dampnable', 'seditious', 'pernicious', 'detestable', 'lewd', 'false', or 'traitorous') texts or material threatening 'the quiet of the realme' and to institute a procedure of licensing books.

Under these procedures, different agents were awarded the task of licensing. There is a range from a town's mayor (Henry, 1546) or a bishop (Henry, 1538) all the way up to the Crown itself (king or queen) or the members of the Crown's Privy Council (Henry, 1538 and again, Mary, 1553). The range of punishments is equally wide: from merely risking her Majesty's 'indignation and displeasure' (whatever this could signal in fact) up to, purely and simply, being decapitated for possession of unlawful books. Elizabeth's fifty-first injunction in 1559 continued this licensing process; in this case, new books had to be licensed either by her in writing, or by other officials, mentioned therein in detail.[8]

As indicated by the charter granted to the Stationers' 'Worshipful'[9] Company in 1557, the methods of censorship and controlling the printing press must have been proven inadequate. The Crown then decided to give in to the regular plea from the Stationers' Company to protect their rights to the copies of the books they were printing against piracy by means of a royal charter. The Crown granted the Stationers' Company a charter under which a lawfully printed book should be recorded in their register. The right to make an entry to the register was confined to the company's members. What the Crown gained was a more effective censorship mechanism and order in one of the realm's trades. The stationers' copyright was perpetual and the author's consent was unnecessary: the author was at the mercy of the stationer who registered the author's work as his own property.[10] Authors, anyway, were not members of the company.

A stationer in possession of the copy of a book which had never been published presented his claim to the Wardens of the Company. The Wardens assigned him the copy as his own, and then the stationer caused the grant to be entered into the Hall Book or Register. This registration was the only proof of his ownership and was accepted as such by all Stationers (Sisson 1969, p. 17). This copyright was an entirely private affair, regulated by the company's ordinances, as was its assignment, sale, or bequest.

The Stationers' Company was incorporated in 1556 and it included at that time 97 members. This meant not only a more formal dignity for their status, but also a better control of the book trade. Perhaps the true bestseller of the Elizabethan period was the ABC with the Catechism, a little book with the alphabet, spelling exercises, psalms, and prayers for schoolchildren.[11] The Bible was, naturally, another bestseller of these times. The ABC was, as expected, constantly subject to piracy, and thousands of copies were unlawfully printed and sold at this time. The plays of Shakespeare were also a favorite printing endeavor for the stationers: the first Shakespeare play printed was *Titus Andronicus* in 1594, and three years later we have the first edition of *Romeo and Juliet*. These editions were also pirated, like the little ABC book. Another publishing standard was ancient Latin classics, such as the *Aeneid*.

The right to print a book was not only secured by stationers' copyright. Another, more prestigious (and profitable) way to achieve roughly the same result was to achieve a printing patent. Printing patents were granted by the sovereign, and their legitimacy was grounded upon the royal prerogative, whose basis was the common law.

The main class of patents was the industrial ones. From 1561 until 1603, 55 industrial patents were classified. They included patents for iron, steel, pit coal, 'aqua composita', 'aqua vitae', vinegar, earth coal, turf, saltpeter, white salt, engines for water-raising, drinking glasses, engines for land drainage, knives, mills for grinding corn, and others (Hulme 1990).

Nevertheless, the printing patent was also among these patents, and led to the printing of almanacs, prognostications, law books, English bibles and psalms, and others. The ABC little reading book was also the subject of a printing patent. General patents covered a whole class of works, whereas limited patents confined themselves to a particular book or work. Patents did not award the right to print a book forever; they usually contained clauses limiting the right to a number or years or, sometimes, for the life of the patentee. The Stationers' Company was also itself a patentee in particular cases. When a conflict arose between a stationers' copyright and a patent for the same work, the patent was deemed, quite reasonably so, as a stronger right. If the stationers' copyright could be characterized as a monopoly, the printing patent was, in a way, the embodiment of monopoly itself. Opposition against these patents was very strong.[12] By the end of the seventeenth century, their significance in comparison to the stationers' copyright was limited.

To return to the much more important, then, stationers' copyright, it meant not only a perpetual right to copy a registered book but also police-like powers of search and seizure of books which were not registered. In this sense, the Crown was using them as ready-made agents for censorship purposes, and it is clear that at that time copyright became an instrument for censorship. A 1566 Star Chamber decree against printing, importing, or selling prohibited books authorized specifically the Stationers' Company to search for these books, wherever they were, and to destroy all unlawful copies. And indeed, we have records of destroying unlawful books in the Halls of the Company. Apart from the damasking of books, other punishments were proved to be no empty promises: John King may well have been only fined two shillings and sixpence in 1559 for printing *The Nutbrowne Mayde*, but William Carter, a printer who also had spent time in prison for activities against these rules, was hanged in the end, for the crime of high treason of printing a seditious book called '*A Treatise of schisme*'.

After the Restoration of the Monarchy in 1660, the Licensing Act was passed, regarding copyrights, in 1662. The Act was entitled: 'An act for preventing the frequent abuses in printing seditious treasonable and unlicensed Bookes and Pamphlets and for Regulating of Printing and Printing Presses'. As easily inferred from its own title, the aim of the statute was not really to safeguard the copyrights of stationers, but to control the press. Nevertheless, just like the earlier proclamations, star decrees, the stationers' by-laws etc., the statute served as a prelude to what copyright became with the Statute of Anne in 1709. The Act was regularly renewed until 1695 (when it lapsed, ending their Golden Age) and the stationers' copyright was, as before, perpetual. A licensed book had to be registered and a copy of the book had to bc deposited, while the procedure was supervised by the Company of Stationers. Powers of seizure etc. continued to exist. The guild's monopoly was once again, secure; 'ignorant and lazy'[13] (and even 'dirty'[14]) the stationers may well have been, but they were also practical and persuasive enough to seek and achieve the protection of their monopoly.

Even after the Licensing Act lapsed for good and before the Statute of Anne was enacted, that is, at a time where, typically, no law prevented anybody from printing any books, the guild's members refrained from printing books which 'belonged' to their brother stationers, because they respected each other's copyrights by custom and also under a special by-law of the company. One can see the same situation long after the enactment of the Statute of Anne in 1709, where sales of copyrights by public auction were, supposedly, open to all, but mysteriously, it was only booksellers who arrived at these auctions.[15] It follows that monopolies (and trade customs) were powerful, both before and after the Statute of Anne, to which we now turn.

b. The Statute of Anne

The Statute of Anne, the first parliamentary Act on copyright, was enacted in 1709 and its title was 'An Act for the Encouragement of Learning, by Vesting the Copies of printed Books in the Authors, or Purchasers, of such Copies during the Times therein mentioned'. The Act was the result of intense lobbying by the stationers to secure somehow their rights to publish books, as the last Licensing Act had lapsed and the market was plagued with chaos. As printing technology advanced, so did pirate copying. Without the old powers of search and seizure of illegitimate books anywhere they were to be found, the stationers remained essentially unprotected. They needed new remedies against pirates. On the other hand, the state was certainly interested in safeguarding order in the book trade by implementing a trade-regulation statute.

The statute was, however, not exactly what the stationers had anticipated. Two major deviations from the past appeared in the statute: firstly, that authors for the first time became right holders and, secondly, that the right to copy, no matter who its beneficiary was, was limited in time. This was a novelty. Another remarkable novelty (Cornish 2000, p. 258) was also that this time limit depended on the author's longevity. The Act signaled therefore a strong blow at the continuation of the booksellers' monopoly – even if this was not entirely clear to everyone until *Donaldson v. Beckett*[16] in 1774. Under this monopoly, the right to publish a book meant the right to continue publishing it forever. Additionally, and much more importantly, the class of persons able to register copyrights was not any more the members of the stationers' company; in fact, *there was no such class any more*, as anyone could now purchase copyrights.

Reasonably enough, the Act refrained from harming the stationers' copyright in published works already in existence, which remained intact and was extended by 21 years. (Of course, one could allege that it *did* harm these copyrights, as it *limited* them to 21 years after its enactment). Equally, the statute did not apply to printing patents, which were allowed to retain their status. But for the right to copies of books to be printed after its enactment, the Act provided that the author or the purchaser (assignee) of these rights was entitled to a period of 14 years' protection and, if the author survived this term, then it was extended for another 14-year period. It is clear in Section XI, which is truly fascinating (Cornish 2000, p. 257) that after this initial 14-year period, the right to copy *returns* to the author, if living. What sustained the rights before the Statute of Anne was trade customs, powers of censorship, and a general understanding of non-interference of persons who were not stationers. But now what sustained the rights was the pure fact of authorship, and any right to a publication had to be traced back to its author.

The formal requirement of registration in the stationers' register remained; order in the book trade demanded, at the time, that one could see which book belonged to whom. But this time, registration was open to all persons, and not only to members of the company, and if the aspiring rightholder was denied registration the statute gave her the alternative of publishing her rights in the *London Gazette*.

The proper interpretation of the Statute of Anne has been the subject of extensive academic commentary, and it seems that there is no consensus. It is supported that the Act did not mean a shift from the older, entrepreneurial copyright to an author's right with the emphasis exclusively on literary creation and its creators (Torremans 2005, 9). The Act should be read, according to another view, as mainly providing a publishers' right, while also regulating trade so as to constrain monopoly (Patterson 1968). Under another view, the primary purpose of the Act was specifically the abolition of the stationers' monopoly (Shirata, date unavailable). Another author sees it as particularly favoring the publishers (Feather 1994). If this is so, then the Statute of Anne is not a truly historic moment in the history of copyright; it only reaffirmed a long-lived status quo, and a monopoly, albeit slightly modified.

Perhaps, though, construction of the Act under a combination of these views is influenced by the indubitable facts that the stationers continued for many years to treat their rights as both exclusive and perpetual, in relation to the authors' rights, and that the courts regularly granted injunctions protecting a common-law right to publish, for the benefit of the stationers, even after the expiration of the statutory term.

Yet another way of interpreting the Act is to stress that its main aim was to ensure that books would continue to be published. Under this view (Deazley 2003a, p. 110), the central plank of the Act was a cultural *quid pro quo*: the author was encouraged to write and the state would give her the right to print the work. Truly enough, the beginning of the Act's title was 'an Act for the Encouragement of Learning ...', which could mean that there were worries about the continuing production of books. After all, following this line of argument, if no worries existed and the book production continued without problems (apart from private disputes of piracy), no new statute to cure a non-existing problem was indeed necessary to be enacted.

The Crown, of course, would not be persuasive as *worrying* whether books were in danger of not being either produced or published at all. What the Crown had shown many times until then was indeed exactly the opposite: that books not favorable to the monarchy or the prevailing religion should certainly *not* be published or circulated and that, anyway, *whatever* was going to be published, it had better be checked beforehand by a particular agent of the Crown. A long list of censorship regulations exists to prove this point.

But it was Parliament which enacted the Statute of Anne. So under the above view (Deazley 2003a, p. 110), Parliament aimed at enhancing the production of books by granting copyrights. But was Parliament worried about books production without the copyrights? Was it enough for Parliament that the booksellers, for their own advantage of course, would constantly bring the argument into play (exactly as today in many respects), that without a strong protection of their investments, they would have to starve and, of course (needless even to mention!), cease publishing?[17] Did Parliament believe the stationers' 'threat', while at the same time, we know that it definitely saw them as greedy monopolists? Did Parliament have a reason to believe, based on some facts, some kind of evidence, that by vesting the right to copy to the author of the work more books than before this rule would be produced – or even that there was a book production failure, which it should address? How could there be a claim of a book production failure, at a time when not even an authors' 'guild' existed and no author's voice was heard, to threat in its turn that, without rights, no works would be produced? How could it be so, since no one at the time argued that without this right there would be no more books printed (Kauffman 1986, p. 395)?[18] The public also was nowhere to be heard, as an outsider's voice to this dispute.

If none of this can be proven, then it is also difficult to prove that the *quid pro quo* deal (copyrights will increase book production) is true, unless it somehow be supported that the Parliament engaged in pure speculation about an author's incentives for the future production of books. But on the beautiful phrase 'an Act for the Encouragement of Learning …', we need concrete evidence that it was, at the time it was written into the statute's title, more than decorative, or hiding an entirely different agenda, or incidentally expressing an idea of the public interest, which was subtly being born.

Today it does not seem very easy to prove without doubt what the Statute of Anne's real purpose was. But one could arrive, perhaps, at some conclusions taking into account a part that was deleted from an initial draft of the Statute. What was deleted was (Shirata, date unavailable):[19]

> … Whereas *the liberty which* Printers, Booksellers, and other Persons have of late frequently taken *in* [the Liberty of] Printing, Reprinting, and Publishing, or causing to be Printed, Reprinted and Published Books, and other Writings, without the Consent of Authors *thereof, in whom ye undoubted Property of such Books and Writing as the product of their learning and labour remains or of such persons to whom such Authors for good Considera(c^)ons have lawfully transferred their Right and title therein is not only a real discouragement to learning in generll which in all Civilized Nations ought to receive ye greatest Countenance and Encouragemt but it is also a notorious lnvasion of ye property of ye rightful* [or] Proprietors of such Books and Writings, to their very great Detriment, and too often to the Ruin of them and their Families …

The monopolistic pressures succeeded in deleting the above from the Statute of Anne. The deleted text shows that the legislative intention was to promote authors' rights, while also abolishing the stationers' monopoly.

Obviously, one cannot accuse modern commentators of a certain inability to agree[20] upon the true meaning of such a little statute of a few articles, hundreds of years after its enactment. Only some decades after the Statute of Anne's implementation, two major judicial decisions, issued only six years apart, arrived at exactly opposite conclusions on the same matter (*Millar v. Taylor*[21] in 1769 and *Donaldson v. Beckett*[22] in 1774). Most notably as well, the 12 Law Lords, dealing with one controversy, were equally in a grave disagreement over what the Statute of Anne meant to achieve in the second of these two cases.

c. Donaldson v. Beckett and the End of the Battle of the Books

For a great while, the London stationers acted in their printing businesses as if the Statute of Anne had never existed.[23] The stationers also managed to secure some judicial injunctions against publishers of books the copyrights in which had, however, expired under the Statute of Anne. The reason was not just the natural inertia immediately following the enactment of a statute which was so disfavorable in essence, to their interests: they had their legal arguments. They claimed that their copyright was perpetual, that therefore they continued to be the right holders and that the Statute of Anne only provided special sanctions for a special period of time. The Statute was, as they saw it, an enforcement tool, enhancing the protection of their rights for a limited time. As this was certainly the view of Lord Mansfield, a most influential Chief Justice of the King's Bench and one of the greatest British jurists, the stationers had a sure powerful ally, when the case of *Millar v. Taylor*[24] was heard by the King's Bench in 1769.

This was an action between publishers of Thompson's *The Seasons,* a pastoral idyll, the copyrights to which had certainly expired under the Statute of Anne when Taylor published it, while Millar had been the text's assignee from the poet in 1730. The controversy directly involved booksellers, especially from

Scotland,[25] who started publishing books freely when the Statute of Anne's copyrights to these books had expired. They were the alleged pirates of these times; against them, the stationers claimed that their copyright was a perpetual common law right. The stationers' view prevailed in *Millar v. Taylor,* although the decision was not unanimous: there was only one dissent, by Mr Justice Yates. Lord Mansfield's eloquent speech, in favor of the stationers, was clear in its natural law roots:

> ... it is just that an author should reap the pecuniary profits of his own ingenuity and labour. It is just, that another should not use his name, without his consent. It is fit that he should judge when to publish, or whether he would ever publish. It is fit that he should not only choose the time, but the manner of publication; how many; what volume; what point. It is fit, to whose care he should entrust the accuracy and correctness of the impression; in whose honesty he will confide. Not to foist in additions, with other reasonings to the same effect ...[26]

Lord Mansfield's arguments – seemingly supporting author's rights but in effect, supporting the stationers' – are very much Lockean in nature: an irony, if one considers that John Locke was a very early and fervent opponent of stationers, whom he characterized as 'ignorant and lazy' monopolists.[27]

Donaldson v. Beckett,[28] the case heard by the House of Lords in 1774, signaled the end of the battle of the books, a 60-years struggle over the question of literary property. The stationers lost: there was no common law right to literary property or, for those Lords who voted that it did exist, the statutory right was above it, as it was granted by the Statute of Anne. After this statutory right expired anyone could print the book in question. And this happened indeed, even pending litigation and, of course, freely after the decision: a multi-volume collection of Shakespeare's works was published by Edinburgh bookseller, John Bell, before the judgment, and after the case's end he also published two multi-volume editions.[29]

In *Donaldson v. Beckett,*[30] one of the points expressed perhaps more directly than ever before was that it would not be just nor efficient to grant perpetual powers of control to booksellers and stationers, while pretending to vindicate the genius of the authors. The booksellers were presented as, sometimes, a very undeserving craft: 'twelve or thirteen booksellers were hovering like eagles over a carcass about the remains of poor Thomson; but he (Sir John Darlymple) hoped that their lordships would protect those remains from such hungry vultures'.[31] The booksellers were also seen as asking 'to exercise their trade with another man's materials' and this 'could not be allowed by reason or natural justice. A miller might grind corn, a carpenter might build a house; but the first was not warranted in grinding any corn but his own, nor the carpenter in building a house with another one's wood'.[32] These 'dirty' booksellers, as exposed by Lord Camden, were themselves so little persuaded that they did enjoy a perpetual common law right that 'in the year 1708 came up to parliament, in the form of petitioners, with tears in their eyes, hopeless and forlorn, they brought with them their wives and children to excite compassion and induce parliament to grant them a statutory security'[33] (which they accomplished with the Statute of Anne). They had become 'instead of salesmen ... engrossers'[34] and in their Registers several extraordinary entries could be found: a book the title of which 'would be sent afterwards' or the translation of a book which was not yet finished: so, wondered Lord Camden, 'all the rest of the world were to be restrained, in the mean time, perhaps for ever, from translating this book?'[35] And did the booksellers forget that until then books were published under privilege or patent (and so, the books were never published otherwise than under privilege or patent, due to a supposed common law right); was this not 'a notorious fact, for which [Sir John Darlymple] could produce a list [of books printed like this] as long as his arm?'[36]

Other considerations also weighed against the booksellers' claims. The power to ask exorbitant prices for books, were this perpetual common law right to be recognized, would forever both strengthen and prove the booksellers' totally undeserving monopoly and also threaten the progress of science and knowledge. Besides, their Company was almost ridiculed, as having adopted too many curious regulations, such as: 1. That no two persons should speak at once. 2. That every member should speak with his hat off and 3. That a member should speak seriously. 'From such important regulations, the importance of the Company might be deduced'.[37] It seems that this was not the kind of Company the Lords were inclined to offer the perpetual monopoly they were asking for.

But despite this dire picture of the booksellers, and the expressed need to deprive them, at last, of the rights they had enjoyed for so long, the Lords engaged in detailed analysis of the nature of property in general, and in particular of literary property. Literary property was presented as 'of too abstruse and chimerical nature to be defined';[38] 'no such property ever existed or ever was claimed to exist in any civilized nation, England excepted, under the canopy of heaven'.[39] What would make James I grant a patent for printing his own translation of the Psalms of David if he had a common law right to the work?[40] Literary property was 'to all intents and purposes indefinable'.[41] The contents of a book were from their very nature incapable of being made objects of common law property, as nothing could be predicated of them which was predicable of every other species of property – ideas did nor bear any similarity to other objects of property and, as incorporeals, they could not be liable to exclusive appropriation.[42] Besides, if a man has a right to his thoughts, when, then, does he part with them? 'Will he claim the breath, the air, the worlds in which his thoughts are clothed?'[43] 'What property can a man have in ideas? Whilst he keeps them to himself they are his own, when he publishes them they are his no longer. If I take water from the ocean it is mine, if I pour it back, it is mine no longer'.[44]

For those, however, who sharply disagreed with these views, literary property did exist and was property beyond that in the materials, the paper and the print; literary property, warranted by principles of solid reason and natural justice, was to be defined and described as well as other matters, and matters which were tangible.[45] The right was like an estate; it was assignable and every man understood what it meant.[46] The series of injunctions by the courts for so long existed to prove that whatever this property was by nature, it was protected in law. Whether it was due to patent, prerogative, private right by charter, there was *something* that had been protected for all those years. And any idea, although it was incorporeal in itself, if it promised future profit to its inventor it was property, because 'property had always been *jus utendi, fruendi, disponendi*'.[47] Everybody agreed that an author had a property interest in his own manuscript, prior to publication, so, 'who could have a greater claim to it afterwards?'[48] Clearly, Lord Mansfield's views, as they were reflected in the speeches of the Lords who disagreed with the final resolution in *Donaldson v. Beckett*,[49] were founded upon powerful arguments from history and natural law.

Donaldson v. Beckett also contains important political discussion of the foundations of copyright. The most aggressive rejection of the legitimacy of the stationers' claims was that of Lord Camden, who summed up 'citations and precedents' offered by the stationers as a 'heterogeneous heap of rubbish': patents, privileges, Star Chamber decrees, the bye laws of the Stationers' Company were all 'the effects of the grossest tyranny and usurpation; the very last place in which I [Lord Camden] would have dreamt of finding the least trace to the common law'.[50] He also accused his older fellow judges of corruption, because they had 'submitted to the arbitrary law of [royal] prerogative'. The desire of the Crown to crush the liberty of the press was also amply presented as the root of the exercise of the prerogative in granting printing privileges and patents; 'the institution of the Stationers' Company [happened] in the reign of Phillip and Mary, princes who ruled in a despotic way ... they, as every other despotic prince, wished to crush the liberty of the press ... and the decrees of the Star Chamber ... were heinous exertions of unconstitutional power'.[51] Therefore, the relationship of copyright with censorship for the Crown's benefit was also not lost in this case.

But the need to control the Press by copyright, as presented in the speeches in this formidable case was not referred to as one of its *past* foundations (and therefore, a way to deny copyright's own legitimacy), but also as a *future* threat to the liberty of the press: 'a despotic minister may buy a copy of a pamphlet, striking at his measures, and secure it as his own, and therefore deprive the public 'of the most interesting information'[52] and therefore, Lord Effingham, speaking last, urged the liberty of the press as the strongest argument against copyright as property. Moreover, when in older cases, the right (to a book) of a stationer was claimed in court by his counsel (Mr. Yorke) as being 'property founded on [royal] prerogative'. Lord Chief Justice De Gray treated this language as 'allowable for counsel but not very admissible by, or [even] intelligible to a judge'.[53] So, arguments such as 'printing belongs to nobody and what is nobody's is of course, the King's' and 'the King pays his judges, *ergo*, he purchases this [copy]right for a valuable consideration' were definitely 'trifling'[54] (although, read today, they do reveal a lot of the legal and political history of these times).

With the end of the battle of the books (or the booksellers[55]), the author emerged as the primary copyright holder and, as time went on, as a professional as well. The acceptance of *Donaldson v. Beckett*, to which jurists such as Lord Mansfield and Blackstone had expressed their opposition, was not absolute – 'indulgences abounded in this respect'.[56] Lord Camden had also eloquently spoken about glory as the only reward geniuses, as authors, really aimed at – certainly not money, nor trafficking 'with a dirty bookseller'.[57] This noble and ideal, no doubt, view was attacked later on, as authors, geniuses or not, also needed to pay 'sordid butchers and bakers'[58] (just like everyone else). But the decision was widely approved at the time of its delivery, and all further efforts by booksellers to secure a new statute, favorable to their interests, failed.[59]

2. THE EVOLUTION OF AUTHORS' RIGHTS IN EUROPE

In Europe, France, Italy, Germany all utilized systems of granting printing privileges from as early as 1469.[60] The republic of Venice granted its privilege for a particular book in 1486.[61] The first in France was probably a privilege granted by Charles III in 1498. Later the French Parliament was also the source of privileges for books. What is important is that, from these early times, *authors*, apart from printers, could ask for and were granted privileges for their own books; and their pleas for protection, as stated in these very old applications, were equal in merit to some of the finest advocacy for copyright of our times:

> [in making and composing his book the petitioner] has thereon employed and spent a great deal of time and expended a large portion of his substance. For this reason, both to communicate the said book to those who shall desire to see it and to profit by it, and also to recover and retrieve part of which it has cost him to make it and compose it, he would gladly have the said book printed, he only and no one else until such time as it shall please us [the King], if it were our pleasure to give him leave him license to do so and to impart to him in this matter our grace and liberality.[62]

Authors, therefore, mentioned the expenditure of time and their costs in 'making and composing their books', and sometimes also the cost of having the book printed. Authors rarely refer to the originality or usefulness of their books, but they do sometimes, and also we find as a reason the public entertainment that the book will cause or, for more serious editions, the benefit to the public (*de la chose publique*).[63] The printers' arguments were similar.[64] The power of an author in respect of his rights to his books in Germany is amply exemplified by the case of Durer, in 1521. He was a famous artist; desperate because of the constant selling of copies of his works, falsely attributed to him, he sued the Nurnberg council for protection which he obtained; later his widow acquired a privilege from Charles V, to her late husband's works.

The various legislative texts protecting intellectual property in Europe around the same time as *Donaldson v. Beckett* was decided in England reveal an equally hesitant and uneven progress (Ginsburg 1990, p. 1006). In France, printing monopoly was a plain fact: the *Comédie Française* had a monopoly over the public performance of classical plays such as those by *Molière, Racine* and *Corneille*. In terms of book publishing, the profession of a printer was reserved to the members of the Paris Book Guild (*Chambre Syndicale de la Librairie et Imprimerie*), the 'brother' of the Stationers' Corporation in London. The Guild had enjoyed a royal privilege to print and distribute all printed matter in Paris. In 1686, Louis XIV decided that the printers in Paris would be limited to 36. Just like in London, to become a printer one was first apprenticed for some years and then, one had to pass the examination of a guild member and the University. Additionally, the successful candidate also had to wait until one of the 36 printers died, then save a lot of money to buy a shop and also pay the high guild membership fees (Hesse 1991, p. 10).

The number of printers had risen to 241 by 1788 (Hesse 1991, p. 10). The legal status of a work to be printed was determined by the official royal censor, the Administration of the Book Trade, and could vary, from an exclusive monopoly to print a work for 10 or 20 years to a total suppression of its printing and publishing, under the threat not only of fines but also of arrest and further penalties.

The intermediate classes of permissions to print were many and very interesting:[65] today, in an almost bizarre *déjà-vu* way, they remind us of the different types of creative commons licenses, at least in the sense that, contrary to the (perhaps necessary) rigidity of copyright laws, there are many ways to allow the use (or publishing) of a work by others. But what we should note here is that special permission existed, in favor of *the author* of a work: the *privilège d'auteur*, under which the administration granted the author or his heirs the monopoly to publish the work forever. Besides, in 1777, the regulation that only printers who were members of the Guild could publish works was amended and the author was added as a possible publisher of his own work.

Pirate editions not bearing the name and address of the registered guild member, the royal 'privilege' and the royal censor's approbation at the back of the book were confiscated. In this, the commerce was as safe as in England in favor of the Stationers' Company. But just as in England, the whole system of royal privilege and censorship was not to last; in 1789, freedom of the press was included in the Declaration of the Rights of Man. Whether or not freedom of *the press* necessarily included the freedom *to print* (there were doubts about this, especially on the part of royal agents, of course[66]), times had changed forever. It was not only royal censors who were anxiously resigning, *en masse*, from their positions, losing their salaries and pensions; the members of the printing guild were equally worried, as the Old Regime died with the French Revolution.

These privileges, though, were the foundation of the law of author's rights in France: as stated by *Louis d'Hericourt* (Pouillet 1908, p. 10), an influential lawyer and author of these times, 'a manuscript, which does not contain anything against religion or against the laws of the State ... consists an interest for the person of the author, which is really his own, because it is the fruit of his work, his own personal work, of which he must have the liberty to dispose at will, so that he may, apart of the honor that this work produces, extract pecuniary benefits'.[67] This natural law foundation of the author's right is therefore not subject to doubt, not it was ever in doubt after the *Fenelon* case in 1777.[68] The right of the author moved progressively into positive law, through the case law of the *Conseil du Roi*. The king himself, Louis XVI, in 1777 and 1778, just one year before the French Revolution, declared by means of these *arrêts* (judgments) that the privileges were temporary monopolies, very rarely perpetual, granted firstly to the authors and, in second place, to their publishers, as compensation for the authors' work.[69]

After the Revolution in 1789, all guilds and privileges were abolished. Two decrees set the scene for authors' rights, one in 1791 and one in 1793. The Decree of 1791, drafted to attack the monopoly of the *Comedié Française*, provided that every citizen had a right to open a theater and to produce plays; moreover, the permission of the author of a play was necessary for its legal production. The decree's reporter, Le Chapelier, wrote then the oft-quoted phrase, 'the most sacred, the most legitimate, the most unassailable ... and the most personal of all properties is the work which is the fruit of a writer's thoughts'. It is true that Le Chapelier clarifies what he means after this phrase (protection of only the right to publish an *unpublished* work – after publication, everything is finished for the author[70]), his statements fully reflect the sentiments of his time and the centrality of the figure of the author in this discourse, a centrality impossible to ignore, even if authors, in order to serve their interests better, represented themselves as servants of the public good, of its enlightenment, in opposition to the private rights of publishers (Hesse 1991, p. 116).

The need to secure authors' rights more firmly, though, meaning securing them even after first publication, was safeguarded in the following decree of 1793; petitions to the competent Committee on Public Instruction by authors referred to piracy of their works and called for their protection from ruin. The Rapporteur of this second decree, *Lakanal*, stated in his speech to the National Convention that the right of the author is, of all rights, the least contestable, a right the reinforcement of which can neither harm republican equality nor violate liberty. This was part of his 'Declaration of the Rights of Genius'. The Declaration of the Rights of Man did not mention the rights of authors, as it was a much more general instrument. In the decree that followed, authors (and their heirs and their assignees) were granted the exclusive right to publish their works; the right lasted for their lifetime plus 10 years. The decree also gave no retroactive protection for the benefit of former holders of privileges, and all works of the past were free for everyone to publish.

There were controversies,[71] naturally, after these two decrees, and it is instructive to see the reasons the French courts had for their decisions. In a case involving sales of unauthorized copies of memoirs, the court stated, 'natural fairness, the first of all laws, sufficiently warned the printers and booksellers that it was not permitted to appropriate the productions of others'. The court did not refer to any public benefit derived from protecting authors; in a later case, *Buffon v. Behemer*,[72] which dealt with copyright protection for works published before the decree of 1793, the court 'first endorsed the notion that authors had property rights in their works as fruit of their labors' (Ginsburg 1990, p. 1019). The question whether the formality of deposition of a work with the National Library was a prerequisite to the birth of an author's rights or served an evidentiary purpose was not firmly resolved in these cases.

In Germany, the passage from publishers' privileges to the author's right was much slower than in England or France. German philosophers, such as Fichte, Putter or Beier and, notably Immanuel Kant, had firmly supported the natural law theory of the author's rights. In Fichte's writings, especially, we see for the first time the author's ideas separated from her expressions – the notion of the material v. immaterial book first emerges (Hesse 1991, p. 153). The General Prussian Code of 1794 established that the consent of the author was a precondition to the legal publication of his work. In 1837, a Prussian statute first recognizes a universal author's right, and in 1871 an act applicable to all German countries was enacted, protecting authors' rights (Koumantos 2002, p. 16).

Therefore copyright's analogue in Germany is *Urheberrecht*, in France *droit d'auteur*, in Italy *diritto di autore* and in Spain *derecho de autor* – all terms referring to author's rights, in the sense of comprising both an exclusive property right and a moral right, the first subject to transfer and the second inalienable. So, the right of the author, as it evolved, was a right of a dual nature, the one part being the *droit patrimonial*, the (clear) property right (mainly: the right of reproduction) and the other one being the moral right (*droit moral*) of the author to control acts such as the time and place of publication (right of publication), and the right of the author to be recognized as the (real) author of a work (right of attribution) and the right to safeguard the work from injurious transformations (right of integrity). No author may resign from her moral rights.

The Berne Convention of 1886 was a major legislative instrument,[73] which included protection of both the economic and moral rights of authors. The duration of (the economic part of) author's rights was set at his lifetime plus 50 years. Especially on moral rights (which lasted in perpetuity), the Convention provided for the right of attribution (the right to claim authorship of the work) and the right to the work's integrity (to object to any adverse transformation of the work which would be harmful to the author's honor or reputation). Later on, all rights were born from the very act of creation of the work; deposition, registration or other formalities previously known were not included in the Convention (Berne Convention revision of 1908 in Berlin).

3. EARLY COPYRIGHT IN THE US

The first rules on copyright on the other side of the Atlantic were certainly easier to draft; after all, the drafters had the benefit of having read similar statutory rules and, later on, the results of cases on copyright such as *Donaldson*. Moreover, their state did not have to endure the adventures (Ginsburg 2006, p. 10) of a Crown granting at times doubtful privileges, creating dangerous monopolies, fighting censorship etc. In this, the new United States was lucky, able to start its life with all the vitality and liberty from this European history would allow. Rules on copyright had at these times (1789–1834) in the US four different sources: statutes from the states, the federal Act on copyright of 1790, the 1787 Intellectual Property (Progress) Clause of the US Constitution and, lastly, the crucial Supreme Court decision in *Wheaton v. Peters*.[74] This mix of rules definitely does not picture with any certainty what the exact nature of early American copyright was, but anyway, even today, there is no unanimity on this matter.

From the state statutes we see that in almost every state the legislator was interested and proceeded to protect the rights of authors to their works; they have been 'accused' of almost having plagiarized the Statute of Anne, but perhaps this is an overstatement. For example, the Massachusetts Act of 1783 provided that the author would have the sole property in his works if the name of the author was printed on the book. The right lasted for 21 years and the author had to donate two copies to the library of the University of Cambridge. Two more states (Rhode Island and Virginia) also adhered to the 21 year limit on copyrights. Most of the states, enacting their laws between 1783–1786, selected a term of 14 years; this term cannot be explained but as harmonious to the Statute of Anne's provisions. The rules on deposit of the work, as a condition of copyright were not uniform: Connecticut, New Jersey, Georgia and some other states made copyright protection conditional on filing the title of the book with the Secretary of State (Patry 2000, p. 20). Other states designated the clerk of the council (Virginia) or 'the prothonotary's office' (Pennsylvania) (Patry, 2000, p. 20). What was to be protected ranged from (only) books to pamphlets, writings, treatises, literary works, maps and charts – we find all these kinds of works in the statutes.

The essence is that from these early statutory laws we can risk the conclusion that the legislators were concerned about protecting the author's natural rights. For example, the preamble to the New Hampshire statute declared, 'as the principal encouragement such persons ("ingenious persons in the arts and sciences") can have to make great and beneficial exertions to this nature must consist in the legal security of the fruits of their study and industry to themselves ... such security is a natural right of all men'.[75] We can probably find in no other *statutory* text such a clear declaration about the nature of the right conferred: a natural right of all people is what copyright is. We can compare this with the preamble to the Connecticut statute (the oldest one, of 1783[76]): 'Whereas it is perfectly agreeable to the principles of natural equity and justice, that every author should be secured in receiving the profits that may arise from the sale of his works and such security may encourage men of learning and genius to publish their writings'.[77] The right belonged properly to the author – only in the statutes of South Carolina and Virginia was the publisher also mentioned as a potential right holder.

The copyright clause of the American constitution soon followed. Sec. 8 cl. 8 of the 1787 Federal Constitution provides that 'Congress shall have the power ... to promote the progress of Science and useful Arts, by securing for limited times to Authors and Inventors the exclusive right to their respective Writings and Discoveries'. The clause ties together the rights of authors and inventors; therefore it is reasonable to assume that the framers considered that these two classes of creators could and should be treated in roughly the same way. In his writings for *The Federalist*, Madison[78] noted that 'the utility of this power [of the Congress] will scarcely be questioned. The copyright of authors has been solemnly adjudged, in Great Britain, to be a right of common law. The right to useful inventions seems with equal reason to belong to the inventors'. There were no dissenting votes on this clause. Copyright and patent are not, as such, mentioned in the text. What was protected was writings and discoveries, and it is a matter of constitutional interpretation to define whether these terms should be broadly or strictly construed.

There is no real evidence about what the framers aimed to achieve through this unanimous adoption of the clause about copyright and patents (Joyce et al. 1998, p. 18). From the text itself we see the purpose of promoting the public interest and protecting the rights of authors and inventors, which should be interpreted as pre-existing, because of the use of the word 'securing'. But the introduction about the progress of 'Science' (at the time this word meant knowledge in general) could correspond to the Statute of Anne's preamble (an Act for the Encouragement of Learning), and so its function could equally be just ornamental (on those who support this view about this preamble, see Kauffman 1998, p. 404). Besides, it seems fair to conclude that the copyright clause is, in many respects, a mirror of the Statute of Anne.

The constitutional language of the copyright and patent clause has been criticized as ambiguous and as reflecting the divided character of the American thought of these times about copyrights and patents (Joyce 1998, p. 18; Joyce & Patterson, 2003, *passim*). On the other hand, it has also been put forward (Patterson 1969, p. 193) that the constitutional clause contains all four basic ideas pertaining to copyright at that time, that is: 1. promotion of public interest (learning: this idea comes from the introduction of the clause); 2. copyright is a grant by the government (this idea comes from the word 'securing'); 3. a rule against monopolies (this idea comes from the words 'for limited times'); and 4. copyright is an author's right and patent an inventor's right (this idea comes from the words 'an exclusive right'). Under this last interpretation, the weight of the constitutional clause fell upon the promotion of learning.[79] From a simple reading of the clause, it seems fair to conclude that is melds public domain and authorial property rationales,[80] although it is less easy to interpret the word 'securing' as reflecting a (new) grant from government ('vesting' or 'granting' perhaps would be far easier – or more correct – to understand this way), instead of a recognition of a pre-existing right.

Without the legislative intervention of Congress the constitutional clause could not have any practical meaning. In 1790, Congress enacted the Copyright Act, which was modeled on the Statute of Anne – the very common, as it had become by then, phrase of 'an act for the encouragement of learning' introduces the rules. The statute provided copyright protection for a period of 14 years, to be renewed for another 14 years if the author was still alive at the expiration of the first period. The statute referred to maps, charts and books (in that sequence) as the subject-matter of copyright. Unlike the constitutional progress clause and seemingly returning to the past, the statute joins authors with proprietors as right holders. Dealing with books that were already published, the statute granted copyright to the authors or their executors, administrators or assignees, citizens or residents of the United States. For maps, charts and books already published, the right belonged (again) to the authors or their executors, administrators or assignees, who, always as residents of the United States, were entitled to publish those works. In the text, the sole right (of authors etc.) is followed by the 'liberty' of printing, reprinting, publishing and vending the work in question – the author had the 'right and liberty' to print.

The Act has been interpreted[81] as clearly creating a statutory right, unrelated to any natural law-like ideas about the rights of an author. It is true that the Act imposes formalities (publication of a copy of the registration record in a newspaper for four weeks, as well as the deposition of a copy with the Secretary of State) and formalities are usually thought of as reflecting a statutory and not a natural right. Also, and perhaps more importantly, the Act limited its protection to authors who were residents of the United States – therefore, not only was pirating foreign editions sanctioned, but also, it made it more difficult to sustain a natural/common law argument in favor of the author: all the mystery and the glorification of the author's genius and all rhetoric about one's most sacred and most personal property right had to vanish, in a way, when it could only be applied in favor of a genius, an author, yes, but *only* if she was a resident of the United States.

The statute was complete as a legislative instrument, as it contained statutory penalties for its breach. Damages were provided for the wronged author (50 cents per infringing sheet found in the infringer's possession), but she was to share this amount with the US government when the action brought was for debt (not so, if the action – on the case – sought further damages). The statute seems to justify the Librarian of Congress's statement in 1897 that copyright under the old law was an annoyance at times, incomplete in its provision and awkward in its administration: as proof one may offer the fact that, whereas between 1790 and 1800 over 15,000 books were published in the United States by resident authors, only 779 works were registered, to acquire copyright (Patry 2000, p. 35).

The difficulties in protecting copyright that the Librarian of Congress complained about were perhaps nowhere more evident than in the case of *Wheaton v. Peters*,[82] the US equivalent of *Donaldson*. The case involved the publication of a work called 'Condensed Reports of Cases in the Supreme Court of the United States', in six volumes. This work was the product of Richard Peters, a reporter for the Supreme Court. But one of these volumes contained Reports by a previous court reporter, Henry Wheaton, Peter's predecessor. Wheaton had not delivered a copy of his Report to the Secretary of State as the Copyright Act dictated (although, under another statute, he had delivered to the Secretary as many as 80 copies).

The difficulty in resolving the case was evident by the fact that the Supreme Court Justices agreed on only one point: that no one could copyright *their* opinions – only marginal notes, syllabuses, the abstract for a case and an index to several cases could be copyrighted. This was not helpful to resolve anything about the case itself. The Justices were careful, however, unanimously and flatly to state this fact.[83] But apart from this, they split four to two.

The majority, headed by Justice McLean, denied any claim by Wheaton to copyright at common law. The majority opinion referred extensively to the British history of copyright (to the cases of *Millar v. Taylor*,[84] *Donaldson v. Beckett*[85] and the Statute of Anne). The opinion said that there was no doubt that an author had a right to his unpublished writings. But publication was another matter; after this, it was impossible to claim a perpetual exclusive property in the work.[86] Congress, by enacting the Copyright Act, created the statutory right of an author. This was the same situation as with patents: the framers, tying copyrights in with patents, meant the same thing, namely, that the author and inventor were to enjoy the rights to their writings and inventions, which rights were not natural rights. The statutory formality of depositing a copy with the Secretary of State was an essential requirement, which would have to be observed. It was not in this case, so Wheaton had to lose. 'All the conditions are important; the law requires them to be performed; and consequently, their performance is essential to a perfect title'.[87]

The dissenting opinion stressed in essence the natural law foundation of copyright, stating that the author had a right to that property as a matter of justice and equity. An extensive analysis of the history of British copyright was also included in the dissenting opinion. The Act protected an existing right and did not create it. On formalities, again, there was disagreement with the majority opinion, in the sense that even if the Act indeed created a new right, it would vest as soon as the author had registered his book.

The presentation of *Wheaton v. Peters*[88] here is necessarily limited. One should not assume that the decisions were as clear as they may seem. On the contrary, it is true that the opinions were 'to put the matter in modern terminology, a mess' (Joyce 2005, p. 328). The opinion of the majority, moreover, reflected 'considerable doubt [and apparently considerable internal confusion within the majority] concerning which of the statutory formalities had to be, and might have been satisfied …' (Joyce 2005, p. 376). This was a tough controversy, probably most disagreeable to the Justices: they had worked closely with both plaintiff and defendant and they must have found it extremely difficult to rule on the matter, while simultaneously avoiding bitterness from both the opponents.

Wheaton v. Peters[89] was the Supreme Court opinion that set the rules about copyright after its promulgation. There were writings, such as courts' opinions, that could not be made subject to copyright. Copyright was a right created by statute for the time defined in the statute; no common law perpetual copyright could exist. Formalities should be observed for the right to accrue. Copyrights were of the same nature as patents. As a result of a later Supreme Court decision, in 1841 (*Folsom v Marsh*[90]), the public and other authors were deemed to have limited opportunities to use passages of a work for reasonable and fair criticism, and the first idea of what later became on the defense of fair use was expressed judicially – again, not easily, as Justice Story, who was also one of the majority Justices in *Wheaton v. Peters*, declared in *Folson v. Marsh*.[91] The first major US copyright codification occurred with the Act of 1909, which included subject-matter rights, rights, remedies and administration rules.

4. BRIEF NOTES ON THE EVOLUTION OF THE PATENT SYSTEM

Patent law is today a standard branch of intellectual property law. It has not always been so, in either the common law world or in the civil one. Although it is reasonable to conclude that people were inventors from the beginnings of history, the historical discussion connecting useful inventions to exclusive rights begins in the Middle Ages. In England, in furtherance of particular industries, the Crown offered grants to foreigners so that they came within the King's power, safely and securely and taught the English about the new industry only they understood. So the Crown gave particular individuals letters patent, meaning an open letter (in contrast to a secret one), sealed with the royal seal, so that anyone could see it. The words letters patent come from the Latin *litterae patentes*. These letters patent conferred the exclusive right or privilege on a particular trade, industry or a 'real' invention (rights to 'real' inventions, as currently used for new, non-obvious useful ideas subject to technological application). This was certainly not always the case for medieval patents.

As early as in 1331 the Crown granted John Kempe of Flanders letters of protection (later to become the letters patent mentioned above) about cloth weaving, so that he could also teach the English his methods. In this same line, letters patent were given to those who possessed *meliorem scientiam* (Hulme 1896, p. 143) about what the Crown wished to promote (soap, 1561; saltpeter, 1561; methods of draining water, 1562; methods of making ovens and furnaces, 1563; making glass, 1567; making clothes, 1569; teaching, printing and publishing works in shorthand, 1588, making flasks for touch-boxes, powder-boxes and bullet-boxes, 1591; and many others). The medieval privilege-based system linked patent law to a normative ideal of public benefit (Drahos 2005, p. 2). The letters patent were the expression of the royal prerogative, and what the sovereign sought was to attract the proper person in possession of new technologies and methods. But as this system developed over the years, favorites of the Crown enjoyed undeserved benefits to the public detriment. For example, the almost outrageous patents for starch, vinegar and playing cards, rightly called the three worst patents of the reign of Elizabeth (Hulme 1896, p. 153) certainly harmed the public interest. Soon this intolerable situation would have to lead to a change, a change not just because the economy was gradually turning from a feudal into a mercantile one.

In the landmark case of *Darcy v. Allein*,[92] in 1603, it was established that there could be no exclusive right to import and sell playing cards in the kingdom, as this consisted a harmful monopoly. Elizabeth had granted a patent to Edward Darcy to stamp playing cards in exchange for an annual payment, perhaps the purpose of the patent was not only to earn the fee for the patent but also as a means for the Crown to know and control a trade which might have become a problem to the Queen's subjects. In this sense, an equivalent of 'censorship' hid behind the playing cards patent, the same way true censorship hid behind the book printing privileges. Allein decided to sell playing cards without paying Darcy for the use of his stamp, and Darcy sued him. The King's Bench held that the grant was void as against common law, restraining the freedom to trade; this was a case of a monopoly and monopolies were harmful, as they raised prices while taking away the incentive to improve a product. Besides, the person who was offered the patent was not the inventor of playing cards. The Case of Monopolies, as *Darcy v. Allein* is also called, consists today a foundation of modern antitrust and competition law.

A few years later, in 1623, the Statute of Monopolies[93] confirmed the illegality of exclusive rights curtailing free trade and competition in commodities and staples. Royal monopolies were prohibited. However, the statute allowed the grant of letters patent for new inventions, lasting 14 years (meaning in essence, two periods of seven years, when 14 years was the usual period needed to train two craft apprentices – seven years each). The grant was offered only for a true and first invention. Also, these grants should not be 'contrary to the law nor mischievous to the state by raising prices of commodities at home, or hurt of trade, or generally inconvenient'.[94] The Statute of Monopolies therefore was an instrument which prohibited monopolies but simultaneously 'legalized' patents under certain circumstances.

In France, the law on patents in 1791 approached the subject differently. The starting point was not to abolish and discredit monopolies, but clearly to recognize that 'all new discoveries are the property of the author; to assure the inventor the property and temporary enjoyment of his discovery, there shall be delivered to him a patent for five, ten or fifteen years'.[95] The patent was granted after no examination whatsoever of what we would call today 'prior art'. On the other side, a caveat was printed on each patent instrument declaring that the French state did not guarantee the merit, success or priority of the invention for which the patent was granted. The period for which the patent would be valid was an open option of the inventor, who could choose between five, 10 and 15 years; an extension demanded statutory intervention. Methods and manufactures were generally patentable subject-matter, but scientific discoveries, for example, were not. The statute of 1791 was amended in 1800 and 1844, with minor alterations. The fees under the 1791 statute were high and depended upon the term selected by the patentee: the longer, the costlier.

Generally, in France, Germany and other civil law countries, patent rights were originally conceived as natural rights of the inventors, in the same way as authors' rights. As early as in 1474 in Venice, when the Venetian patent system was reorganized by two patent laws, it is fair to conclude from their texts that inventors had an inherent right to patent protection, and not merely an inconclusive hope of a grant (Prager 1952, p. 133). Under the statute, the inventor could, if he wished, obtain exclusive rights status for a term of 10 years. Much later, in 1873, in the Congress of Vienna for Patent Reform, grand language was used about the natural rights of inventors and the need to have these rights protected by the laws of all civilized nations (Drahos 2005, p. 2).[96]

4. LESSONS FROM HISTORY

a. Meeting a Wide Divergence of Academic (and other) Opinion

The temptation to explain history in support of a particular position is to select the 'bits' of history that seemingly tend to prove that position. As 'torturing' numbers is a sure way to make them 'confess' to anything, one can 'torture' history enough and history will also 'confess' to everything (this is of course an exaggeration). But copyright's[97] history is especially suitable for this end, due to a sort of general accord that it is obscure, 'metaphysical', that the cases it deals with demand answers to 'embarrassing' questions, that the lines to be carved are thin and help no future claimant, as no general principles can be formed.

And indeed, the history of copyright has been analyzed to confess to almost everything. For example, some commentators believe (and use arguments from history to support their belief) that the Statute of Anne had as its primary purpose to protect the public from the monopoly of the stationers.[98] Others explain the Statute as stressing authors' rights, as being the first statute where the author appears as a right holder, and her rights are tied to her longevity – therefore, a statute which does not mainly enact a publisher's right (Patterson 1968, pp. 143–50). Still other views insist that the value of the Statute was to secure that a copyright is a grant, a privilege from government for a limited period. Cornish (2000, pp. 254–70) disagrees with both Patterson's (1968, pp. 143–50) and Feather's (1980, p. 3) views. And, lastly, the Statute has also been explained as a clear effort to promote the public's interests.[99] Perhaps it is better to adhere to the sincere view, which simply states that it is hard to say whether Parliament was resisting a clear theory of authors' rights put forward in the previous decade (Rose 1993, p. 48).

The (generally accepted) idea that the civil law of authors' rights is centered on the author has been criticized as warranting substantial amendment (Ginsburg 1990, p. 1031).[100] The same commentator claims that the two revolutionary French and American systems share much, not only in theory but also in practice (Ginsburg 1990, p. 1031). The dominant view of American copyright may truly be instrumental in character, meaning that 'copyright is seen as a means by which the general welfare is advanced through the provision of economic incentives to creators of new works of the intellect' (Joyce et al. 1998, p. 26).

But it is less evident that this result is firmly founded upon American's copyright history, in the pages of which we find very often quoted phrases like Madison's: 'the copyright of author's has been solemnly adjudged in Great Britain to be a right of common law. The right of inventors seems with equal reason to belong to the inventors. The public good fully coincides in both cases with the claims of individuals'.[101] So perhaps it is not easy to assume without reservation that 'the Founding Fathers understood the nature of copyright as a monopoly that was granted for administrative purposes to promote the sciences' (Shirata, date unavailable).

Accordingly, the language of the constitutional clause does not support *the hierarchy* of the public's interests as *superior* to the author's or the inventor's: no certain precedence can be proven in this case and it is probably right that 'little is known about what precisely the Framers had in mind when adopting this provision' (Joyce et al. 1998, p. 18). The stress on the promotion of science and literature, which we have seen in President Washington's review of intellectual property in 1790,[102] may well have meant that by protecting works and artists by copyright, the state showed its respect and wish to recognize the importance of these works to the public good.[103] The focus in the subsequent replies from both the Senate and the House, that the promotion of science and literature would contribute to the security of a free government, seems to fall upon the idea of science and literature as foundations of freedom.

The same divergence of opinion among commentators appears when the question about the nature of the American constitutional provision about patents and copyrights arises: there are views (or even court opinions) claiming that it is obvious that this is an anti-monopolistic provision, or that the public's interest is paramount.[104] We also see, conversely, its main aim as being to secure the author's and inventor's rights. The constitutional clause on patents and copyrights, which has provoked so much commentary, does not contain the answer to whose (the public's? the publisher's? the author's?) interest (if someone's) is the most important one and, therefore, prevails.

The state statutes, before the federal Copyright Act, stress the natural law rights of authors. Whereas in their titles many of these statutes have copied the Statute of Anne's famous phrase, 'an act for the encouragement of learning', or a similar phrase, their contents definitely support a natural law approach to literary property. The famous preamble 'for the encouragement of learning' did appear in the federal Copyright Act of 1790 but was not repeated in the Copyright Act of 1831 and it has never reappeared (Kauffman 1986, p. 415).

The most important judicial controversies relating to copyright have been adjudicated upon by the greatest jurists of their time, and yet they found themselves in acute disagreement and confusion; they have produced voting results such as 6-5 (*Donaldson v. Beckett*[105]) and 4-2 (*Wheaton v. Peters*[106]). There is no agreement today about not simply what *Donaldson* really meant, or upon what doctrine the case was adjudicated, but not even on whether the votes on this case's question 1 were 10 to one (Whitcher 1981, p. 128; Kauffman 1986, p. 403; and Patterson 1968, p. 175) or eight to three (*Wheaton v. Peters* at 656; Rose 1993, p. 109). As regards the most crucial question 3 (did the statute take away the common law right?) which side was supported by six votes? The side for or against the survival of the common law right?[107] On this sort of uncertain facts (not interpretations), it is indeed quite a task to attempt to rationalize *Donaldson*'s outcome.

It is also intriguing to fantasize what the result for the whole copyright system would be if this one judge had voted differently, in *Donaldson* perhaps meaning the recognition of a perpetual common law copyright. Other judges have also noted the great difficulty of adjudicating on cases involving copyright.[108] But the point here is that history seems to be an unstable foundation of any purported stable conclusions about copyright theory.

What is certain, in such an uncertain discussion, is that copyright, when recognized as such by statute, was in both cases (civil and common law copyright) and from the very beginning *tied to the author's life* (in England, author's life plus 14 years, in France author's rights plus 10). What one can make of this undeniable fact will perhaps follow the usual path of a great divergence of opinion. But, again perhaps, it can have no other meaning but that the right stems inextricably from the person of the author. Also, the historical development and existence of inalienable moral rights in the civil law world (which today in the common law system are also protected via other legal institutions and also legislatively[109]) points toward the same direction: that copyright is very tightly tied to the person of the author. Copyright in both systems, common and civil law, lasted, at some early point in history, for the *whole* of the author's life (and more) – this also could portray its nature as a natural law right.

b. The Currently Dominant Incentive Theory and Copyright History

The currently dominant American intellectual property doctrine,[110] that copyright and right to an invention are necessary because they function as a mechanism supplying the necessary *incentives* to authors and inventors so that they produce, is not easy to detect as such in the major accepted historical sources of common and civil copyright law.[111] We do not see in these texts a fully developed argument that, for example, without copyright, people will write *no more*, that if a society does not offer copyright as an exclusive right *fewer* works will result or that copyright is necessary to enhance an artistic or industrial production *which is deemed unsatisfactory and inadequate*.[112] On the contrary, the natural law concepts which inspired common law copyright and early copyright statutes remained part and parcel of copyright jurisprudence (Yen 1990, p. 531).

We also do not see in these texts an argument that the best possible society is a society 'drowned' by the creations of people, and so we need to have *as much as possible* (Yen 1990, p. 531). No historical vision of society where *everyone* is a writer or an inventor as the best society exists in the texts.[113] And besides quantity (the more the better), we do not even see in these texts the argument that *no matter what* one writes or what one invents (the quality question), the best possible society is the one where we have as much of (whatever) intellectual objects as we can have – hence copyright and patents are needed as *incentives*.

The notion of an 'incentive' is regarded here as stronger than mere 'encouragement', a word we have seen in the old copyright statutes, because this is how current intellectual property doctrine seems also to regard it. An incentive is different from a just due – a reward (a simple act of encouragement or expressing support). An incentive is clear when, for example, a state offers double the salary for a teacher to work at a school lost up in the hills of a very poor province of a country; an incentive, legally, is clear when a legislator offers monetary benefits to people who want to start up a particular kind of business with uncertain profits but necessary for a particular place; and incentive is clear when an airline is offered tax cuts if it adds flights to remote airports usually serving small numbers of inhabitants. An incentive, in short, in this sense, comes to cover an acknowledged social need for more (such as the need Elizabeth wanted to satisfy with importation patents). Moreover, an incentive covers a need so acute that it must not be left without specific legislative intervention (should not be left entirely, for example, to the market). In copyright's case, this acute need could be a need that only strong copyright rules could cover.[114]

English judges speak of 'glory as being the reward of science',[115] of the value of geniuses such as Locke, of 'favoured mortals' and 'sublime spirits',[116] of the most sacred and most personal of all rights – of very different concepts of creativity and creators, of justice and morality being the foundation of the common law author's right. The statutes of the colonies of the United States are focused almost in their entirety upon the natural rights of the author.[117] It is difficult to maintain that there was genuine anxiety that no works would otherwise be produced (if no copyright was offered as an incentive), to the detriment of society, because no shortage of works has been denounced as necessitating legislative intervention.

The discussion in terms of the supply of necessary incentives is probably normal in today's industrial world, in the world where we see works as information and where so many creators are 'content providers'. The idea of copyright as a means of serving the public's welfare is a standard part of copyright history, but this public service has not, as a rule, been expressed in terms of the supply of incentives. It has been mostly expressed in terms of securing reasonable access and the distribution of creative works and inventions to people, for people's benefit.[118] And access means, for example, not allowing monopolists like the stationers to conquer and reign over the whole of the book market, demanding whatever price they want for Shakespeare's works and prohibiting Scottish booksellers from underpricing them. And the same is true for the Paris Book Guild, before the French Revolution.

Probably many people do create in order and only because they aim to gain monetary benefits, and will not create otherwise. It would be most instructive if we could have some scientific evidence about the psychological reasons for which people write or create in general, as we know for example, at least from anecdotal evidence, that (at least some) people write because it is impossible for them not to. Most artistic masterpieces in the history of civilization appear to have been created at times when no copyright existed at all and the creators did not care enough to sign their works.[119] Perhaps the reasons for creation vary as much as the characters of the creators themselves.[120] Creators today vary and are certainly not always individual artists. Most certainly, modern big pharmaceutical corporations, which demand a very early patent for a drug they have just started to investigate, given the large investments consecrated to this endeavor, would not be interested in proceeding with the drug trials without a patent.

But copyright and patent history does not appear to support the view that rights were secured mainly because without copyright and without patents people would *stop* writing and inventing; in short, copyright history seems comprised mainly and mostly of a series of rules dedicated to regulating copyright and patents after a work or an invention is born (what today would be after fixation), published or unpublished, and not so much before an intellectual work existed at all.

The question of what is just, in the case where a free rider (here we start using modern intellectual property terminology) rips off the creator of his right dues is of course mentioned (in different terms) in copyright's and patent's history. But it is mainly dealt with as a matter of natural justice – that another should not be allowed to take advantage of the creator's labors – not as a matter of possible *diminishing* of the number of creative works due to a free riding. Along the same lines, in 1773, when Samuel Johnson elaborated, in a passage very often quoted by copyright historians, on the harms of the perpetuity of copyright in relation to the interest in learning, he was careful to note, '[the right of the author] should from its nature be perpetual … but reason and *the interests of learning are against it; for were it to be perpetual, no book however useful, could be universally diffused amongst mankind, should the proprietor take it into his head to restrain its circulation*'.[121]

Johnson, therefore, seems to construe the 'interest of learning', as opposed to perpetual copyright, in terms of securing *the dissemination* (not the production) of works. And this may support the view that property and perpetuity were not properly separated by early copyright cases; because in the eighteenth century perpetuity was a *sine qua non* of property; the jurists, having to select in *Millar* and *Donaldson* between a perpetual right, which would lead to the stationers' monopoly, and no common law right at all, were finally obliged in *Donaldson* (not all of them; again, it was a six to five decision) to uphold the latter.[122]

Similarly, more than 50 years later and in another continent, the angry voice of Wheaton exclaiming 'who would have undertaken the expense and the risk of publishing an edition [of judicial reports]' if they 'might be encountered the next day by a piratical edition?'[123] was not answered in the lengthy opinion, or even the dissent which strongly supported *his* view about his natural law rights, with the (standard today) economic justification that, if creators are deprived of their copyright, fewer works will be created.

Lastly, what is also not easy to detect in the history of copyrights and patents is the notion that an author's and inventor's rights perhaps merit somewhat 'less' recognition or protection than one would have thought originally, because works and inventions are creations founded upon the former creations of other authors and inventors. This issue, especially important today with the current debate about the importance of the public domain, is certainly not even close to the center of the discussions of (for example) *Donaldson v. Beckett* or its American counterpart, *Wheaton v. Peters*.

NOTES

1. 'Patents and copyrights approach nearer than any other class of cases belonging to forensic discussion to what may be called the metaphysics of the law, where the distinctions are, or at least may be, very subtle and refined, and sometimes, almost evanescent': *Folsom v. Marsh*, 9 Fed. Cases 342, 344 [C.C.D. Mass. 1841[(No. 4901) (per Story J. at 344).
2. See (on copyright) Yen (1990): 'Oddly enough, the story of copyright begins with a strange partnership of censorship and commercial interest', at 524.
3. For example, most commentators present the Statute of Anne (1710) as a starting point of the history of (Anglo-American) copyright; however others start as far back as Roman Law. See Versteeg 2000, '[the Romans] did develop the legal rules of property, contract and liability, that have shaped many of the essential building blocks of American copyright law' (p.523).
4. 'Monks were heavily involved in the reproduction and preservation of the literature that had been inherited from earlier writers – writers whose works had been accepted as classics. The Rule of St. Benedict, for example, contained a specific instruction that a certain number of hours in each day were to be devoted to labor in the sciptorium. The monks who were not yet competent to work as scribes were to be instructed by the others': see Yu (2006) p.7.
5. See also Cornish (2000), 'Copyright law is not simply a response to technical advance. There is always a political and social dimension to it': p.255.
6. 2 Brown's Parl. Cases 129, 1 Eng. Rep. 837; 4 Burr. 2408, 98 ER 257 (1774).
7. But see Feather (1980) p.39 note 3, stating that the correct year is 1710.
8. The other licensing agents were the six members of the Privy Council, or the Bishop of London or the Chancellors of Oxford and Cambridge and the Bishop and Archdeacon of the place of printing: see Patterson (1968), p.37.

9. The name of the Company was 'The Worshipful Company of Stationers and Newspaper Makers', the 47th Livery Company of London.
10. One should note, however, that one-third of copies actually printed were never registered, a fact which reduces the significance of registration (Sisson 1969, at 8, 9, referring to Sir Walter Greg). Moreover, some maintain that at that time the mere publication of a book established copyright, or that publication was necessary to establish copyright firmly: Sisson (1969) 9.
11. See Anders (1936) 37, 'the little ABC-book was an exceedingly profitable, perhaps the most profitable book on the market'.
12. For example, in 1577 the company filed a petition against printing patents to Lord Burghley, arguing that patents such as those granted to particular persons for Bibles, Testaments, the ABC and Almanacs and Prognostications were threatening to ruin all the company's members (at the time, 157): see Patterson (1968) pp. 92–3.
13. As characterized by the philosopher John Locke, a fervent opponent of the Licensing Act and the stationers' monopoly, in his letter to Edward Clarke (Jan. 2, 1693), in Rand (1927).
14. See speech of Lord Camden in *Donaldson v. Beckett*, available at: www.copyrighthistory.com/donaldson.html, last accessed April 30, 2009: 'it was not for gain that Bacon, Newton … instructed and delighted the world; it would be unworthy of such men to traffic with a dirty bookseller'.
15. The booksellers themselves actively sought this exclusivity: as late as in 1769, 60 years after the Statute of Anne was implemented, Donaldson, a Scotsman, was sent a note that his presence at the 'public' sale of the copyrights for Thomson's Seasons was not desired: see Patterson (1968) p. 152.
16. 1774, 4 Burr. 2408.
17. See for example the content of one of the stationers' petitions to the Commons in 1694: 'if their Property should not be provided for by the said Bill [which the House of Lords was contemplating at the time] not only the Petitioners, but many Widows, and others, whose whole Livelihood depends upon the Petitioners' Property, will be utterly ruined': XI H. C. Jour. 305–306, cited at Patterson (1968) p. 139.
18. 'There is nothing to show that the public goal of encouraging learning was Parliament's primary purpose in passing the Statute of Anne … there is no evidence whatever if any decline in book production prior to the Statute Likewise there is no evidence that the Parliament predicted an imminent decline': Kauffman (1986) p. 395.
19. See Shirata (date unavailable).
20. Besides, writings in this area include texts 'from the perspective of lawyers, printers, authors, literary theorists, Marxist theorists, post-modern writers and industrial critics': Bowry (1996) p. 329.
21. 4 Burrow 2303, 98 ER 201 (K.B., 1769).
22. 2 Brown's Parl. Cases 129, 1 ER 837; 4 Burr. 2408, 98 ER 257 (1774).
23. 'The great consequential issue in the Battle of the Books … was also rooted in the inherited practices of the Stationer's Company. Its members continued to deal with the Copy-rights in their Books as indeterminate property capable of assignment in whole or in part': Cornish (2000) p. 259. 'But even after the passage of this Statute, the major London booksellers continued to treat literary property-including works by such classic English writers as Shakespeare and Milton-as perpetual properties, and they regularly secured injunctions against those who would reprint such classic texts': Rose (2003) p. 77.
24. 98 ER 201 (K.B. 1769).
25. But also from Dublin, Amsterdam and other provincial cities: see Tompson (1992).
26. 98 ER 210 (1769), 252. See also id. at 220 (opinion of Aston J.), id. at 218 (opinion of Willes J., 'it is not certainly not agreeable to natural justice, that a stranger should reap the beneficial pecuniary produce of another's work'. See also Cornish (2000), p. 264 and Rose (2003).
27. Letter from John Locke to Edward Clarke (Jan. 2, 1693), in Rand (1927): 'I wish you would have some care of book-buyers as well as all of booksellers and the company of stationers, who having got a patent for all or most the ancient Latin authors (by what right or pretense I know not) claim the text to be theirs, and so will not suffer fairer or more correct editions than any they print here, or with new comments to be imported without compounding with

them, whereby most useful books are excessively dear to scholars, and a monopoly is put into the hands of ignorant and lazy stationers'.

28. 1 ER 201 (K.B. 1769).
29. Bell's British Theatre in 21 volumes (1776–1780) and Poets of Great Britain, in 109 volumes: see Rose (2003) p. 77.
30. 2 Brown's Parl. Cases 129, 1 ER 837; 4 Burr. 2408, 98 ER 257 (1774).
31. From the speech of Sir John Darlymple, attorney for the Appellants in *Donaldson v. Beckett*, see (all speeches in) http://copyrighthistory.com/donaldson.html, last accessed April 30, 2009.
32. Speech of Mr Justice Narres, id.
33. Speech of Lord Camden, id.
34. Speech of Lord Camden, id.
35. Speech of Lord Chancellor Apsley, id.
36. Speech of Sir John Darlymple, id.
37. Speech of Sir John Darlymple, id.
38. Speech of Mr Attorney General Thurlow, id.
39. Speech of Sir John Darlymple, id.
40. Speech of Sir John Darlymple, id.
41. Speech of Attorney General Thurlow, id.
42. Speech of Mr Baron Eyre, id.
43. Speech of Lord Camden, id.
44. Speech of Sir John Darlymple, id.
45. Speech of Judge Ashurst, id.
46. Speech of Mr Justice Willes, id.
47. Mr. Solicitor General Wedderburn, id.
48. Mr. Solicitor General Wedderburn, id.
49. 2 Brown's Parl., id.
50. Speech of Lord Camden, id.
51. Speech of Sir John Darlymple, id.
52. Last speech, by Lord Effingham, id.
53. Speech of Lord Chief Justice De Gray, id.
54. Speech of Lord Camden, id.
55. Biller (1899) p. 99.
56. Ginsburg (2006).
57. Speech of Lord Camden, id.
58. Macauley (1774) 15.
59. See Patterson (1968) p. 178.
60. Privilege for Johannes de Spira, September 1469, from the government of Venice, threatening anyone who tried to start a press with fines and with the confiscation of his tools and his books. See Armstrong (1990) p. 2.
61. Ibid., p. 3.
62. From the application of Eloi d'Amerval to Louis XII, Letters Patent granted in 1508. Armstrong (1990) p. 79.
63. Ibid., pp. 82–83.
64. Ibid., p. 88.
65. For example, the 'permission simple' meant that the publisher could print the work only once. The 'permission tacite' gave the work no legal sanction but insured that the authorities would permit its publication and the 'tolerance' meant that the work was illegal but the authorities would tolerate, its circulation for the times they considered necessary: Hesse (1991).
66. An argument used by the Parisian royal agents to deny the application by a Mlle Louise de Kerallio to establish a printing shop in Paris. See ibid., chapter, 'The Declaration of Press Freedom'.
67. Translation from the French text by the present writer.
68. Where it was held that the renovation of the privileges presupposed the consent of the heirs of the authors: see Colombet (1999) p. 3.

69. See generally Gaudrat (2001) p. 19. For general treatises on author's rights and its origins in France see (among others) Lucas & Lucas (2001), Edelman (1999), Colombet (1999) and Bertrand (1999).
70. See Ginsburg's comment here, '[Le Chapelier's passage] is taken out of context … According to Le Chapelier, the main principle is the public domain and its exception at the right place': Ginsburg (1990) p. 1007.
71. Ginsburg collected 37 controversies of these times: ibid., p. 1016.
72. Judgment of 29 therm. an 11, Cass. civ., [1791] 1 Dev. & Car. 1.851.
73. See Ricketson (1987) pp. 1–35.
74. 33 U.S. (8 Pet.) 591 (1834).
75. Copyright Enactments: Laws Passed in the United States Since 1783 Relating to Copyright at 8, Copyright Office Bulletin n. 3, revised, 1973.
76. See Rudd (date unavailable).
77. US Copyright Office, Copyright Laws of the United States of America 1783–1862, 1962.
78. Madison, *The Federalist Papers* (no 43). The text continues: 'The public good fully coincides in both cases with the claim of individuals. The States cannot separately make effectual provision for either of the cases, and most of them have anticipated the decision of this point, by laws passed at the instance of Congress': id. Madison's view must have been influential in the attaching of the case for copyright and patent protection in the same clause.
79. 'The dominant idea of the framers of the Constitution seems to have been the promotion of learning': Patterson (1969) p. 193.
80. Ginsburg (2006) p. 21.
81. Patterson (1968) pp. 200–201.
82. 33 U.S. (8 Pet) 591 (1834).
83. Ibid., at 668.
84. 4 Burrow 2303, 98 ER 201 (K.B., 1769).
85. 2 Brown's Parl. Cases 129, 1 ER 837; 4 Burr. 2408, 98 ER 257 (1774).
86. Ibid., at 658.
87. Ibid., at 664.
88. 33 U.S. (8 pet) 581 (1834).
89. Ibid.
90. 9 F.Cas. 342, 6 Hunt Mer. Mag. 175, 2 Story 100, No. 4901, Case No. 4901, 2 Story, 100.
91. Ibid. Justice Story's first sentence characterizes the controversy as giving rise to an intricate and embarrassing question, (a controversy 'in which it is not easy to arrive at any satisfactory conclusion': id., due to its peculiar nature and character).
92. 77 ER 1260 (King's Bench, 1603).
93. Available at http://ipmall.info/hosted_resources/lipa/patents/English_Statute1623.pdf, last accessed April 30, 2009.
94. Id., section 6(e) of the Statute.
95. See generally Hilaire-Pérez (1994).
96. Drahos however stresses that the Convention for the Protection of Industrial Property (Paris Convention) that was signed by 11 countries in 1983 committed those countries to comparatively little (2005, p. 2).
97. We use the term to include both Anglo-American copyright and civil law author's rights.
98. '[T]he modifications of the statutory copyright are explained as efforts to destroy the monopoly in the book trade. Making the copyright available to all was a move directed to the monopoly of the company itself … the author was used as a weapon against monopoly': Patterson (1968), p. 147.
99. For example, Deazley (2003a, pp. 106–33 and 2003b. pp. 270–79) has stated that copyright is not and has never been a common law right.
100. Ginsburg states: 'the characteristic modern portrayal of French revolutionary copyright as an unambiguous espousal of an author-centric view of copyright requires substantial amendment … If U.S. copyright's exponents sought to promote the progress of knowledge, they also recognized that the author's labors are due their own reward' (1990 p. 1031).
101. Madison, *The Federalist Papers* (no 43). We have to note here, though, that Madison in a letter to Jefferson expresses a different sentiment about monopolies (in particular), namely

that they, as encouragements to literary works and ingenious 'discoveries ... are too valuable to be renounced': see quotation in Patry (2000) p. 23.

102. See Patry (2000) p. 18.
103. 'Nothing ... can better deserve your patronage than the promotion of science and literature', as cited by Patry (2000) p. 18.
104. *Twentieth Century Music Corp. v. Aiken*, 422 U.S. 151 (1975).
105. Id.
106. (1834), 33 U.S. (8 Pet.) 591.
107. The 6-5 refers to the answer to question no. 3 posed to the Judges, namely whether even if a common law right had existed, it was taken away by the Statute of Anne (held: yes, by 6–5). If Lord Mansfield had also voted, the vote would have been an intolerable 6–6, unless one accepts Rose's account (1993, pp. 98–99), that the tally was 6-5 in favor of the common law right; but this was lost, as the clerk recorded wrongly the vote of Justice Nares. Deazley (2003b, p. 272) displays tables with different interpretations of what the judges voted in this case. He concludes that 'a majority of the speaking judges, seven, acknowledged the existence of a common law copyright ... a majority of the judges (six) considered this common law right pre-eminent over the Statute of Anne': id.
108. For example, see Justice Story in *Folsom v. Marsh*, 9 F. Cas. 342 (C.C.Mass. 1841), note 1.
109. And have started appearing even in statutory instruments such as VARA (the Visual Artists Rights Act of 1990): see extensively Liemer (2005).
110. We will mention here, due to limits of space, only some of the early supporters of current dominant intellectual property doctrine: Breyer (1970), Hurt & Shuchman (1966), Fisher (1988), Landes & Posner (1989) and Gordon (1989).
111. Meaning here the first constitutional and statutory instruments on copyright (both common and civil law copyright) and the texts and opinions of (concurring or dissenting) judges on major historical copyright cases (again, both common and civil law copyright). We certainly do not include here as a source of patent law the letters patent by Elizabeth to foreigners so that they would immigrate and bring to England their knowledge of, for example, glass making: they have been called 'importation patents', belonging to a time before they were regulated by a source of law (the source was the royal prerogative) and most certainly, aimed at providing incentives to the recipients by granting them monetary benefits.
112. See also Kauffman (1986) p. 387: 'Copyright rhetoric [of the past] speaks of encouraging authorship; and yet, it has never been suggested that any legislator ever proposed a copyright bill because "authors were not writing enough". Moreover, neither Parliament nor Congress has ever passed copyright legislation due to an actual decline in book production. To be sure, copyright legislation appears when there is a massive invasion of the natural right: plagiarism, unauthorized performance, and literary and record piracy are prime examples'. It follows, perhaps, that the very old words 'encouraging authorship' perhaps meant something different from what they mean under the currently dominant intellectual property doctrine.
113. For example, the text of the Statute of Anne refers to the encouragement of 'Learned Men' to compose 'useful books'.
114. See the comment of the Registrar of Copyrights Abraham Kaminstein in 1965 that 'The basic purpose of copyright is the public interest, to make sure that the wellsprings of creation do not dry up through lack of incentive, and to provide an alternative to the evils of an authorship dependent upon private or public patronage. As the founders of this country were wise enough to see, the most important elements of any civilization include its independent creators – its authors, composers and artists – who create as a matter of personal initiative and spontaneous expression rather than as a result of patronage or subsidy. A strong, practical copyright is the only assurance we have that this creative activity will continue': quoted in Patry, p. 24. Kaminstein appears, though, to reach his conclusion about strong copyright (or otherwise, no works will be produced) too fast and without appropriately supporting it by arguments from copyright's history. Indeed, the simultaneous acknowledgement that artists create as a matter of personal initiative and spontaneous expression and that without a strong copyright the creative activity will cease appears almost controversial.
115. Speech of Lord Camden in *Donaldson v. Beckett*: see http://copyrighthistory.com/donaldson.html, last accessed April 30, 2009.

116. 'If there be any thing in the world common to all mankind, science and learning are in their *nature* publici juris, and they ought to be as free and general as air or water. They forget their Creator, as well as their fellow creatures, who wish to monopolize his noblest gifts and greatest benefits. Why did we enter into society at all, but to enlighten one another's minds, and improve our faculties, for the common welfare of the species? Those great men, those favoured mortals, those sublime spirits, who share that ray of divinity which we call genius, are intrusted by Providence with the delegated power of imparting to their fellow-creatures that instruction which heaven meant for universal benefit; they must not be niggards to the world, or hoard up for themselves the common stock', *Donaldson v. Beckett*, speech of Lord Camden, http://copyrighthistory.com/donaldson.html, last accessed April 30, 2009.
117. As accepted, for example, by Patterson (1968) pp. 183 and 186 ('the purpose of the statutes according to their preambles was to secure profits to the author … the theory upon which it was based was that of natural rights of the author' and Patry (2000) at 18. This is so even if in their preambles we see our well-known 'encouragement of learning' or something similar (it exists in the titles of six of these statutes). For a chart of all these preambles see Shirata (date unavailable), who disagrees with this conclusion and argues that most statutes 'provided the character of copyright as a monopoly or an exclusive right that would be allowed specially for the promotion of science and literature'.
118. Compare this with the following: the 'motivation must ultimately serve the cause of promoting broad public availability of literature, music, and the other arts': *Twentieth Century Music Corp. v. Aiken*, 422 U. S. 151, 156 (1975).
119. This was a standard rule of Byzantine art, since all works were considered the result of divine inspiration.
120. On this debate, as discussed in modern times, see Breyer (1970) (the incentive theory does not work), Tyerman (1971) and Breyer (1972).
121. Italics ours. Johnson cited by Rose (1993) pp. 85–6.
122. See Kauffman (1986) p. 398, who refers to this as 'the perpetuity accident' and who explains the great ambiguity around a common law copyright because the right was codified by the Statute of Anne before the common law courts were able properly to define copyrights, as the question had never reached them, as the Stationers resolved their disputes internally (391).
123. Wheaton's Pre-Argument Memorandum A.: see Joyce (2005) p. 365.

REFERENCES

Armstrong E. (1990), *Before Copyright, The French Book Privilege System 1498–1526*, Cambridge: Cambridge University Press.

Anders H. (1936), 'The Elizabethan ABC with the Catechism', *The Library*, 4th ser. XVI.

Bertrand A. (1999), *Le droit d'auteur et les droits voisins*, Paris: Dalloz, 2e édition.

Biller A. (1899), *Seven Lectures on the Law and History of Copyright in Books*, London.

Bowry K. (1996), 'Who's Writing Copyright History?', *EIPR* 322.

Breyer (1970), 'The Uneasy Case for Copyright: A Study of Copyright in Books, Photocopies and Computer Programs', 84 *Harvard Law Review* 281.

Breyer S. (1972), 'Copyright: A Rejoinder', 10 *UCLA Law Review*, 75.

Colombet C. (1999), *Propriété littéraire et artistique et droits voisins*, Paris: Precis Dalloz, 9e ed., n. 4.

Cornish W. (2000), 'The Author's Surrogate: the Genesis of British Copyright', in Katherine O'Donovan and Gerry R. Rubin (eds.), *Human Rights and Legal History: Essays in Honour of Brian Simpson*, New York: Oxford University Press.

Deazley R. (2003a), 'The Myth of Copyright at Common Law', *Cambridge Law Journal* 62 (1) 106.

Deazley R. (2003b), 'Re-Reading Donaldson (1774) in the Twenty-First Century and Why it Matters', *EIPR* 270.

Drahos P. (ed.) (2005), *Death of Patents*, London: Lawtext Publishing and the Queen Mary Intellectual Property Research Institute.

Edelman D. (1999), *La propriété littéraire et artistique, coll. Que sais-je ?,* Paris: Presses Universitaires de France (PUF), 3ème édition.

Feather J. (1980), 'The Book Trade in Politics: the Making of the Copyright Act of 1710', 8 *Publishing History* 19.

Feather J. (1994), *Publishing, Piracy and Politics: An Historical Study of Copyright in Britain*, London: Mansell Publications.

Fisher W. (1988), 'Reconstructuring the Fair Use Doctrine', 101 *Harvard Law Review* 1659.

Gaudrat P. (2001), *Propriété Littéraire et Artistique*, coll. Droit Fondamental, Paris: Presses Universitaires de France (PUF), 4ème édition.

Ginsburg J. (1990), 'A Tale of Two Copyrights: Literary Property in Revolutionary France and America', 64 *Tulane Law Review* 991.

Ginsburg J. (2006), 'Une Chose Publique? The Author's Domain and the Public Domain in Early British, French and US Copyright Law', 65 *Cambridge Law Journal* 636, also available at: papers.ssrn.com/sol3/papers.cfm?abstract_id=928648.

Gordon W. (1989), 'An Inquiry into the Merits of Copyright: the Challenges of Consistency, Consent and Encouragement Theory', 41 *Stanford Law Review* 1343.

Hesse C. (1991), *Publishing and Cultural Politics in Revolutionary Paris, 1789–1810*, Berkeley: University of California Press, 1991, also available at: http://ark.cdlib.org/ark:/13030/ft0z09n7hf/.

Hilaire-Pérez L. (1994), *Inventions et Inventeurs en France et en Angleterre au XVIIIe siècle*, Lille : Université de Lille.

Hulme W. (1896), 'The History of the Patent System under the Prerogative and at Common Law', 12 *Law Quarterly Review* 141.

Hulme W. (1900), 'The History of the Patent System under the Prerogative and at Common Law – A Sequel', 16 *Law Quarterly Review* 44.

Hurt R. and R. Shuchman (1966), 'The Economic Rationale of Copyright', 78 *Am.Econ. Assoc.Papers & Proc.* 421.

Joyce C. (2005), 'A Curious Chapter in the History of Judicature: *Wheaton v. Peters* and the Rest of the Story (of Copyright in the New Republic)', 42 *Houston Law Review* 325, also available at: SSRN: http://ssrn.com/abstract=801226.

Joyce C. and L.R. Patterson (2003), 'Copyright in 1791: An Essay Concerning the Founders' View of the Copyright Power Granted to Congress in Article I, Section 8, Clause 8 of the US Constitution', 52 *Emory Law Journal* 909, also available at: SSRN: http://ssrn.com/abstract=559145.

Joyce C., W. Patry, M. Leaffer and P. Jaszi (1988), *Copyright Law*, 4th ed., New York: Matthew Bender & Co.

Kauffman G. (1986), 'Exposing the Suspicious Foundation of Society's Primacy in Copyright Law: Five Accidents', 10 *Columbia-VLA Journal of Law and the Arts* 381.

Koumantos G. (2002), *Copyright*, 8th ed., Athens: A. Sakkoulas.

Landes W. and R. Posner (1989), 'An Economic Analysis of Copyright Law', 18 *Journal of Legal Studies* 325.

Liemer S. (2005), 'How We Lost Our Moral Rights and the Door Closed on Non-

Economic Values in Copyright', 5 *The John Marshall Review of Intellectual Property Law* 1.
Lucas H. and H.J. Lucas (2006), *Traite de propriété littéraire et artistique*, 3ème édition, Paris: Litec.
Macauley C. (1774), *A Modest Plea for the Property of Copyright*, Bath.
Patry W. (2000), *Copyright Law and Practice*, Washington, D.C.: Bureau of National Affairs, also available at: http://digital-law-online.info/patry/patry5.html.
Patterson L.R. (1968), *Copyright in a Historical Perspective*, Nashville: Vanderbilt University Press.
Pouillet E. (1908), *Traité de propriété littéraire et artistique*, Paris: Marchal et Billard, 3ème édition.
Prager F.D. (1952), 'The Early Growth and Influence of Intellectual Property', 34 *Journal of the Patent Office Society* 106.
Rand B. (ed.) (1927), *The Correspondence of John Locke and Edward Clarke*, Oxford: Oxford University Press, pp. 366–401.
Ricketson S. (1987), *The Berne Convention for the Protection of Literary and Artistic Works: 1886–1986*, London: Kluwer.
Rose M. (1993), *Authors and Owners, The Invention of Copyright,* Cambridge, MA: Harvard University Press.
Rose M. (2003), 'Nine-Tenths of the Law: The English Copyright Debates and the Rhetoric of the Public Domain', 66 *Law & Contemp. Problems* 75.
Rudd B. (date unavailable), 'Notable dates in American Copyright', available at: http://copyright.gov/history/dates.pdf.
Shirata H. (date unavailable), 'The Origin of Two American Copyright Theories – A Case of Reception of English Law', available at: http://orion.mt.tama.hosei.ac.jp/hideaki/twocopy.htm.
Sisson C.J. (1960), 'The Laws of Elizabethan Copyright: the Stationers' View', *The Library*, 5th ser. XV.
The Federalist Papers (1937). No 43 (Madison) (Modern Library Ed. at 279), available at: http://thomas.loc.gov/home/histdox/fed_43.html.
Tompson R. (1992), 'Scottish Judges and the Birth of British', 37 *Copyright, Juridical Review* 18.
Torremans P. (2005), *Holyoak and Torremans Intellectual Property Law*, 4th ed., London: Oxford University Press.
Tyerman B.W. (1971), 'The Economic Rationale for Copyright Protection for Published Books: A Reply to Professor Breyer', 18 *UCLA Law Review* 1100.
Versteeg R. (2000), 'The Roman Law Roots of Copyright', 59 *Maryland Law Review* 522.
Whicher J.F. (1981), 'The Ghost of *Donaldson v. Beckett*: An Inquiry into the Constitutional Distribution of Powers over the Law of Literary Property in the US-Part I', 9 *Bulletin of the Copyright Society of the U.S.A.* 102.
Yen A. (1900), 'Restoring the Natural Law: Copyright as Labor and Possession', 51 *Ohio State Law Journal* 517.
Yu P. (2006), 'Of Monks, Medieval Scribes and Middlemen', 35 *Michigan State Law Review* 1.

3. The US and European legal regimes: a critical overview

The legal norms aiming at a universal application of intellectual property rules are many and have existed for quite some time. In the field of industrial property, the 1883 Paris Convention for the Protection of Industrial Property covers patents for inventions, industrial design rights, trademarks and unfair competition protection. Copyright's 'Magna Carta', the 1886 Berne Convention for the Protection of Literary and Artistic Works, has been a very significant starting point, even if the US joined the Convention more than 100 years after its conclusion. Another international convention on copyright was the 1952 Universal Copyright Convention. Also important, for copyright, is the 1961 Rome Convention for the Protection of Performers and Broadcasting Organizations.

The European Patent Convention was signed in Munich in 1973. Many European Directives, enacted during the last 15 years, deal with intellectual property rights; they cover particular areas such as, for example, the harmonization of certain aspects of copyrights (Directive 2001/29/EC) or the legal protection of biotechnological inventions (patent rights, Directive 98/44/EC). Many more legal norms of supranational character have been promulgated, with varying degrees of success; the same is true of the European Directives, which, however, at times, Member States have refused to implement or have done so in ways contrary to the very purposes of the instruments, such as unification.

Directive 2004/48/EC on the (civil) enforcement of intellectual property rights is applicable to the protection of all kinds of intellectual property rights. As such, it unites all patents, copyrights and trademarks. It does not, however, deal with any substantive intellectual property law matters, but remains in the domain of procedure.

The principle of territoriality, meaning that each Member State must grant nationals of the other Member States the same rights and protection as it grants its own nationals, is a common theme in the conventions of Paris, Berne and the Universal Copyright Convention. It is also contained in the Agreement on Trade Related Aspects of Intellectual Property Rights (TRIPs) of 1994. TRIPs is an international agreement on intellectual property rights which all members of the World Trade Organization are obliged to adopt, under penalty of severe enforcement measures against them.

Intellectual property, as evident from the above multiplicity of sources at national, but also supranational, level has ceased long ago to be a matter of internal state regulations and has acquired an international economic character and a clear political dimension.

1. PATENTS

Patents are regulated at international, constitutional, federal (for the US), and national (for each separate state of the US and each state for European and other countries) level. We see, therefore, an interplay of legal sources of varying power, and also an interplay among classic common law sources such as judicial precedent, and others, such as statutory laws and the decisions of the administrative bodies dealing with patents (patent offices). The growing economic importance of intellectual property rights we have seen in recent decades has reinforced this multiplicity of types of regulation. The willingness to strengthen the protection of inventions by patent laws also varied according to the status of the country facing the dilemma: developed countries (producers of inventions) were much more prone to offer strong patent protection than developing countries (mostly users of industrial property).

Globalization has not functioned as a factor working towards simplification of these regimes. Obviously, the interests of inventors, who are often strong multinational corporations, could be best served by a single patent procedure, where the patent issued would have universal validity without necessitating the filing a series of patent claims. This is certainly not the case today.

a. The US Regime Today

The most fundamental US legal clause on patents is Art. 1 par. 8, cl. 8 of the US Constitution.[1] This reads:

> The Congress shall have power … to promote the progress of science and useful arts by securing for limited times to … inventors the exclusive right to their … discoveries.[2]

'Discoveries' (in today's terminology, inventions) are constitutionally protected as inventors' rights, for a limited time, to be set by Congress. The purpose of this grant and the limitation of 'limited times' constitute clear constitutional constraints, binding Congress not to legislate in contravention of these fundamental principles. The constitutional provision allowing federal legislation on patents has the potential to pre-empt any state statutes, which may not be in harmony with the constitutional clause.

The Patent Act, which executed the constitutional mandate in 1793, was amended in 1836 and in 1952. The current Patent Act of the United States is a statute of 1952 (66 Stat. 792), considerably amended at times by Congress. The codification of the 1952 statute is contained in Title 35 of the US Code. Under this statute, patents must refer to a new, useful and non-obvious process or product. Whoever invents or discovers any new and useful process, machine, manufacture or composition of matter may obtain a patent therefore (U.S.C. 35 Section 101). If these requirements are met, then an exclusive right to the invention is granted for a term not exceeding 20 years from the filing date (this term was, until very recently, 17 years). No patent rights exist before they are formally acknowledged by the Patent Office, after an examination of the claims of the applicant.

The main features of (any) patent system are (a) the subject-matter (what is patentable?) (b) utility (is this patent useful?) (c) novelty and non-obviousness (is this patent new and non-obvious?) and (d) infringement (when is a patent infringed and what are the consequences?) These topics will be now analyzed.

I. Patentable subject-matter

i. General Principles

The question of what may be patented is probably the most crucial question of the law of patents. It is also the question which has fired the most vigorous debate, internationally as well as nationally, especially in the field of biotechnology patents (sometimes called life patents) and, secondly, software patents.

Section 35 of the U.S.C. par. 101 allows patents for processes, machines, manufactures and compositions of matter. Commentators divide patents into two classes: product patents and process patents. Machines, manufactures and compositions of matter all fall under this rough classification within product patents, as they logically do not have any relation to any process, but describe a sort of an end-result of a process, that is a product. A process, on the contrary, is a means to an end; a way of doing something.

In theory, pure ideas cannot be patented; only their application can. This idea/application distinction exists as a cornerstone of the whole intellectual property system, both in the US and Europe, although it has been gradually more and more difficult to claim that it is applied practice. The examination of whether what is claimed as an invention to be patented is in fact an (unpatentable) abstract idea is undertaken in the case of an application for a process patent (as of course, an abstract idea cannot be, simultaneously, a product).

ii. Software and Business Methods Patents

One of the first modern US cases where the Supreme Court rejected such an application is the well-known case of *Gottschalk v. Benson*.[3] The claimant asked to patent a process for converting binary-coded decimal numerals into pure binary numerals. The Court held that what the claimant was really asking for was a patent over an algorithm running a computed program. An algorithm, however, was an abstract idea and was not patentable. The Supreme Court restated the non-patentability of software algorithms six years after *Gottschalk*, in *Parker v. Flook*.[4] In *Parker*, the Court held that a formula for computing an updated alarm limit was what the claimant had asked to patent, but this was unpatentable.

The problem of software patentability in the US has been addressed by granting patents for 'computer implemented inventions', which is, according to some, just another way of patenting algorithms. This evolution started with the famous Supreme Court decision, *Diamond v. Diehr*,[5] in 1981. There the Supreme Court held that the respondent claimed a patent for a method of curing rubber by controlled heating, which involved the transformation and reduction of an article to a different state. That this transformation was aided by a computer program should not exclude patentability; the focus was upon the transformation and not upon the help of a computer program.

Claims for patents for computer programs flooded the Patent Office after *Diamond v. Diehr*. Thirteen years after *Diamond*, in *In re Alappat*,[6] a case from the Court of Appeals for the Federal Circuit, the Court substantively accepted software patents and overturned a long-held policy of the Patent Office not to grant patents to 'inventions that could be functionally implemented in software' (as the attorneys for the claimants described this particular software).[7] The case involved a claim to an improved display screen, similar to a television screen. Alappat's mathematical algorithm had the effect of improving the clarity of the picture. The majority saw the invention in this case as a machine and heavily criticized this policy of the Patent Office for being out of place 'in a world that has become totally dependent on technology'.[8] The majority also stressed that computer programs are patentable because they limit a general-purpose computer to a specific purpose. In contrast, the dissent stressed that the claimed invention performed the (admittedly new) algorithm using standard electronic devices, so it was unpatentable.

Ever since, there has been no question that in the United States, in essence, software is patentable in various cases as an invention, even if many opponents of this policy have stressed that software is in fact a composite of algorithms and expression that should not be patentable.

Another important question about patentability is whether business methods are patentable. In the famous case of *State Street Bank & Trust Co. v. Radio Corp. of Am*,[9] the Federal Court, relying on *Alappat*, granted a patent for a particular method of doing business. This case is also relevant to software as a patentable invention;[10] in a sense, the case combines the software with the business methods patentability question. In *State Street* it was held that a software program was patentable as producing a tangible result when its output was a useful number that a set of calculations produced.[11] This result of this machine was a final output value, even if it existed only as a set of numbers; it was concrete and tangible enough to override the 'mere algorithm' exception.

In a dispute between the Internet-operating companies Amazon.com and Barnes and Noble about the patent Amazon had secured for its one-click service to customers ('a method of placing an order to purchase an item on the internet'), Amazon was initially granted a preliminary injunction against Barnes and Noble. The case was settled in 2002 and therefore there was no final judicial resolution of this matter.[12] But in 2007, the US Patent Office rejected Amazon's one-click patent.[13]

IBM has secured a great number of Internet business methods patents, such as patents for storing data in an interactive network, adjusting hypertext links with weighted user goals and activities and ordering items using an electronic catalogue. In 2006, IBM sued Amazon for patent infringement,[14] a suit which (just like the Amazon/Barnes suit) ended with a settlement which included the cross-licensing of patents from both sides. No matter how the cases were resolved and what the real motive was, patents for Internet methods of doing business have been issued in thousands by the US Patent Office.

Clear cases of unpatentable ideas, such as, for example, Einstein's formula E=MC2 and so many other true laws of nature, of course do exist. These are abstract principles which in a sense, have 'been there' all along, so they are barred from patentability. The same is true for physical phenomena: they cannot be patented. However, inventions that apply the laws of nature (for example, a pendulum clock which applies the law of gravity) may be properly patented.[15]

iii. Medical Procedure Patents, 'Life' Patents-patents and Biotechnology

Most medical technologies are patentable. Drugs are clearly patentable, meaning the *method* of producing a drug. The drug may well be the result of more than a very costly decade of research and conducting trials. Obviously, there are very high costs involved in pharmaceutical research and the corporations definitely count on patents in order to recoup their heavy investments. Questions about drugs and patents have been raised especially when developing countries, suffering badly from AIDS, claimed that the high prices of antiretrovials, coupled with the illegality of distributing generic AIDS drugs, rendered any help to the AIDS victims there impossible. The drugs' high prices were attributed to drug patents. This controversial and emotional debate continues today.[16]

People have also tried to patent particular new medical/surgical procedures. The whole subject is quite controversial.[17] In many states of the US, several hundred patents for medical procedures are granted every year; medical procedures have generally been patented in the US since 1954, when the US Patent Office held that medical and surgical methods were patentable.[18] After a case where an eye-surgeon sued another for the use of his patent in performing cataract surgery, the American Medical Association pressed for and had passed an amendment to the Patent Act, so that medical procedures might be patented but liability for their infringement by a practitioner was eliminated (35 U.S.C. par. 287 c).

More disputes have also arisen in biotechnologies. Before 1980, patents were not issued for any life forms. The Patent Act allowed patents for compositions of matter or new and useful processes, but life forms were not, until 1980, conceived as (mere) compositions of matter. In 1980, the US Supreme Court held (*Diamond v. Chakrabarty*,[19] 5-4) that a 'live, human-made microorganism' could be patentable subject-matter. In this case, a microbiologist had added to his patent claims a separate claim to patent bacteria which, as the Supreme Court accepted, were not a non-naturally occurring manufacture or composition of matter: the bacterium *Psudomonas* was genetically modified, in the laboratory, to consume oil slicks, and so definitely *not* naturally occurring. Nothing in the Patent Act was seen by the majority opinion to preclude patentability for a certain composition of matter merely because this composition of matter happened to be alive.

This expansionist interpretation of the Patent Act (as in *Chakrabarty*, where the majority held that anything under the sum made by man could be patentable) opened the doors for patents for living organisms,[20] the most important of which now are gene patents and, more recently, patents to sequences of DNA that were only segments of a gene. Specific guidelines of the US Patent Office direct claimants how to claim these DNA sequence patents.[21] Patents have also been issued for stem cells from many different organisms, such as monkeys. The US Patent Office's policy on patentability of genes and DNA sequences is enormously broad.[22] Patents have been granted for 'non-naturally occurring' animals such as polyploid oysters[23] and a genetically altered mouse (called 'oncomouse', allegedly useful for cancer research).[24] These 'non-naturally occurring' patented animals are 'useful' (in patent terms) as research tools, possibly enabling further disease research.

A distinct class of patents is plant and design patents, which are allowed under sec. 161 and 171 of the Patent Act (35 U.S.C.A.). A plant may be patented if it is new, distinctive and non-obvious and only in order to protect a distinct new variety of an asexually (meaning no seeds are involved) reproducing plant. In 2001, the Supreme Court held[25] that patents for plants are also available under the (classic) utility patents (and not only under the stricter conditions of 35 U.S.C.A). A design patent may be issued to protect an original, new ornamental design for an article of manufacture (functional article). Computer icons and fonts may be patented as design patents. In this case, the patents cover only the ornamental features of an object and not its functions (which could, however, be the subject of a utility patent).

II. Utility

'A patent is not a hunting license', wrote the late Justice Fortas in *Brenner v. Manson*[26] in 1966.[27] In this case, the claimant wanted to patent a chemical process, which did not appear to produce a demonstrable useful result. Therefore, the Court held that the claim should fail on the ground that the requirement of utility (of the patent) had not been met. This requirement is a constitutional one (the patent clause expressly refers to the *useful* arts) and also a federal one (the Patent Act gives protection only to *useful* inventions: 35 U.S.C.A. sec. 101). What Justice Fortas described so clearly was that a patent may not cover a whole field without any specification of why this particular patent produces a specific and demonstrable (in the patent application) benefit. This condition also has the result that no patent may encompass a whole range of unknown applications (and, hence, more an idea than a concrete application of an idea) as no 'monopoly of knowledge'[28] is allowed. The Patent Office, however, may not demand the proof of particular commercial feasibility (proof, that is, that the invention has any real commercial value in trade) before accepting that an invention is useful in the sense of patent law. The question of usefulness arose as particularly important when scientists filed repeatedly for the patenting of DNA sequences in the US, starting with Graig Venter's application in 1991.[29] The first such patent was granted in 1998 for Human Kinase Homologs.[30] Utility, therefore, has been accepted in US patent law for DNA sequences as inventions.[31]

Utility as a concept is, in theory, also designed to preclude illegality and immorality. For example, dangerous machines with no beneficial use are, as a rule, not patentable. One of the oldest rulings on this point was Justice Story's in *Lowell v. Levis*,[32] where he, a trial judge at that time, interpreted the statute's word 'useful' as preventing the patenting of a mischievous or immoral device: an invention should not be frivolous or injurious to 'the well-being, good policy, or sound morals of society'.[33] The Court of Appeals for the Federal Circuit in 1999 rejected[34] the rule that an invention's deceptive intentions should bar patentability and allowed a patent for a post-mix beverage dispenser, which was designed to make buyers believe that it was in fact a pre-mix beverage dispenser. The Court stated that the battle against deceptive commercial practices belongs to other agencies, such as the Federal Trade Commission, and not to the Patent Office, whose purpose is entirely different.

Due to the utility condition, an invention presenting mere novelty or curiosity cannot sustain an application for a patent. That a patent is useful must be affirmatively proven before the patent is granted; utility must be specific, substantial, credible and may not be presumed. Under the Patent's Office Utility Guidelines of 2001, the disclosure in the patent's claims of at least one specific, substantial and credible utility is necessary (the proposal that, in gene patent cases, the mere disclosure of a DNA sequence should in and of itself satisfy the utility condition of patentability, as carrying an inherent value and enabling endless uses, was rejected).

III. Novelty and non-obviousness

Non-obviousness of an invention (which is not synonymous with novelty of an invention, as an invention may be novel but also obvious to a person skilled in the relevant field of technology) has been a requirement of patenting even before it was expressly incorporated in the 1952 US Patent Act (sec. 103). Before the Act, that is, the question of novelty and non-obviousness was examined as necessarily included in the proper construction of the word 'invention' itself; after all, 'invention' is the word in the US Constitution and the 'object' for which the Constitution allows a monopoly by granting a patent for it. But for many years, the question of novelty/non-obviousness had not been dealt by the courts, interpreting 'invention' in an entirely objective and uniform way. This gave rise to many complaints for insecurity. This is why the new, at the time, Patent Act attempted statutorily to clarify this important matter.

Under 35 U.S.C. sec. 103, an invention is non-obvious if a person skilled in the art (or technology etc.) to which the claimed invention 'belongs' would not know how to achieve the advance over prior art that this invention claims to represent. In 1966, the US Supreme Court articulated[35] a three-step standard of non-obviousness: 1. a survey of the scope and content of the prior art; 2. an examination of the differences between the invention and the prior art; 3. a determination of the level of ordinary skill in the art; and 4. objective evidence of non-obviousness. What is important, therefore, is to examine the scope and content of prior art, the level of ordinary skill in the art, the differences between the prior art and the claimed invention and the extent to which any objective indicia of non-obviousness.[36] As objective indicia of non-obviousness, the claimant may present evidence about commercial success, long-felt but unsolved needs, the failure of others to solve the problem the particular invention allegedly solves, the fact that experts in the particular field show disbelief at the discovery's announcement and the very existence of a well-established prior art. This prior art comes from either printed publications or testimonies and statements by experts and skilled practitioners in the field the claimed invention belongs to. Domestic prior art is distinguished from foreign prior art and foreign prior art does not defeat a patent application (Art. 102 par. a).

The combination of known elements can also be considered obvious, leading to an 'invention' failing the non-obviousness test. For a combination to be patentable as a whole, it must create something new and non-obvious. So, a claimed invention may be based on a combination of teachings of the prior art, but in this case there must be, as a requirement of patentability, evidence of some teaching, suggestion or reason to combine the references.[37] The absence of a suggestion to combine rules out a determination of non-obviousness and, of course, of patentability. This test, of teaching/suggestion/motivation reframes the non-obviousness question as 'whether an person of ordinary skill in the art, possessed with the understandings and knowledge reflected in the prior art and motivated by the general problem facing the inventor, would have been led to make the combination recited in the claims'.[38]

The primary purpose of the teaching/suggestion/motivation test is to ward off impermissible hindsight bias. One should not just pick any number of prior art references and combine them together as a new invention to be patented. But the application of this test seems to have been not always in line with the *Graham* test. The Court of Appeals for the Federal Circuit (competent to hear all patent appeals cases) has dealt with the 'suggestion' test severely, reaching the point where to defeat a claim of obviousness the invention must be explicitly 'suggested' in prior art, otherwise a patent must be issued. Moreover, this Court had for a number of years elevated secondary considerations (for non-obviousness, such as commercial success etc.) to primary status: the courts had to consider these indicia of non-obviousness (they did not just enjoy a discretion to do so) and also, the burden of proof that commercial success of a patent was *not* due to the use of the claimed invention fell upon the party asking for the annulment of a patent.[39]

However, in 2007, the Supreme Court in *KSR v. Teleflex*[40] reaffirmed that the *Graham* principles controlled the non-obviousness test of patentability. The Court held that the teaching/suggestion/motivation test of non-obviousness must not be rigidly applied and that the obviousness analysis cannot be confined by a formalistic conception of the words teaching, suggestion and motivation or by overemphasis on the importance of published articles and the explicit content of issued patents. Thus, the 'shortcut' for a non-obviousness analysis that the use of the teaching/suggestion/motivation represented until 2007 is no longer available.

IV. Infringement of a patent

Patents are issued for processes or devices; the patentee has the exclusive right to make, use or sell the invention (35 U.S.C.A. par. 154). To infringe a patent, a device or a process must perform the same work in substantially the same way as the patent and they must accomplish substantially the same result as the patented process or device, without a license by the patentee.[41] Exactly when this happens is not always clear. The rule is that someone is liable for infringement if he has made, used, sold, offered to sell or imported an infringing invention or its equivalent. 'Equivalent' inventions are prohibited as much as 'same' ones, as it is important to prevent an infringer from 'stealing the benefit of the invention'.[42] This is the essence of the 'equivalents doctrine', under which no absolute identity between an issued patent and a possibly infringing process or device is necessary to be proven before a claim for infringement may stand.

It is irrelevant whether the patentee has himself engaged in producing, selling, using etc. the invention because under US laws the patentee is under no obligation to exploit his invention in any way. A suit for patent infringement is possible for 20 years after the issuance of the patent, as this is now the patent term in the US.

The patentee is bound by the claims filed to acquire the patent. He is also bound by any narrowing of patent claims to which he has agreed before the patent examiner. Therefore, the file wrapper estoppel will defeat a patent infringement claim by the patentee, when the claim lies upon a broader interpretation of what the patent covers than the one accepted by the patentee before the patent was granted.

Infringement may be direct, indirect or contributory. Anyone who makes, uses or sells the invention is a direct infringer; a direct infringer may infringe a patent innocently. Anyone who induces another to do the same is an indirect infringer. Anyone who knowingly supplies another with a non-staple item for which the only or predominant use is in connection with a patented invention is a contributory infringer. All these classes of infringers are subject to liability for patent infringement. Contributory infringement allocates liability even if what the infringer sells is in the public domain and has no patent protection itself. To the extent that the only use of the item sold is in connection with an infringing device or process, liability is ascertained. In this way, patent protection is necessarily extended and covers items not only unpatented but also completely unpatentable. Good faith on the part of the infringer is a defense only against contributory infringement. In *Aro Manufacturing Co. v. Convertible Top Replacement Co*,[43] buyers of Ford cars who did not know that the sellers did not have a valid license from their patentee to use the convertible tops of the cars were held to be not liable for contributory infringement of the patent.

Remedies for patent infringement include an injunction (against future infringements), award of a reasonable royalty (equivalent to a reasonable amount for the licensed use of the patent, under current market rules) or damages (for lost profits and treble damages in case of willful infringements, attorney's fees in some cases and court costs).

One of the most famous patent infringement cases ever in the field of biotechnology was the Canadian case of *Percy Schmeiser and Schmeiser Enterprises Ltd. v. Monsanto Canada Inc. and Monsanto Company*.[44] In *Monsanto,* the company had patents over a chimeric plant gene that conferred resistance to glyphosate herbicide and to plant cells that contained the chimeric plant gene. But Canadian patent laws do not allow patents for plants *qua* plants. The farmer Schmeiser was sued by Monsanto for saving and planting seeds and then harvesting and selling plants which contained patented genes and modified cells making up the plants. The question was whether his activity involved an object that included a patent component or not. The Supreme Court held that the infringement of the Monsanto patent did not require use of the patented gene or cells in isolation and held for Monsanto. Schmeiser claimed that the seeds blew onto his land and he did not know that these were 'Monsanto's seeds'.[45] However, Schmeiser had noticed the presence of Roundup resistant seeds and then isolated them and saved them for planting next year. The Court also clarified that the protection of a patented gene or cell extends to its presence in a whole plant, even while the plant itself, as a higher life form, cannot be patented. Whether this is an entirely reasonable conclusion is an open question. The dissenters offered many reasons against it and openly declared that patent claims to genes and cells cannot be interpreted to extend patent protection to entire plants.

b. The European Patent Regime Today

What would truly 'count' as European patent law today? As the European Community has dealt with patents in a number of ways, including for example, Green Papers etc. It is closer to the (legislative) truth to maintain that as sources of European patent law today, one should definitely include (at least) a. the European Patent Convention of 1973,[46] b. the 1998 Directive on Biotechnology, and c. the 2006 Regulation on compulsory licensing of patents relating to the manufacture of pharmaceutical products for export to countries with public health problems. Apart from these sources, the European Court of Justice's jurisprudence is also, of course, a source of European patent law, and also the case law of the Boards of Appeal of the European Patent Office. And we also have the case law on patents by the national courts of the European countries, which, until it is replaced (if it ever will be) by a European court such as envisioned in the discussions and proposals about the European Community Patent, offer us a picture of what really is protected as part of a European patent right in Europe, and what is not.

The most crucial subjects of the debate about patents in Europe are software patents (and – secondly – business method patents), 'life' (biotechnology) patents and drug (pharmaceutical) patents. The first matter has led to an (perhaps temporary) end to all projects to award software patents on a large scale, as the European Parliament dictated in 2005. Admittedly, though, and most importantly, the European Patent Office is reported to have issued more than 30,000 patents for computer-implemented inventions, even if the very text of the Convention clearly states that no patents for computer programs are possible.[47] The matter of 'life' patents, that is biotechnology gene patents, stem-cell patents, DNA sequencing patents etc., is regulated in a special Directive. And, lastly, the question of drug patenting in connection with exports for very important reasons of public health is regulated by a special Regulation. Around these issues, many legislative or legislative-like instruments exist, such as, for example, the Community Patent Convention.

I. The European Patent Convention

If one were to understand the European patent regime as a regime which deals with patents and is applicable to all European countries, granting inventors, via a single patent application procedure, a single Community-wide patent, enforceable throughout Europe, one would be mistaken. This has clearly, of course, been an (admittedly distant) objective behind legislation such as (most notably) the European Patent Convention of 1973, although at the same time, it was obvious that no 'true' Community patent existed. What existed and still is true is, instead, a 'method' of filing for a European patent with the headquarters of the European Patent Office in Munich or one of the other offices competent to accept European patent applications, such as in The Hague. If the application for the European patent is accepted, the patentee acquires a bundle of national patents in common form, for such participant countries as designated in the application. The European Patent Office granted 63,000 patents in 2006 and the average time before the grant is 44 months.[48]

In cases of infringement, the national courts protect the rights of the patentee in the countries where the infringement arose. Clearly, no cross-border injuction from a national court is enforceable in other countries. The European Court of Justice has held[49] that European patents are national rights, to be enforced (only) nationally. If an infringement, therefore, has occurred in many countries, the patentee has to follow separate legal procedures in each and every country. The European Patent Convention has been signed by 31 European countries, Latvia being the more recent signatory, on July 1, 2005.

Another kind of a patent, which is sometimes confused with the European patent under the European Patent Convention, is the Community patent. The Community patent was supported under the Community Patent Convention signed at Luxembourg in 1975 (which never entered in force). This patent was to be the embodiment of the above objectives, as it could be enforced within all European countries. All patent grievances would be heard by a special court, 'attached' to the European Court of Justice and the Court of First Instance, whose decision would then be enforceable throughout the European Community. These plans, which had at times reached somewhat satisfying legislative progress (e.g. with the 2000 Community Patent Regulation Proposal), are currently stalled, mainly due to the multiple and complex problems created by the multiplicity of European languages.

These procedural, yet very important, matters aside, what the European Patent Convention provides as substantive law requirements of a patent is described in Art. 52(2), under which:

> European patents shall be granted for any inventions which are susceptible to industrial application, which are new and which involve an inventive step.

The Convention then proceeds with exceptions to patentability: discoveries, scientific theories and mathematical methods, aesthetic creations, rules and methods for performing mental acts, playing games or doing business and programs for computers and presentations of information are not patentable under the Convention. Also not patentable (for policy reasons) are methods of treatment of the human or animal body by surgery or therapy and diagnostic methods practised on the human or animal body, inventions contrary to *ordre public* (public order) or morality and plant or animal varieties and essentially biological processes for the production of plants and animals.

In these provisions, therefore, are included all the substantive requirements for a patent, as well as the exceptions to a *prima facie* case for patentability. Novelty is a requirement of patentability. An invention is deemed new under the Convention if it does not form part of the 'state of the art'. The state of (any) art is everything made available to the public by means of a written or oral description, by use or in any other way, before the date of filing of the European patent application. The content of the patent applications as filed before the date of filing of the patent application in question is considered as comprised in the state of the art. Under Art. 56, an invention shall be considered as involving an inventive step (a requirement, again, of patentability) if, having regard to the state of the art, it is not obvious to a person skilled in the art. Under Art. 57, an invention shall be considered as susceptible of industrial application if it can be made or used in any kind of industry, including agriculture.

Art. 100 provides that an opposition to a European patent may be filed on the ground that the subject-matter of the European patent is not patentable, or the European patent does not disclose the invention in a manner sufficiently clear and complete for it to be carried out by a person skilled in the art or if the subject-matter of the European patent extends beyond the content of the application as filed.

If the patent application is successful, then a European patent is granted for 20 years from the filing date.

i. A Note on Computer Programs

The Guidelines for examination in the European patent of 2003[50] refer, *inter alia*, to the most important question of the patentability of computer programs.[51] A reasonable thought would be that the main text of the Convention, especially ruling out patentability for computer programs in Art. 52(2), could not be clearer. On the other hand, the 2003 guidelines contain an analysis of the patentability of computer-implemented inventions. While 'programs for computers' are included among the items listed in Art. 52(2), if the claimed subject-matter has a technical character it is not excluded from patentability by the provisions of Art. 52(2) and (3). The guidelines continue that if a computer program is capable when running on a computer, of bringing about, a further technical effect going beyond the normal physical effects, it is not excluded from patentability, irrespective of whether it is claimed by itself or as a record on a carrier. This further technical effect may be known in the prior art. Also, the requirement of technical character is satisfied, if technical considerations are required to carry out the invention, which technical considerations must be reflected in the subject-matter.

As the Patent's Office Board of Appeals has decided (Cases T–1173/97 and T–0935/97), this 'further' technical effect as a requirement of patentability means that the alleged technical effect must exceed the 'normal' physical interactions between program and computer.[52] If this can be found, a computer program may not be excluded from patentability. In 1997, a 'potential technical effect', in addition to a (proven) technical effect, was accepted as possibly satisfying the standard of patentability, an interpretation which enlarged the domain of patents for computer-implemented inventions.[53] An achieved reduced memory access time or better control of a robotic arm are examples of this 'further' technical effect. Interestingly, in 2002 alone, a total of 6,856 patent applications in the computing field were filed.

An effort over many years to arrive at a special Directive for the legal protection of computer programs with patent rights seems now to have been abandoned, after stern opposition throughout the European Union. A Directive proposal in 2002, under the title 'EU Directive on the patentability of computer-implemented inventions' would have established common rules before Europe's national courts but was overwhelmingly rejected by the European Parliament in 2005.

ii. A Note on Business Methods

On business methods, however, the European Patent Office has been very stirct and declined to follow the US Supreme Court decision in *State Street.* In the case of *Pension Benefit Systems Partnership*/T–0931/97, for example, it held that 'methods only involving economic concepts of doing business are not inventions' because the lack a 'technical contribution'. The European Patent Office has remained faithful to the unpatentability of business methods, although some view some of its granted patents as, in essence, business method patents.[54] Recent decisions by the Office's Boards of Appeal (like T–641/00 and T–258/03) stress the requirement of inventive step so much so as to render the patentability of inventions with no technical features (such as business methods) impossible. Claims may consist of a mixture of technical and non-technical features, but for the European Patent Office novelty and inventive step can only be based on technical features.[55]

II. European patents and biotechnology: the European Patent Convention and Directive 98/44/EC

Patents in the field of biotechnology are regulated by the European Patent Convention in conjunction, though, with the Directive on legal protection of biotechnological inventions, Directive 98/44/EC.[56] The decisions by the European Patent Office are also crucial. According to many critics of biotechnological patents, this Office has repeatedly broadened the scope of patentability and undermined existing restrictions to patenting.[57]

Biotechnological inventions are patentable under both the European Patent Convention and the subsequent *ad hoc* Directive 98/44/EC. Under the European Patent Convention (Rule 23c), biotechnological inventions shall be patentable if they concern (a) biological material isolated from its natural environment or produced by means of a technical process, even if it previously occurred in nature; (b) plants or animals if the technical feasibility of the invention is not confined to a particular plant or animal variety; and (c) microbiological or other technical process, or a product obtained by means of such a process other than a plant or animal variety.

The Preamble to the Directive on biotechnological inventions of 1998 contains a series of recitals which are very useful to its interpretation. For example, it is recognized that, particularly in the field of genetic engineering, research and development require a considerable amount of high-risk investment and that, therefore, only adequate legal protection can make them profitable (recital 2). Throughout the text, it is also clear that harmonization of relevant national laws is a key purpose, as differences in the legal treatment of biotechnological inventions constitute, amongst other, severe barriers to trade within the European Union.

Biotechnological inventions patentable under the Directive are those inventions which concern a product consisting of or containing biological material or a process by means of which biological material is produced, processed or used. The term 'biological material' means, under Art. 2, any material containing genetic information and capable of reproducing itself or being reproduced in a biological system. As there is a special Directive on patents and biotechnology, it serves as a supplementary means of interpretation of the European Patent Convention's rules on patentability of biotechnological inventions. Biotechnological inventions may be patentable even if they concern biological material which is isolated from its natural environment or produced by means of a technical process even if it previously occurred in nature (hence, biological material may be considered patentable even if it alrealy occurs in nature).

Under Art. 3 of the Directive and in combination with the above, biotechnological inventions which are new, which involve an inventive step and which are susceptible to industrial application shall be patentable. But plant and animal varieties and essentially biological processes for the production of plants or animals are not patentable (Art. 4 of the Directive). Inventions which concern plants or animals shall be patentable if the technical feasibility of the invention is not confined to a particular plant or animal variety. Most importantly, the human body at the various stages of its formation and development and the simple discovery of one of its elements, including the sequence of a gene, cannot consitute patentable inventions (Art. 5).

An element isolated from the human body or otherwise produced by a technical process which is susceptible to an industrial application, including the sequence or partial sequence of a gene, may constitute a patentable invention even if the structure of that element is identical to that of a natural element. Such an element is not *a priori* excluded from patentability since it is, for example, the result of a technical process used to identify, purify and classify it and to produce it outside the human body, techniques which human beings alone are capable of putting into practice and which nature is incapable of accomplishing itself (Recital 21 of the Directive). The industrial application of a sequence or a partial sequence of a gene must be disclosed in the patent application. These provisions are identical to the relevant parts of the European Patent Convention.

Where the commerical exploitation of an invention would be contrary to *ordre public* or morality, then the invention is unpatentable (Art. 6). The notion of public order should reasonably be construed in connection with the protection of individual security and physical integrity, whereas the notion of morality should be interpreted in view of currently held beliefs about right and wrong in Europe. The Directive contains concrete examples of unpatentable inventions under the prohibition of violation or *ordre public*/morality: processes for cloning human beings, processes for modifying the germ line genetic identity of human beings, uses of human embryos for industrial or commercial purposes and processes for modifying the genetic identity of animals which are likely to cause them suffering without any substantial medical benefit to man or animals, and also animals resulting from such processes. These are identical to the European Patent Convention's exceptions to patentability, which also bar patentability for patents which are against *ordre public* or morality.

The story of the patent on a certain kind of laboratory-made mouse, the 'oncomouse', shows how the European Patent Office grants 'life' patents and the role of morality in these cases. Harvard Univeristy had acquired a US patent for a mouse, the 'oncomouse', a transgenic mouse 'created' in the laboratory that was supersusceptible to breast cancer as it contained an oncogene (a gene able to cause cancer). In 1984, Harvard Univeristy filed for a patent for 'its' mouse before the European Patent Office. The Office refused to grant it because, as it then stated, the patent would violate Art. 53(b) of the European Patent Convention; it was, that is, a patent for a new variety of animals, which was expressely forbidden. After an appeal by Harvard, claiming that oncomices were not a new variety of animals, but a new kind of animals transcending varietal classification, the application was returned[58] by the appeals board to the examiners for a review. This time the review was not to check the application for conformity with Art. 53(b) but with Art. 53(a), whether the patent was or was not against morality. The examiners were asked to balance whether a patent on the oncomouse would be unethical, if it could increase the suffering of animals (as animals with cancer were created on purpose) and whether oncomice were also an environmental danger (if the oncogenes somehow escaped from the laboratory and 'infected' the general mouse population). These matters were to be weighed against the possible benefit for humankind if research with oncomice increased the possibility to cure breast cancer. In the end, the examiners allowed the patent.[59]

The Technical Board of Appeal of the European Patent Office has stated[60] that exceptions to patentability, in relation to plants and animals, must be construed narrowly. Seeds and plants should not be regarded as unpatentable because they are living matter or because they should remain 'common heritage of mankind', but the check on patentability should proceed on a case-by-case basis. On the legislative demand that a biotechnological invention may not be granted if it clashes with public order, the Technical Board of Appeals has stated that subject-matter claimed as a patentable invention may not be patented if it is likely that it will seriously prejudice the environment.[61] The words 'likely' and 'serious' (prejudice) necessarily constrain the cases of unpatentability. In short, the policy of the Board of Appeal is to patent these inventions.

III. Regulation (EC) 816/2006 on pharmaceutical products for export to countries with public health problems

Regulation 816/2006 is not the only Regulation issued on patent-related themes, but it seems the most important one.[62] It concerns one of the most severe problems of the international community, the problem of access to life-saving drugs which are, however, either not available or so expensive as to be prohibited to patients suffering, for example, from AIDS. The Regulation establishes a procedure for the grant of compulsory licenses in relation to patents and supplementary protection certificates concerning the manufacture and sale of pharmaceutical products, when such products are intended for export to eligible importing countries in need of such products in order to address public health problems (Art. 1). As it is a Regulation of the European Community, Member States do not have to implement its rules into their internal legal system with some statutory instrument (as is the case for a Directive): its force is direct upon all Member States.

The Regulation is not limited to any particular diseases. It does not refer to any kinds of disease for which a compulsory license must be issued. The European Community has adopted a special program for action: 'accelerated action on HIV/AIDS, malaria and tuberculosis in the context of poverty reduction';[63] this program focuses on these diseases as they are killing more than five million people each year, mostly in developing countries. The 2006 Regulation which covers all diseases also extends to all medicinal products to which a compulsory license may apply. What is also notable is that the issuance of a compulsory license is not at the discretion of a state; the Member States shall grant a compulsory license to any person applying for one, under Art. 6 and subject to the conditions of Arts. 6–10. The person to whom the compulsory license is granted may manufacture and sell for export the pharmaceutical/medical product (drug etc.) in question. Normally, this person, the applicant, must provide evidence that she tried to obtain authorization from the right holder and that these efforts were unsuccessful. This is however not required in cases of national emergency or other circumstances of extreme urgency or in cases of public non-commercial use. The Regulation also provides for the remuneration of the right holders (Art. 10 par. 9).

c. A Comparative Perspective of Patent Law in the US and Europe

It is clear from the above discussion that the two patent systems share many common rules. In both systems, an invention must have some kind of novelty to be patentable, a novelty which is 'checked' against prior art. In both systems, an invention must involve an inventive step (for the US this is the statutory test of non-obviousness, for Europe the condition of inventive step imposed by Art. 56 EPC).[64] Inventions must be subject to industrial application in both cases. The term of the patent is in both cases 20 years. In the US, the consequences of the infringement of a patent are deliniated in the patent federal law and apply throughout the states, but in Europe, these consequences etc. are dealt with by the national laws of each Member State (EPC Art. 64).

One of the initial differences we note is about the meaning of prior art ('state of the art' for Europe). In the US law, prior art means prior art *only within the United States*: foreign knowledge and use of the claimed invention do not mean that there is prior art defeating the application for a patent (sec. 102a, Patent Act: an invention will be anticipated if it is known in the US). This is sharply in contrast to the European rule, under which foreign prior knowledge counts as the state of the art, and defeats the application for a patent (Art. 53 par. 2).

Many problems arise when an applicant in the US asks for a patent for something that is, however, well known abroad. One example of this is the controversial case of the patenting of the neem tree, a tree indigenous to India. The neem tree produces substances from which, among others, entirely natural pesticide products are made. One of these European patents on these products, granted to W.R. Grace, was invalidated after a challenge by two Indian non-governmental organizations, as it was discovered that the Indians had known these qualities of the neem tree for centuries.[65] But the US patent stood, as foreign previous knowledge does not 'count' as prior art; domestic knowledge is distinguished from foreign. The same difference supported the granting of a patent for a particular blood test for the HIV virus in the United States in 1984, even though a patent for the same test had been already patented in France.[66]

In the very important matter of exceptions to patentability, the US Patent Act does not in itself contain specific exceptions to patentability. On the contrary, the European Patent Convention specifically enumerates the cases of unpatentability (as in the example in Art 52 par. 2, discoveries, scientific theories etc.). Art. 53 (a) also excludes patents which are against *ordre public* or morality and (b) excludes patents for animal and plant varieties or essentially biological processes for the production of animal or plant varieties as such. One major difference between the systems is that the public morality argument is feeble in American patent law, although, at times, it was more strongly developed.[67] In Europe, the question of morality in relation to patenting is not only a matter of common public discussion, but has entered the very text of the law, therefore commanding the observance of harmony between the granting of patents and morality.

The unique problems about morality and patenting rising from patents to DNA sequences perhaps have not been met by the EU Directive on biotechnological inventions. The European Patent Office was and still is granting patents to DNA sequences, both before and after the Directive.[68] The 'real' differences in patentable subject-matter between the US Patent Office and the European one seem to lie with business-method patents, and secondly with software patents, with the reservation that the European Patent Office does grant patents to computer-implemented inventions (which for some is equal to software patents). The total rejection of the proposal for a software patent Directive, however, in Europe in 2005 indicates a general hostility towards this particular kind of patent. Plant varieties are not patentable in Europe, as they are in the US; but in Europe, inventions related to plants *in general* will be patentable. If follows that these distinctions may end up being superficial as, for example, a plant variety may not be patentable as such in Europe, but if this plant variety contains a patented gene it constitutes a patentable invention. The same comment could sound true for software patents (unpatentable) and computer-implemented inventions (accepted).

As no 'real' European Community patent exists, the necessary co-function of all national patent systems in Europe, simultaneously with the European Patent Convention and the European Patent Office, is a fundamental barrier to a true and uniform European patent law. And because this is the case, obviously the road towards a uniform *international* patent law is also very long.

2. COPYRIGHTS

Copyrights, like patents, are regulated at international, constitutional, federal (for the US) and national level. The interplay of legal sources of varying power we saw for patents is equivalent for copyrights. The decisions of the courts coupled with the decisions of the Copyright Office (mostly for the US) also belong to the fabric of the copyright legal world. In Europe, more Directives have sought to harmonize copyright rules than patent rules; we have, today, no fewer than seven Directives on copyright-related matters, whereas only one deals with patents (the biotechnology patents Directive 98/44/EC). Directive 2004/48/EC on enforcement covers both fields, and also trademarks.

Copyright is a right 'attached' to a work when the work is born; no registration is today a condition for copyright protection. This is also a major difference from patent rights, where an application must be granted by the state before a right to a patented invention may exist. Copyright has not developed an administrative examination before registration, a prior check whether concrete legal conditions have been met for a certain product of the mind, a work, so that an exclusive property right to this work may accrue.

Copyright in the Anglo-American system means an exclusive property right to a work, to an original 'writing' of an author. The notion in the European civil law system is somewhat different: it is the right of the author to her work which has, however, two sides, the property right to control (mainly) the copies of the work in the economic sense and also, most notably, the moral right to safeguard other aspects of the work such as its integrity, the timing of its publication etc. These interests are also protected in the Anglo-American system, however not always as features of copyright law itself.[69]

a. The US Regime Today

The most fundamental legal clause on copyright of US law is Art. 1 par. 8 cl. 8 of the US Constitution. This reads:

> The Congress shall have Power ... To promote the Progress of Science and useful arts by securing for limited Times to Authors ... the exclusive Right to their ... Writings... [What is omitted here refers to patents].

The writings of authors, then, are constitutionally protected as authors' rights, for a limited time, to be set by Congress. An author is one to whom anything owes its origin: the originator, the maker, one who completes a work of science or literature.[70] A writing is any physical rendering of the fruits of the author's creativity.[71] A work cannot be copyrighted unless it is fixed in a tangible medium of expression. A work is fixed in a tangible medium of expression when its embodiment in a copy or phonorecord, by or under the authority of the author, is sufficiently permanent or stable to permit it to be perceived, reproduced or otherwise communicated for a period of more than transitory duration.[72] Fixation, therefore, is a condition of copyright, quite compatible with the idea/expression dichotomy: works existing solely in the mind of the author are not subject to copyright. The constitutional term 'writings' has come to be very broadly construed, indeed very far away from the small list of books, maps and charts provided as protected by the first American statute on copyright in 1790[73] (musical works, paintings and drawings were at the time, for example, totally omitted).

In 1991 the Supreme Court further clarified[74] that the term 'writing' also embodies the requirement of *originality* as a constitutional condition before copyright may be granted. Therefore, unoriginal writings are not properly subject to copyright. The standard of originality, however, is left to Congress and to the courts, although it is fair to assume that it cannot be as low as to be practically nil.

That the term of protection must be limited is also a constitutional requirement. The interpretation of what limited (times) really means came under intense debate in 2003, when the Supreme Court decided[75] (not unanimously) that the steady extension of the copyright time limits by Congress (such as the extension by the challenged Sony Bono Copyright Term Extension Act) still related to a limited, set term and could cover pre-existing works in line with the Constitution.

The text of the Constitution does not mention any other condition of copyrights, such as the aesthetic quality of the work. Also, registration of the work with a state office or notice that the work is copyrighted upon the work itself is no longer a condition of copyright. These requirements were however added with the first Acts and generally remained federal law until very recently, when the US joined the Berne Convention on March 1, 1989. The Copyright Act of 1790 was substantially amended four times – in 1831, 1870, 1909 and 1976. The changes always meant extension of protection, both in terms of time limits and of subject-matter. All these Acts have required deposit or registration of a work with a court or an office; formalities such as these declined in significance over time. Unlike the case with patents, no formalities are today to be kept as prerequisites to a valid copyright.

The main features, therefore, of a copyright system which deserve some further discussion are a. the subject-mater (what is copyrightable?); b. originality (is the work original?); c. the boundaries of copyright: exceptions of copyright in favor of third parties and the public (what justifies access to the whole or parts of a copyrighted work without permission/payment?); d. infringement (when is a copyrighted work infringed?). These topics will now be analyzed.

I. Copyrightable Subject-matter

i. General Principles

Under the 1976 Copyright Act, 17 U.S.C.A sec. 102(a), copyright protection subsists 'in original works of authorship, now known or later developed'. The statute does list a number of copyrightable kinds of works, but these come as 'included' (as protectable subject-matter of copyright) works and not as an exclusive list. These listed works are: literary works, musical works including any accompanying words, dramatic works including any accompanying music, pantomimes and choreographic works, pictorial, graphic and sculptural works, sound recordings and architectural works (sec. 102, Subject matter of copyright: in general). Compilations and derivative works are also copyrightable, under specific rules.[76]

The debate about copyrightable subject-matter in the past concerned the copyrightability of software. Although it never reached the intensity with which people opposed (and continue to oppose) software patents, it did constitute in the past an uncertain domain of copyright. In the end, software copyright was accepted.

The software problem reflects a major issue of copyrightability: the separation between an idea and the expression of that idea. This is so because with software it is evidently difficult to separate the idea behind a computer program and its expression in code. An idea is not copyrightable; only its expression is. This is a fundamental principle of copyright law, clarified[77] in 1879 in *Baker v. Selden*,[78] a US Supreme Court case dealing with the alleged illegal copying of an accounting method. Selden's idea underlying his system of accounting was not copyrightable, only its expression was. As the Court noted, 'no one has a right to print or publish (another's) book, or any material part thereof, as a book intended to convey instruction in the art, any person may practice and use the art itself which he has described and illustrated therein'.[79] The current value of this idea/expression distinction has been (and is) discounted in parts of the copyright scholarship (in the sense of the impossibility to distinguish between these two in particular cases and not only in software ones), but is a fundamental copyright principle. Its equivalent in patents is the idea/application distinction.

Facts are also not copyrightable – 'the most fundamental axiom of copyright law is that no author may copyright his ideas or the facts he narrates'.[80] They do not owe their origin to any individual and they may not be copyrighted, as they are parts of the public domain available to every person.[81] Generally, in no case does copyright protection for an original work of authorship extend to any idea, procedure, system, method or operation, principle or discovery, regardless of the form in which it is described, explained, illustrated or embodied in such work.[82]

Another area of discussion is the copyrightability of useful works/objects, noting a division between utilitarian objects (not copyrightable) and non-utilitarian objects (copyrightable). This was, for example, the question which arose with lamp-bases designed as art-works but still performing their function as lamps; in 1954, in *Mazer v. Stein*,[83] the Supreme Court held that copyright existed for the aspect of these lamp-bases (statuettes) which was non-utilitarian. Risking an oversimplification of the judgment, what it meant was that one could 'dissect' the lamps' function, separating useful from beautiful (simply meaning that one could always turn off the lamp and only enjoy its design). These statuettes were recognized as original expressions of their designer's ideas, hence, copyrightable. After *Mazer*, the Copyright Office amended its regulations, although very carefully, and determined that registration of copyright in a work of art would not be affected by 'the use of the work, the number of copies reproduced or the fact that it appears in a textile material or textile product'.[84]

It follows that fabric designs, fashion designs and jewelry designs etc. may or may not be copyrighted, depending upon whether one can separate the design itself from its utilitarian aspect. The Copyright Act allows copyright for pictorial, graphic and sculptural works only to the extent that the design involved incorporates pictorial, graphic or sculptural features that can be identified separately from and are capable of existing independently of the utilitarian aspects of the article.[85] So, objects which solely perform a utilitarian function are not, as such, copyrightable; they may, however, be patentable if the conditions of patentability are, of course, met. In general, when the courts examine copyrightability, they also check whether a different form of legal protection is more fitting, such as protection by utility or design patents. A positive answer to this question is a factor towards denying copyright protection.

ii. Software and Copyright

Before 1980, it was not certain in the US that a computer program could be copyrighted. As a creation, software evidently did not present any immediate similarity to a book or a musical composition, or other copyrightable work. Nor was the mood of the initial software 'authors' towards protection from copying: on the contrary, the ethos in early times was an ethos of sharing and improving other people's codes.[86] Anyway, the Copyright Office decided in 1964 to accept the registration of computer programs, but under the 'rule of doubt', meaning that registration did not by itself award a definite copyright to the program registered.

In 1980 however, the Copyright Act was amended and for the first time permitted copyright for software,[87] accepting the recommendation of the National Commission of New Technological Uses of Copyrighted Works (CONTU). A computer program, under the amendments, is a set of instructions to be used directly or indirectly in a computer in order to bring about a certain result. The law made it explicit that a computer program could embody an author's original creation and be a proper subject of copyright. A computer program, whether in object code (machine-readable only code) or in source code (human readable code, to be translated into object code), is a literary work under the Copyright Act.[88] Also, as well as the individual instructions (code), the structure, the sequence and organization of a program deserve protection – the non-literal components of the program (unlike the literal one, which is the object code and source code).[89] Still, a computer program lacking minimal originality or embodying the only way to achieve a particular result is not copyrightable.

The question whether user interfaces are copyrightable has also in the past received a positive answer, as the 'look and feel' of a computer program was held protectable.[90] User interfaces are very important features of computer programs as they often dictate the programs' usefulness and their possibility of commercial success. In 1991, however, it was held that the literal copying of the menu and command sequence was not infringing because the command identifiers were essential to operation and, therefore, they were a method of operation and not a protectable expression of ideas. In 1995, the Supreme Court affirmed[91] that a menu command hierarchy is uncopyrightable subject-matter, because it is a method of operation, the means by which a person operates something. These opinions, crucial for an entire sector of industry, have never been unanimous.

Under the Semiconductor Chip Protection Act,[92] mask works fixed in a semiconductor chip product (for example, code fixed in read-only memory) are protected by a special kind of intellectual property protection, borrowing from both copyright and patents. Semiconductor chips, expensive to design but cheap to copy, consist of layers composed of metallic and insulating materials on which patterns are etched or deposited. Chip protection safeguards the product mainly against copying by a photographing process. Protected chips must be registered within two years of commercial exploitation and the protection lasts for 10 years; for 10 years, the right holder enjoys an exclusive right to reproduce the mask work by any method, as well as to import or distribute a semiconductor chip that embodies the mask work. Reverse engineering is allowed as an exception to the exclusive right.

iii. Compilations-Databases

The 1976 Copyright Act affords protection to compilations, continuing the protection of the older Copyright Act of 1909. A compilation is 'a work formed by the collection and assembling of preexisting materials or of data that are selected, coordinated, or arranged in such a way that the resulting work as a whole constitutes an original work of authorship'.[93] The term compilation includes collective works. A factual compilation is eligible for copyright if it features an original selection or arrangement, but the copyright does not extend to the facts themselves.[94]

Disputes about copyright in compilations had led to court decisions in as early as the middle of the nineteenth century.[95] Ever since and until the 'famous' 1991 *Feist*[96] decision of the Supreme Court, it was thought that under no other condition did a collection of works or facts for which (only) 'sweat of the brow' could be proven (that the author devoted his labor to the creation of a compilation) and not 'real' originality, deserve copyright protection. With *Feist*, which rejected copyright protection of a telephone book, it was clarified that a mere collection of facts (such as telephone numbers) which showed no originality in the selection and arrangement of these facts (telephone numbers) was not copyrightable. In the most important and long database dispute after *Feist*, the Westlaw databases (on-line reports of court decisions) were held[97] not copyrightable, in both aspects of content (judgments are in the public domain) and also its 'own' star pagination system (enabling the reader to identify precisely where in the usually long texts of the judgments is the page break).

The modern successor of 'compilations' is databases. The legal protection of databases, which today definitely are one of the most valuable commercial products demanding substantive investments, has been the subject of intense debate in the US (as in Europe etc.). It has led to a series of draft bills introduced for discussion, with first the 1996 HR3531, Database Investment and Intellectual Property Antipiracy Bill.[98] In almost every one of the subsequent years, relevant draft bills have been introduced for discussion,[99] without any success. After the belated 2005 European evaluation[100] on the success (or rather failure) of the 1996 European Directive for the protection of databases, it seems that the whole American movement for the copyright protection of databases via statute has ceased, as no bill has been introduced since.

II. Originality

The fundamental condition of copyright protection, originality, is mingled with the question of the copyright subject-matter. Obviously, many kinds of human 'creations' are not copyrightable subject-matter, exactly because they fail the test of originality: non-original (in the sense of the organization and arrangement of their contents) databases are one example. But it is also true that a work may very well fall within copyrightable subject-matter (for example, a photograph), still simultaneously be denied copyright protection because it lacks originality (for example, when anyone using a camera would arrive at exactly the same photograph as the one for which copyright is claimed). The *sine qua non* of copyright, as stated by the Supreme Court in 1991,[101] is originality. But the question remains: what *is* originality?

The example of the photograph is indeed appropriate here, as at first glance a photograph is not perceived as a creation, an intellectual work, but more often than not a mere reproduction of a natural object or person. But in the US, as early as in 1884, the Supreme Court held,[102] dealing with a photograph of Oscar Wilde, that it was a 'writing', under its constitutional meaning and also 'new, harmonious, characteristic and graceful'. Most notably, the photograph was its creator's original mental conception, as he posed Oscar Wilde in front of the camera, selected and arranged the costume, draperies and other various accessories. It was the photographer, therefore, who was entitled to the copyright in Wilde's photograph.

The purpose of the work (e.g. is it commercial?) or its aesthetic value (e.g. should the work be really valuable aesthetically?) is irrelevant to the fundamental copyright condition of originality. Chromolithographic advertisements of a circus, portraying a ballet, a number of persons performing on bicycles, and groups of men and women whitened to represent statues, were declared by the Supreme Court[103] in 1903 proper subjects of copyright, even if their purpose was solely to advertise the circus show and they, certainly, had no connection to the fine arts. Ever afterwards, the courts were prevented from assessing the artistic merit of any artistic creations for which copyright was claimed, and focused on originality in the sense that these creation originated from a claimant.

Reproductions of works of art are also copyrightable, even if at first glance it seems as if the only true 'author' is the one who made the work of art being reproduced. If a copyist can demonstrate that he added something, not merely trivial, to the work of art reproduced, then there is no barrier to copyright.[104] Reproductions are derivative works under the Copyright Act (sec. 103a) and are separately protected as such.

Originality is seen many times through another lens of the copyrightabilty question: the 'sweat of the brow' standard. The 'sweat of the brow' is another approach to originality and it means that the author is rewarded for her significant efforts and labor towards her creation with copyright. 'Labor, skill and judgment' (a usual expression) put into the creation of a work must be proven before the exclusive copyright is granted.

In the US, where the 'sweat of the brow' approach to originality enjoyed a long history of judicial application, it was finally settled in 1991, with *Feist Publications Inc. v. Rural Telephone Service Co.*[105] that a copyright work must display some creativity in order to be regarded as an intellectual creation. Copyright protection was denied to a telephone directory, which contained people's names and telephone numbers in an alphabetical order, as this 'garden-variety white pages directory was devoid of even the slightest trace of creativity'.[106] The Court did note that what was required was a minimal creative spark, but at least, this minimal spark was required.

III. Boundaries of copyright: the fair use limitation

In every copyright system, the exclusive right to a work is not absolute, in the sense that for public interest reasons others are, under certain conditions, allowed to access and copy parts or even the whole of the work. In the US, the Copyright Act provides in sec. 107 the defense to a charge of copyright infringement of fair use. The section is the codification of the pre-existing doctrine of fair use, which originates from a decision of 1841, *Folsom v. Marsh*.[107] The four fair use factors, which were codified in 1976, come from this famous opinion of 1841 by Justice Story.[108] There is no definition in the statute of the limitation of fair use and each case is to be judged on its own facts.

The four factors to be taken into account in order to estimate whether a particular use is an unauthorized use of a copyrighted work are:[109] a. the purpose and character of the use, including whether such use is of a commercial nature or is for nonprofit educational purposes; b. the nature of the copyrighted work; c. the amount and substantiality of the portion used in relation to the copyrighted work as a whole, and d. the effect of the use upon the potential market for or value of the copyrighted work. The fact that a work is unpublished does not by itself bar a finding of fair use if such finding is made upon these four factors. These four factors, however, are not examined in isolation, but in combination with copyright's purpose of promoting science and the arts.[110] Section 107 on fair use is the main general limitation on exclusive rights, but the statute continues with some special cases, such as reproduction by libraries and archives (sec. 108), exemption of certain performances and displays (sec. 110), secondary transmissions (sec. 111) and others.

Fair use legalizes, therefore, a number of uses of another's work, such as quotation of excerpts in a review for criticism for purposes of illustration or comment, quotation of short passages in a scholarly or technical work, for illustration or clarification of the author's observations, use in a parody of some of the content of the work parodied, summary of an address or article, with brief quotations in a news report, reproduction of a work in legislative or judicial proceedings or reports, incidental and fortuitous reproduction in a broadcast and other uses.[111] There is no limit to the types of unauthorized uses of a work which may appear, and technology here plays a major role in enabling new and unforeseeable uses and reproductions of works.

The question of fair use is a mixed question of law and fact. The Supreme Court has dealt with fair use four times since the enactment of the Copyright Act. In the famous Betamax case, the *Sony* case, the private use of the machines to record ('copy') copyrighted broadcast television programs for later viewing was recognized as a fair use of these copyrighted programs, because viewers were anyway invited to watch these copyrighted programs for free at earlier times than they selected.[112] The amount of the copying here (the whole work) did not jeopardize the fair use finding. However, the unauthorized publication of (only) 300/400 verbatim quotations taken from the as yet unpublished copyrighted memoirs of former President Ford constituted unfair use because, even if insubstantial as a portion of the protected work, the passages were substantial from a qualitative point of view and played a key role in the infringing article in *Campbell.*[113]

The third Supreme Court case on fair use had to do with the well-known (and copyrighted) song 'Oh Pretty Woman', which members of the rap group 2 Live Crew chose to parody with another similar song, named 'Pretty Woman'. The Supreme Court allowed[114] in *Harper v. Row* the use as fair use, and more specifically as parody of the song. It may well have had a commercial purpose as well, but the main purpose was parody; also, the copying was not excessive in relation to the song's purpose (parody). Moreover, the second song as a rap version of the first one was unlikely to harm any potential market, as the two works served different markets. Lastly, under the fourth case's judgment,[115] the distribution and publication of a derivative work during the copyright renewal term of a preexisting work incorporated into the derivative work infringes the rights of the owner of the preexisting work where the author of that work agreed to assign the rights in the renewal term to the derivative work's owner, but died before the commencement of the renewal period, and the statutory successor does not assign the right to use the preexisting work to the owner of the derivative work.

The jurisprudence on fair use, apart from these Supreme Court cases, has been extensive, though not necessarily producing a safe guide for those aiming to invoke a fair use defense to copyright infringement. Actually, the malleability of fair use emerges starkly from the fact that all three cases (meaning *Sony, Harper* and *Campbell)* were overturned at each level of review, two of them by split opinions in the Supreme Court.[116] This is not exactly a clear guide for prospective fair use allegers. To add to these difficulties, sometimes the suit for infringement itself has a hidden agenda,[117] namely of freezing constitutionally protected free speech and not, properly, protecting economic interests. These cases have been resolved favorably for the defendants; however, they do complicate the matter further.

On top of these difficulties, the doctrine and application of fair use entered a brave new world when the question arose in connection with digital works. The recent Digital Millennium Copyright Act of 1998 (DMCA[118]) did specify that nothing in the Act would alter, among others, the fair use provisions of the 1976 Copyright Act. At the same time, however, the act of circumvention of technological protection measures protecting digital copyrighted works was outlawed and threatened with severe penalties, irrespective of whether the access achieved could be privileged as fair use or not. Whatever is fenced lies out of the reach of anyone without the 'key'.

So in this sense, any accessing of another's digital work, when it entails the circumvention of technological measures, is either legal because it is authorized by the copyright owner (and means for example, that one has the password to circumvent) or is, purely and simply, illegal 'no matter what'. Under these circumstances, it is difficult to speak of fair use of another's digital, but also technologically protected, work, as legal theorists have been quick in analyzing, demanding change and stressing threats to First Amendment values. Others search for a technical way to implement fair use by design, meaning that current digital rights management (DRM) technology, fencing copyrighted content, should also incorporate technology mimicking the intent of the law on fair use.[119]

In 2003, the Supreme Court rejected the argument that the First Amendment (freedom of speech) qualifies as independent grounds of legitimizing the unauthorized use of another's work (*Eldred v. Ashcroft*[120]). In this seminal case, the Court accepted that fair use, the limited term of copyright protection (in the sense of 'not perpetual'), together with the principle of idea/expression dichotomy appropriately safeguard the public interest in access to copyrighted works.

IV. Copyright infringement

In order to answer the question 'when is a copyright infringed?', one must know the exact content of the right to a work, secondly, what constitutes impermissible infringement and, thirdly, who may be held responsible. But from the outset it should be made clear that copyright infringement does not imply good or bad faith on the part of the infringer. Innocent infringement is as much illegal as intentional infringement. As such, liability for copyright infringement is a sort of strict liability. The defendant's state of mind does, however, play a role in determining whether the infringement in fact occurred and, secondly, in assessing damages. Infringement may also be direct or indirect; in this second sense, contributory liability may rise when a party substantially participates in an activity, knowing that copyright infringement is the probable result.

i. Exclusive rights

The Copyright Act lists in sec. 106 six exclusive rights of the copyright holder. These are: a. the reproduction right; b. the derivative work right; c. the distribution right; d. the performance right; e. the display right; and f. the digital transmission performance right. Infringement occurs, therefore, when any one of these six exclusive rights is violated. The three first exclusive rights cover all kinds of works: these are the rights of copying, recording, adaptation and publishing.

Reproduction is central in copyright law; it has been the main act for which, historically and for very many years, copyright was sought. Under 17 U.S.C.A. 101, reproduction means the right to produce a material object in which the work is duplicated, transcribed, imitated or simulated in a fixed form from which it can be perceived, reproduced or otherwise communicated, either directly or with the aid of a machine or device. The right includes copying in phonorecords, which are not copies under the statute. Display of the work is not reproduction. Reproduction presupposes that the fixation of the work in tangible form is sufficiently permanent or stable to permit it to be perceived, reproduced or otherwise communicated for a period of more than transitory duration. To constitute an actionable copy, an expression need only be a material object permanently cast in some intelligible form.[121] Temporary recording also needs the permission of the copyright owner, as reproduction, so 17 U.S.C.A sec, 111 (b) (c) specifically allows transmitting organizations (television, radio etc.) temporarily to record works for later transmission.

Derivative works include translations, arrangements, dramatizations, fictionalizations, films, recordings, abridgements, condensations or any other form in which a work may be recast, transformed or adapted (17 U.S.C.A. sec. 101). It follows that the legislative intent was expansionist: to enforce copyright to any kind of derivative work. The inclusion of derivative works in the domain of protected copyright became clear only with the 1976 Copyright Act; before then, the courts were not entirely consistent in their judgments. Translation of another's work was held not protectable in 1853, when the seminal work *Uncle Tom's Cabin* was translated, without the author's permission, into German.[122] Only in the Copyright Act of 1870 were translations included in copyright.

The distribution of copies of the work to the public by sale or other transfer of ownership or by rental or lending is the third right of the copyright owner. This is also the content of the 'first sale' doctrine, under which, once a first sale of the work has been executed, the copyright owner parts from the work so that the new owner may recognize the object embodying the copyrighted expression as her own. The object (for example, a book) is, therefore, released for any further sale, rental and lending, unless it is a phonorecord or a computer program. In this case, the industry has achieved a statutory exception to the doctrine, so that commercial further sale etc. is restricted without the permission of the copyright owner (17 U.S.C.A. sec.109 (b) (1)). The uploading of a digital file with a copyrighted work on the Internet so that anyone can download it constitutes public distribution, necessitating the author's permission.[123]

The copyright owner controls the public performance of her work. Public performance applies to literary, musical, dramatic, choreographic, pantomime, motion picture and other audiovisual works. Sound recordings are not included. To perform a work is, for example, to read a book aloud, dance a ballet, act a theatrical play. In the case of a motion picture or other audiovisual work, public performance is to show its image in any sequence or to make the sounds accompanying it audible. (sec. 101). Publicly means performing to a substantial number of persons outside the normal circle of a family and its social acquaintances. Also, acts that transmit or otherwise communicate a performance or display of the work to the public by means of any device or process, whether the members of the public are capable of receiving the performances or display in the same place or in separate places and at the same or at different times, are included (sec. 101).

ii. Infringement

What copying amounts to impermissible appropriation is not always easy to detect. The defendant may have been using public domain sources and not the plaintiff's work; in this case, there is no liability. Ideas are free; expressions are not. The clear case of copyright infringement is the unauthorized reproduction of the whole of the work as it is. But this is not always the case, as parts of a work may be copied verbatim (fair use and other limitations come into play here) but also some features of a work may be copied, such as for example, a part of a plot, a character who is or looks like the defendant's character, some musical lines, etc. These are harder cases, reminding us of Judge Story who referred to copyright as the metaphysics of the law.[124] The abstraction/subtraction approach to copyright infringement means that, before comparing two works, one has to subtract from the alleged infringing work the elements of this work which belong to the public domain or are otherwise unprotected, and then check whether what remains is so similar (or even identical) to the first work as to infringe.[125] Also, one should check whether the total concept and feel of the second work is the same as those of the first one; this is also important to a finding of infringement.[126]

In literary works, a plot may or may not be protectable, depending largely upon its character. As a plot becomes more detailed and complex, the chances that it will be held protectable also increase. When it comes to characters, they too become more protected if they are detailed. 'The less developed the characters, the less they can be copyrighted; that is precisely the penalty an author must bear for marking them too indistinctly'.[127] Characters at some point may assume personalities, so they are definitely protected. Cartoon characters, like Mickey Mouse, are also protectable.[128]

The infringement of musical works is also not always easy to clarify. The main elements used to compose music are of course in the public domain – the seven notes and generally all the building blocks of music, the kinds of rhythms etc. One may, however, recognize a musical phrase 'taken' from a song one has heard before in a way that disallows a coincidence.

Proof of infringement generally includes proof of access to the allegedly infringed work and also proof of substantial similarity to this work. On this second point, expert opinion may be used in support of an action for infringement.

V. A note on moral rights

Copyright in the US is not a two-pronged right, divided into a property right and a moral right for the author of the work (as is the case in Europe). The moral right in Europe consists of a bundle of important rights which are inalienable (are not proper 'objects' of legal transfers or waivers) and may not be inherited (in principle, moral rights 'die' with the author). The right of attribution is a moral right; so is the right of integrity. The right of attribution guarantees that the author's name as the creator of a work must always remain intact (no misattribution is allowed). The right of integrity means that the creator of a work may disallow any distortion, alteration or change of her work. Moreover, the moral right includes the right of first publication of a work and the right of withdrawal.[129] Moral rights protect personal and reputational values of the works to their creators.

The rights of (only) certain authors to attribution and integrity of their works (which rights are parts of the more general European moral right of the author) are however directly protected, by sec. 106A of the Copyright Act (after an amendment of that Act). This section is known as the Visual Artists Rights Act (VARA) of 1990 and it applies only to visual art. The Act protects (only) the rights to attribution and integrity. Any intentional distortion, mutilation or other modification of a work, if that distortion is likely to harm the creator's reputation, is unlawful.

Visual art includes: paintings, drawings, prints, sculptures and photographs, existing in a single copy or a limited edition of 200 or fewer signed and numbered copies. In the case of a sculpture, the right refers to sculptures in multiple casts, carved or fabricated sculptures of 200 or fewer that are consecutively numbered by the author and bear the signature or other identifying mark of the author. VARA also applies to photographs; a still photographic image for exhibition purposes only, existing in a single copy that is signed by the author, or in a limited edition of 200 copies or fewer that are signed and consecutively numbered by the author.[130] The destruction of a work covered by the Act is forbidden.

Apart from the VARA provisions protecting rights to visual art, there are several other possible legal mechanisms, which could be used as legal foundations to protect the moral rights of authors. For example, the alteration or distortion of a work could be regarded as a new, illegitimate derivative work from the original. A suit could be filed, then, claiming breach of the Copyright Act. The laws of privacy, defamation, the doctrine of misappropriation and the Lanham Act (which regulates unfair competition and trademarks) can be and have been used as rules protecting the moral interests of authors.[131] Some states also have enacted statutory protection of the moral rights of authors.

When the US joined the Berne Convention in 1988, it was obliged as a member state to follow Art. 6*bis* of the Convention, which explicitly protects moral rights. The US, however, stated that there already existed proper protection of moral rights, via other preexisting laws. Therefore, the US insisted that it did not have to engage in a specific amendment of the Copyright Act so as to 'fit' the Berne Convention on this particular point. This was very clearly stated in the 1988 House Report on the Berne Implementation Amendments, which concluded that existing (federal and state) law satisfied the requirements of the Convention on moral rights,[132] listing in the legislative sources the Lanham Act.

In 2003, the Supreme Court rejected[133] the application of the Lanham Act in a 'moral rights' case. In the case of a work which had passed into the public domain and which was remade and sold without any attribution to the original work, the Supreme Court held that there was no violation of Sec. 43(a) of the Lanham Act in the sense of a reverse passing off (a false designation of origin, false or misleading description of fact which was likely to cause confusion as to the origin of the goods). The term 'origin' in the Lanham Act was held to refer only to the origin of the physical goods sold and not to the intangible ideas contained in the physical goods (e.g. in a videotape). The Court stated that to hold otherwise would be to create perpetual patents and copyrights, which Congress may not do. From a public domain perspective, the decision definitely promoted the uninhibited enrichment of the public domain with new works, without the burden of finding and attributing the works used to all potential creators of these works. The conclusion, however, puts into grave doubt the allegation that the US fulfills the Berne requirements that it protects the moral rights of (all) authors.

Lastly, it should be noted that in the US there is no federal provision aiming at the protection of an artist's resale right. This is the European *droit de suite*, the resale right, under which an artist retains a right to claim a 5% royalty when her work is resold by a commercial entity like Christies'. The Copyright Office, after a long consultation and public hearings, decided against the implementation of this right, as it found no sufficient economic and copyright policy justification for the extension of the resale right in the US.[134]

b. The European Copyright Regime Today

European countries have sought to harmonize copyright rules from as far back as in 1886, when the Berne Convention for the Protection of Literary or Artistic Works was signed. The French *Association Litteraire et Artistique Internationale* (ALAL) founded in 1878, engaged in long efforts to produce a draft for this Convention. Today, all European Member States are bound by the Berne Convention, which is also *acquis communautaire*, and therefore necessarily binds every future Member State as well. The literary and artistic works of every author, a national of one European Member State, are similarly protected within the jurisdiction of all signatories to the Berne Convention. Moreover, under the Berne Convention, no registration of a work or any other formality is a condition of copyright. The Convention recognized both economic/property rights to protected works and moral rights for their creators. In this sense, it moved more towards the French *droit d'auteur* than the Anglo-Saxon copyright. Copyright lasted for 50 years after the author's death (this duration was extended with the 1993 special Directive on harmonizing the term of copyright). Every signatory may enact specific limitations and exceptions to copyright, but these exceptions and limitation must be confined to certain special cases, they must not conflict with a normal exploitation of the work and they must not unreasonably prejudice the legitimate interests of the creator (or right holder). This is the well-known 'three-steps test', which was afterwards included in other international Treaties, like TRIPs and the WIPO Copyright Treaty.

The Berne Convention is in force in a great number of countries outside the European Union, in Africa and Asia etc. The United States, bothered for more than a century by the elimination of registration as a requirement of copyright and by the moral rights provisions, finally joined the signatories in 1987.

A number of European Directives harmonize copyright. Perhaps not surprisingly, the first Directive, in 1991, dealt with copyright protection of computer programs. The course of European copyright harmonization by Directives moved from the specialized regulation of a particular kind of work or right (computer program, rental right, databases etc.) towards the general regulation of copyright (2001 EU Copyright Directive), or of all intellectual property rights together (adding patents and trademarks to copyrights: Directive on enforcement of all intellectual property rights, in 2004).

The judgments of the European Court of Justice dealing with the interpretation of the Directives also form part of European copyright law.

I. Copyrightable subject-matter

i. General Principles

Under the Berne Convention (Art. 2), all works in the artistic, scientific and literary domain are protected by copyright. As such, the Convention includes all productions of a literary, scientific and artistic nature. Specifically, Art. 2 provides that the expression 'literary and artistic works' shall include every production in the literary, scientific and artistic domain, whatever may be the mode or form of its expression, such as books, pamphlets and other writings; lectures, addresses, sermons and other works of the same nature; dramatic or dramatico-musical works; choreographic works and entertainments in dumb show; musical compositions with or without words; cinematographic works to which are assimilated works expressed by a process analogous to cinematography; works of drawing, painting, architecture, sculpture, engraving and lithography; photographic works to which are assimilated works expressed by a process analogous to photography; works of applied art; illustrations, maps, plans, sketches and three-dimensional works relative to geography, topography, architecture or science. This is, indeed, a very exhaustive list. Translations, adaptations, arrangements of music and other alterations of a literary or artistic work are also protected. The list is, moreover, only indicative, leaving open the possibility of protecting new kinds of works.

The news and simple journalistic information are not protected (Art. 4 par. 8). More generally, and as a principle of copyright law, ideas are not protected. Only the expression of these ideas may be. This is a key element in copyright law, with old roots in the European jurisprudence.[135] The European Directives on copyright do not contain a specific provision. However, under TRIPs, Art. 9(2) and the WIPO Copyright Treaty, Art.2, copyright protection extends to expressions and not to ideas, procedures, methods or operation or mathematical concepts as such.

ii. Software and Copyright

Directive 91/250/EC provides for software copyright. Software entered the class of protected works as belonging to the larger category of literary works. Obviously, this was not a result achieved easily or quickly. On the contrary, it was the end of a long procedure. In comparison with patent protection or the creation of a *sui generis* right to software, copyright protection offered the guarantee of widespread application under the Berne Convention; also, patent protection necessitated the intervention of the state with the grant of a special license (the patent). Art. 10 of TRIPs also states that software is protected as a literary work. Along with the software program itself, its preparatory material is also protected (Art. 1 par. 1 of the Directive).

Ideas and principles of a software program and the program's interface are not protectable subject-matter (Art. 1 par. 2 of the Directive). The Directive has been implemented in all Member States and the Report by the European Commission on its success was positive, noting a fall in software piracy after its implementation.

iii. Compilations-Databases

The Berne Convention protected compilations, in the sense of collections of literary or artistic works, like encyclopedias, which due to their original selection and arrangement consist intellectual creations (Art. 2 par. 5 of the Convention). In 1996, Directive 96/9/EC was enacted, dealing exclusively with databases. A 'database' under the Directive is 'a collection of independent works, data or other materials arranged in a systematic or methodical way and individually accessible by electronic or other means' (Art. 1 par. 2). The protection is extended to databases in any form (Art. 1 par. 1). Therefore, the definition of a database is extremely broad, covering databases in both electronic and non-electronic form. There is no requirement in the Directive that the aim of the database be to offer an information product to the public, which allows the retrieval of information.

The Directive creates a distinction between original and non-original databases, offering however copyright protection to both classes of databases. In the case of original databases, copyright exists in the original selection and arrangement of the database for 70 years after its creator's death. In the case of non-original databases, collections of data, materials etc., which are the result of substantive investment, the database's maker is entitled to a 15-year term of protection.

II. Originality

Originality carries great importance in copyright law. Along with the question of subject-matter, it determines, as a rule, which work will be protected and which not. Issues on originality not only derive from the very meaning of a 'work' of an 'author': the very notion of a 'work of authorship', as stated in Art. 1 par. 1 of the Berne Convention, necessarily internalizes an implicit requirement of 'originality'. Therefore, under the Convention, mere factual accounts cannot be said to fulfill the elementary condition of a 'work of authorship'. Besides, Berne precludes protection for news of the day or miscellaneous facts having the character of mere items of press information (Art. 2(8)). That copyright protection of various collections is not granted to the data or material itself is plainly stated also in TRIPs Art. 10(2) and in the World Copyright Treaty (Art. 5).

Originality should not be confused with novelty; a new work may be original enough to enjoy copyright. The work must originate from the author but, moreover, it must show some individuality. This standard is closer to the French and German tradition than to the British one. In the UK, notions like the exercise of 'skill, labor and judgment' of the author in the creation of a work still play an important role and differentiate the legal interpretation of originality from the continental one. Copyright there is more tied to the condition that a work must not be a copy of another's work to be protected (but no more is necessary).

The concept of originality is variable, as it also depends on the nature of the work examined for originality. It is also a concept which is transformed in relation to the social and cultural aspects of a particular society. The Directives, joining all Member States under the same legislative umbrella, abstained from providing a definition of originality, with the exception of software, photographs and (only in a way) databases. The result is that every Member State does demand originality as a requirement of copyright, but the construction of the term in the UK, for example, in comparison to that in France, cannot be said to be the same.

In the very important case of software, Directive 91/250/EC states that a software program is original if it is the intellectual creation of its author ('the author's own intellectual creation'). This, admittedly, lowers the standard of originality for software, in the sense that it grants copyright protection to every software program that is not the work of another person.

On photographs, Art. 6 of Directive 93/98/EC provides that photographs which are the photographer's own intellectual creation are protected by copyright. The protection of all other photographs rests with the discretion of the Member States.

On databases, Directive 96/9/EC separated two classes (without using these exact terms): original databases and non-original databases. Originality here means that the creator of a database exercised his judgment in the selection and arrangement of the materials. The Directive provides that copyright is afforded to databases which, by reason of the selection and arrangement of their contents, constitute the author's own intellectual creation. This is the same phrase we have seen in software and photographs, and takes us back to the sole condition that a work is not a copy of another's work. However, especially on databases, the maker's *sui generis* right to a non-original database is so strong (it lasts for 15 years but the term starts running again every time the database is being updated etc.) that it is fair to comment that we have a case where the strongest copyright protection is granted to the least original work, in the classical sense of the word in the intellectual property world.

III. The boundaries of copyright: exceptions and limitations

The boundaries of copyright are another crucial matter for the legislator as they delineate where copyrights end and public domain/free private uses begin. Until 2001, the European legislator had abstained from entering this area in a general way, but with the Information Society Directive an exclusive list of exceptions and limitations was promulgated.

In the national *droit d'auteur* systems, exceptions and limitations have always been strictly defined and closed.[136] The Information Society Directive naturally adhered to this mode of regulation. The harmonization of limitations, however, proved to be a highly controversial issue, which explains in large part the delay experienced not only in the adoption of the Directive itself but also in its implementation by the Member States.[137]

The implementation of the limitations in the 2001 Information Society Directive (also called the EU Copyright Directive) is entirely left to the discretion of the national legislators. These legislators could, as it follows, enact none of these exceptions and limitations and keep the exceptions and limitations already existing in their separate national statutes. Additionally, special mandatory exceptions and limitations are found in the Directives on software and database protection and on the rental right. In these cases, the limitations of the Information Society Directive are not applicable.

i. The Exceptions List in the Information Society Directive

A Member State may enact any one or more exceptions or limitations of the list included in Art. 5 of the Information Society Directive. The list has the meaning that it is exhaustive; no other limitations may be enacted after the Directive, although the Directive, wisely, did not annul in any way different limitations that the Member States already had in place.

An exception for teaching and scientific research is, first, applicable for the sole purpose of illustration and as long as the source, including the author's name, is indicated and for a non-commercial purpose. Uses for the benefit of people with disabilities, which are directly related to the disability and have no commercial nature, may also form an exception. Another possible exception covers use for reporting current events. The following exception for quotations is subject to the condition that (a) the purpose is criticism or review and (b) they relate to a work or other subject-matter which has been lawfully made available to the public; (c) the author's name is indicated, unless this is impossible and (d) their use is in accordance with fair practice and to an extent required by the specific purpose. There are exceptions for public security, for use in political speeches, for religious celebrations, for use of works of architecture or sculpture located in public places (as an incidental inclusion).

Exception (j) allows uses in advertising public exhibitions or sales of artistic works, again to the extent necessary to promote the event and excluding any commercial use. The next exceptions permit uses for caricature, parody and pastiche, use in connection with the demonstration and repair of equipment, for the reconstruction of buildings, for research or private study (allows use by communication or making available to individual members of the public by dedicated terminals on the premises or establishments, of works and other subject-matter not subject to licensing terms which are contained in their collections) and for uses in cases of minor importance, where exceptions and limitations already exist in national law, provided that they only concern analogous uses.

Another major exception is the provision on transient copies (Art. 5 par. 1), allowing the act of Internet caching and browsing.

The Directive does not deal with the problem of whether the limitations, when enacted, constitute *ius cogens*, that is whether they are or not subject to any contractual modification. Therefore, in the Information Society Directive, the resolution of *Copyright v. Contract* in the important matter of exceptions was left entirely to the discretion of Member States. In the Database and the Computer Programs Directives, where the lawful user is guaranteed a minimum of mandatory exceptions, the opposite is true.

Art. 6(4) par. 1 of the Directive provides that, in the absence of voluntary measures taken by the right holders, including agreements between the right holders and other parties concerned, Member States must take appropriate measures to ensure that right holders make available the means of benefiting from a certain number of limitations, to the extent necessary to benefit from these limitations and where the beneficiary has legal access to the protected work or subject-matter concerned. These provisions show the European Commission's stance on the need to promote contractual agreements as a preferred method of regulating the use of copyright protected works, when it comes to exceptions.

Lastly, the exceptions are in fact not applicable to on-demand services. Under Art. 6(4)4, the provisions shall not apply to works or other subject-matter made available to the public on agreed contractual terms in such a way that members of the public may access them from a place and at a time individually chosen by them. As a justification for this exclusion, the Directive (Recital 53) projects the need to secure a secure environment for the provision of interactive on-demand services, when such services are offered under a contract.

ii. Exceptions and Software

Directive 91/251/EC on software contains certain limitations of copyright (Arts. 5 and 6). A lawful user of software may create one copy of the program for safety reasons – any contractual clause to the opposite effect is void. Also, a lawful user may engage in reverse engineering of the software, in order to study the ideas and the principles etc. of the computer program and acquire information on its compatibility with other computer programs. This exception is mandatory.

iii. Exceptions and Databases

A lawful user of a database may extract and reutilize insubstantial parts of the database. This exception is mandatory. However, in combination with this exception, a lawful user of a database may not engage in acts which conflict with the normal exploitation of the database or cause damage to the legitimate interests of the maker. The Member States, under the Database Directive 96/9/EC, could provide exceptions for the extraction and reutilization of substantial parts of a database only in the case of non-electronic databases, for research and teaching or for administrative and public security purposes.

iv. The Three-Steps Test

The provision of certain exceptions in the legislation of the Member States must be construed in combination with the well-known three-steps test of the Berne Convention. The test is also included in the Information Society Directive (Art. 5 par. 5) and in Art. 13 of the TRIPs agreement.[138] Therefore, even when an exception or limitation exists and may be invoked, the act may not conflict with the normal exploitation of a work and may not cause unjustified damage to the legitimate interests of the right holder.

The interpretation of these terms (normal exploitation, unjustified damage etc.) and, generally, the application of the three-steps test rest with the judiciary. The trend is, in Europe's *droit d'auteur* system, to interpret the limitations and exceptions narrowly and in the end to give precedence to the author's rights.

IV. Copyright infringement

Copyright infringement depends on the scope of the rights that the law confers on the right holder. These rights have been constantly expanded ever since the 1710 Statute of Anne. Generally, these rights are: the right of reproduction of the protected work, the right of distribution, the rental or lending right, the public performance right, the right to communicate a work to the public, the right of adaptation and the right to make derivative works. These rights are exclusive, in the sense that they belong only to the right holder, who has a right against any third party to preclude or punish infringement. As a result of the EU Duration Directive, these rights endure for the life of the author plus 70 years. The nature of these rights had to change along with technology, leaving the legislator in a constant race with technological possibilities which made, for example, the reproduction of works as fast as the click of a mouse.

i. Exclusive Rights

a. The right to reproduction The right of reproduction of a work is at the heart of copyright. It is protected in the Berne Convention (Art. 9) and the Rome Convention (Art. 1e). The meaning of reproduction of a work has changed with the years, due to the development of new technology, resulting in a very inclusive definition of what reproduction is in the Information Society Directive, Art. 2 sub. A. There, the European legislator opted for a very extensive definition of reproduction, joining direct and indirect reproduction, temporary or permanent reproduction and reproduction by any means and in any form, in whole or in part, as falling within the absolute and exclusive right of the author.

The Database and the Software Directives contain different provisions for the reproduction of these particular protected works, appearing narrower than the 'sweeping' Information Society Directive on reproduction. On databases, the Directive's terminology is new, referring to the exclusive right of extraction and re-utilization of parts of a protected database. The need to re-characterize copyrights in this way remains unclear. The extraction right could be interpreted as the well-known right to reproduction, as extraction is termed the permanent or temporary transfer of the contents of a database to another medium by any means and in any form.

Digitization of a work, a most significant act, must be construed as constituting a reproduction of that work under the Directive. Therefore it is fair to say that we now have a broad-ranging reproduction right in Europe. Transient and incidental copying have been the subject of a limitation in the Directive, under Art. 5.1, in order to legitimize acts like internet browsing and caching.

b. The right to adaptation of the work The right to adaptation of a work remains largely unregulated at the European Community level. Only the Directive on the protection of computer programs expressly provides for the exclusive right of adaptation, translation or arrangement of a protected computer program (Art. 4b). The right to adaptation is left to the separate regulations of the Member States, which have, however, all introduced its protection, for example as a separate restricted act or as part of the more general reproduction right.

The boundaries of an adaptation of a work are defined in strict relation to the originality standard that a particular Member State uses in order to offer protection to works of authorship. An adaptation of another's work is a derivative work, which, in principle, necessitates the author's consent.

c. The right of distribution The Information Society Directive includes broad distribution rights. The author is entitled to authorize any distribution to the public by sale or otherwise of her work (Art. 4). Distribution here entails distribution in tangible form. The Rental and Lending Directive also provides for broad distribution rights to the benefit of performers, phonogram producers, film producers and broadcasters. Another way of expressing the same notion is the 'making available' right, which we see in the Renting and Lending Directive; this clearly signals the distribution right. The same right is also provided in the Directives dealing with software and databases. On databases, the special terminology used there, on the right of re-utilization of parts of a database, poses some questions, but re-utilization in the sense of selling physical copies of a database could be construed as distribution of this database. There are here, however, problems of interpretation.

d. The rental/lending right The rental and lending right of a work has been harmonized mainly by the Rental Right Directive (92/100/EEC), although the right applies only to the rental and lending of physical copies of a copyright work. The rental and lending right is in essence part of the wider distribution right. The right does not apply to works of applied art, buildings and databases protected by the *sui generis* right. The Computer Programs Directive also protects the right of making available for use, for a limited period of time and for profit-making purposes, a protected computer program, and therefore we must deduce that this also refers to a right to lend a protected computer program. Authors, performers, phonogram producers and film producers are beneficiaries of the rental/lending right.

The lending right may be exercised only when the lending of the work is done by public institutions such as public libraries and archives, school libraries, research libraries and the like, for non-profit purposes. The European Court of Justice has ruled that, when a Member State (in this case, Portugal and Spain[139]) has incorporated an exception for the benefit of public libraries so that all public libraries (all archives, all educational and academic institutions) are exempt from paying any remuneration for public lending, then the Directive has not been correctly implemented. The Court demanded that a valid exception cannot apply to all the institutions of a kind, such as all academic libraries. The obligation to pay remuneration for public lending may also not be limited in time.[140]

Libraries' organizations, such as the International Federation of Libraries Associations and Institutions, have voiced their opposition to the public lending right,[141] as they see the obligation to pay remuneration for public lending of books as important barriers to the fulfillment of their purposes.

e. The public performance right Public performances apply to literary, dramatic and musical works. These acts are restricted and controlled by the copyright holder of these works. These works may, therefore, not be shown or broadcast in public without the copyright holder's permission. The definition of what a 'public' performance is may present problems, as, for example, playing music to a group of 10 friends is not playing it to the 'public'. The public performance may be direct (when the public is present at the time of the performance) or indirect (when the work is performed as a film, a video etc.).

When the exact definition of 'the public' came before the European Court of Justice, in a case where hotel owners had installed TV sets in every room (is this a private or a public place? do the guests of this room constitute 'public'?), the Court declared that the cable and satellite Directive did not define whether that act amounted to a communication to the public and that this was a matter for national law.[142] This led, as expected, to a variety of definitions by the Member States.

f. The right to communicate a work The right to communicate a work to the public is provided in the Information Society Directive, Art. 3. It entails communication of literary, musical and artistic works, sound recordings, films and broadcasts to the public and it covers a general right of communication to the public by any means or process other than the distribution of physical copies of the work to the public. The difference between the right to communicate a work to the public and the right to a public performance of this work is that, in the case of the right to communicate a work to the public, the public is not present at the place where the communication originates (recital 23 of the Information Society Directive).

g. The 'making available' right Under Art. 3(1) and (2) of the Information Society Directive, authors, performers, phonogram producers and producers of films and broadcasting organizations enjoy the right to make their works available to the public in such a way that the public may access these works from a place and at a time individually chosen by them. This is called 'the making available right', again a sub-species of the much older right of distribution/communication of a work to the public. The distribution in this case occurs through interactive networks such as, of course, the Internet. The right is designed in such a way as to cover all forms of transmission that allow for a degree of interactivity. Music downloads at will as well as listen-only services are covered. The right in the Information Society Directive originates from the WIPO Treaties (WIPO Copyight Treaty Art. 8, WIPO Performers and Phonograms Treaty, Arts. 10 and 14).

The 'making available' right marked a further expansion of rights for copyright holders, as the previous state of the law, mainly governed by the Berne Convention, did not specifically include the recipient-initiated transmissions covered by exclusive rights.

h. The resale right The resale right, or the *droit de suite* (the right to 'follow a work') has been implemented in Europe after a rather long deliberation by Directive 2001/84/EC on the resale right. The resale right is sometimes classified as a moral right and not an economic one.

This right originates from Art. 14*ter* of the Berne Convention. The right secures for the creator of a work of art a royalty for that work when it is resold. The aim is to protect artists who have sold their works at low prices, but who later one become famous, only to see their works being resold at high prices, to which they have no claims. The right applies to any works of graphic or plastic art such as pictures, collages, paintings, drawings, engravings, prints, lithographs, sculptures, tapestries, ceramics, glassware and photographs. Copyright in the work must not have expired. The sale must involve a gallery, a saleroom, an art dealer, a professional auction house (such as Christies'); sales between private individuals remain unaffected by the resale right, irrespective of prices. The artist is entitled to a percentage of the price which Member States may define in a changing scale, depending on the total price of the work (this percentage is usually a 4% of the price achieved, when this price is over 50,000 euros). The resale right is inalienable; it may not be transferred to third parties, except to the artist's heirs upon her death. Any contractual provision to the contrary is null and void. Therefore, the right seems to be a property right, as it involves right to remuneration, but its personal character is equally difficult to ignore.

i. Moral rights The discussion of the author's moral rights in the European copyright system deserves to be somewhat longer than in the American one, because in Europe moral rights constitute an integral part of the author's rights, whereas in the US, for example, the Visual Artists Rights Act recognizes moral rights only in particular cases. Generally speaking, in the European national legislative schemes moral rights rank as a category at least the equal of economic rights.[143]

The author's moral right to her work (the term coming from the French *droit moral*) is recognized in various European Member States and originates in Europe (mainly France and Germany). In reality, the moral right encompasses a set of rights, namely the right to paternity (also called the right of attribution, meaning the right to be recognized as the creator of a work), the right to integrity (the right to safeguard the integrity of the work), the right to first publication of the work, the right to access one's own work and the right to withdraw a work from the public (for example, when the creator has written a book which no longer properly expresses her views). A state may have incorporated the author's moral rights not as a 'set', including all of the above; usually, the main features of a moral right are the right to attribution (paternity) and the right to integrity. In different European jurisdictions we also find the author's moral right either as a generally expressed right or as a detailed set of different moral rights.

Moral rights cases in France have appeared from as early as 1845. In *Marle v. Lacordaire*,[144] a writer (Marle) edited and published a book entitled *Les Conférences de l'abbé Lacordaire*, which contained sermons by the abbé Lacordaire, published without his consent. The Court ruled for the abbé Lacordaire, explaining that the author's right to his moral personality had been violated (this would be properly termed today the violation of the moral right to first publication of a work). In another old French case, in 1867, by the Supreme Court, *Delprat v. Charpentier*,[145] it was decided that a writer was the absolute owner of his work, which might not be modified, or even more so, distorted without his knowledge and consent. Therefore in this case it was held that the editor of a journal was not allowed to modify an author's text without securing the author's approval, prior to publication. The same rule in a different setting, which concerned the publication of cartoons of an author altered (for example, the dialogue was changed) by another one was again confirmed in 1899, in *Agnes Dit A. Sorel v. Fayard Frères*.[146] A very interesting case was the *Camoin* case,[147] where (almost unbelievably) pieces of pictures thrown by the painter in the rubbish as unacceptable were found by a rag picker, joined together and sold many years later by art collectors. The battle between the ownership over the physical object incorporating the works (clearly the art collector's, as throwing anything to the bin legally means an abandonment of property) and the painter who claimed the right to the work itself was resolved in favor of the artist. His personality was held to have been violated, as an artist has a right to his work, unrestrained, as an expression of his thought, his talent, his art and in philosophical words, his individual self.[148]

As important as the moral rights of the author may be in the national legislations of the Member States and as long as their history may have been, there has been no harmonization of the moral right at the European level by a Directive or as part of a Directive. The reasons for this arguably important omission are generally twofold: firstly, the European Commission's competence in regulating economic rights is beyond doubt, a fact not as easy to state as regards harmonization in the realm of culture and, secondly, the author's moral rights are rooted more firmly in the continental legal systems but not in the UK or Ireland. From the *acquis communautaire* we can deduce that the European Commission has kept a clear distance from any real attempt to harmonize intellectual property rights apart from the strictly economic ones, that is, moral rights. The debate about the substantial desirability of strong moral rights in theory and in various settings, as these rights for many people represent an undue strengthening of the bargaining position of an author, to the detriment of the entrepreneurs undertaking to exploit the work. Agreement on these matters seems far away at the moment.

However, the Berne Convention is clear in Art. 6*bis*, and provides that, independently of the author's economic rights, and even after the transfer of the these economic rights, the author shall have the right to claim authorship of the work and to object to any distortion, mutilation or other modification of, or other derogatory action in relation to, the work which would be prejudicial to the author's honor or reputation. This was a discretionary provision in the Rome version of the Convention in 1928, which became obligatory in the Brussels version in 1948. Thus, the Berne Convention protects the two main features of an author's moral rights: the right to attribution and the right to paternity.

Some countries such as Greece have implemented, quite apart from any legal obligation to implement a Treaty etc., an author's moral rights as a more complete set, including the right to first publication, the right of withdrawal and the right to access the work after it has been sold. Comparably, in the UK, the 1998 Copyright Act defines four distinct moral rights, namely: the right to be identified as author or film director, the right to object to derogatory treatment of a work, the right against false attribution of a work and the right to privacy in private photographs and films. In some countries, moral rights endure as long as the economic rights to a work; in others, the moral rights survive the expiration of the copyright term. In general, there are Member States where an extensive protection of a variety of moral rights has been recognized.

ii. Infringement

Actions violating any one of the above exclusive rights or the moral rights of the authors constitute copyright infringement. Under the 2004 Intellectual Property Enforcement Directive, the Member States are required to institute special procedures under special rules before the courts to enforce (all) intellectual property rights. The Directive marks a clear European tendency towards a 'holistic' approach to all rights to protected works (copyrights), patents and trademarks, along with the will of the European legislator to tighten protection of these particular rights.

The separation of idea/expression, the public domain nature of facts, ideas, methods of operation, mathematical axioms, etc. also constitute boundaries of copyright infringement. The European standard for originality, a compromise between the typical copyrights of Member States (Cyprus, Malta, Ireland and the United Kingdom) and the *droit d'auteur* continental systems, is that the work must be the author's own intellectual creation (an expression we find in, for example, the Directive for the protection of software, the protection of photographs as works etc.). Only in Europe, however, can we find copyright protection of a collection of unoriginal facts as a database, using as a standard the substantiality of a particular investment. Infringement here is unrelated to any notion of an author's own intellectual creation.

c. A Comparative Perspective on Copyright Law in the US and Europe

The view that common law copyright is founded on economic-utilitarian considerations, while civil law copyright is more oriented towards the protection of the natural law rights of the authors seems today to deserve closer examination. It is evident from the recitals and the texts of the European copyright Directives that the European Commission is mainly concerned with the strengthening of the European copyright industry in a competitive global market. Investments towards the creation of information products are seen, in the recitals and the texts of the Directives, as primarily worthy of legal protection, the protection of laws which always offer stronger copyright protection, never less. Additionally, we lack studies on the balancing of costs and benefits, costs to the public domain and to the interests of the public in obtaining access to information. The stories told in the recitals and the texts are stories about the dangers of piracy to the production of information products, about the necessity to safeguard costly industry investments in the creation of information goods, about the threats that the new digital copying technologies pose to remuneration for investments etc. This is not 'natural law', '*droit d'auteur*' like prose – it is purely an economic-utilitarian one.

The European Commission is entitled to intervene, legislate and harmonize laws of the Member States in order to promote the free circulation of goods and services within the Community. It is in this legal context that the Directives were promulgated. As a major purpose of the new legislation, a purpose sometimes confessed in writing, was to equal or, if possible, to surpass the US production of information goods (such as databases or software), the invocation of economic-utilitarian arguments is not an entirely surprising result. It clearly fits the picture of a competitive market for information products, an environment where pictures of the deserving artist-genius, tied to her work as a mother to her child, does not fit. The degree of closeness that the European legislator will allow to this bond depends not upon the just rights of the creators, their just remuneration for their work, but upon the necessities of a functioning market for information goods.

The refusal of the European legislator to harmonize (or even to refer to) the moral rights of authors again marks, among other things, an (willful or not) approach to the US copyright system. Moreover, it necessarily signals that the European legislator did not see the matter of the protection of moral rights as equally deserving of protection, as obviously the clearly economic exploitaiton rights. In this, the European legislator again seemed to side with the interests of publishers and generally the representatives of the content industries, and not with the interests of the creators themselves, as persons. The diplomatic way in which the European legislator escaped the delicate and major problem of how to award the initial copyright to the natural person who created a computer program and not, directly, to the company who hired her also shows one more deviation from the classic *droit d'auteur* system, with its known concern for and focus on the rights of the creator, in favor of one much closer to an economic-utilitarian one. While perhaps risking an overstatement (but perhaps not), it is true that in his effort to harmonize the two internal tendencies within the European Member States, one towards the *droit d'auteur* and one towards common law copyright, the European legislator favored the latter.

And in some ways, actually, the European legislator went even further than his American counterpart. The Digital Millenium Copyright Act definitely restricts fair use in the digital environment with its anti-circumvention rule in a very important way.[149] But the Information Society Directive goes further. It criminalizes even mere possession of anti-circumvention devices, threatening possession of the devices with the same punishment as for the circumvention itself. And it prohibits anti-circumvention irrespective of whether the purpose is access or copying, whereas the DMCA prohibits it only when it aims to gain unauthorized access and not when the act circumvents, for example, printing limitations protected by code. Also, the European legislator seems content with the provision that the exceptions and limitations of copyright should be respected by the right holders, who now bear a (simple) duty to safeguard their exercise by the users by taking voluntary measures.[150]

The French *Cour de Cassation* ruled, in the *Mullholand Drive* case,[151] that the exceptions and limitations are not users' rights, in the technical sense of a right. The French Supreme Court's interpretation of copyright's exceptions as not users' rights is bound to be influential at least in Europe. This interpretation may lie behind the decision of a small District Court in Finland. The decision of this court protected a user, who used an anticircumvention device (the

DeCSS). This protection was achieved not by engaging in difficult philosophical and legal constructions of whether a user has what rights towards a protected work and what an exception is. The protection was the result of simply declaring that DeCSS was not an 'effective' technological protection measure, because it was widely available online. Therefore, the use of the DeCSS was not prohibited by the law: the law prohibited *effective* technological measures. It is too early to judge whether this decision will survive attack in higher courts. Yet it did give rise to articles entitled 'keep on hacking'[152] etc. In the US, conversely, the argument about ineffectiveness ('but this device is everywhere!') only produced a comment that it is unacceptable.[153] But in this case, it was not an argument connected to the very wording of the statute in question.

The US Digital Millennium Copyright Act does not go so far as to prohibit circumvention, when that Act does not aim at gaining access to the protected work (for example, when its purpose is, after gaining legal access to the work, to use and reproduce the work). Access is the center of the section on circumvention, not reproduction or use. Legal access, then, but circumvention of technological protection measures in order to be able, for example, to print an article does not fall within the anti-circumvention provision of the DMCA, while it certainly does when it comes to applying the Information Society Directive's Art. 6.

The US distance from the natural law rights of authors is further accentuated with the final rejection by the Copyright Office of the implementation of the resale right, the European *droit de suite*. Again, Europe enacted a whole Directive on the resale right, after many controversies, but again the arguments put forward kept a distance from the natural law rights of authors. Curiously enough, almost as a matter of a habit impossible to abstain from, the European legislator justified the resale right with mostly economic-utilitarian arguments. One wonders whether, without these economic foundations, the resale right, a right so closely tied to natural law rights of authors, this inalienable, unassignable, sometimes classified even as a clear *moral, personal* right would be left unjustifiable.[154] The US, after a long procedure of deliberations, rejected the resale right, again mainly on economic-utilitarian justifications.

Indeed, the European Commission goes even further than the US when it comes to the protection of unoriginal collections of facts, databases, with *sui generis* copyright protection, which according to many results in a stronger protection of data than the copyright protection of a literary work. It is in the recitals and the very wording of this Directive, the Directive on database protection (96/9/EC), that the terminology and justification are almost absolutely pure economic-utilitarian (the purpose is to strengthen the European database market *vis-a-vis* the US one; the method is to award a *sui generis* right to the maker of an unoriginal database because of *substantial investment*; exceptions and limitations only in favor of an lawful user of the database etc.).

The discussion on database protection in the US seems to have stopped, after the steady failure of various draft bills, proposed to the Congress. But the European Commission remained loyal to economic-utilitarian justifications for database protection even when, under the Report on the success or failure of the Directive, the Report turned out definitely negative. Five years after the enactment of the Directive, the production ratio of databases between US and Europe was even worse for the European Community than before the Directive (a one to two database production rate in favor of the US in 1996 worsened for the European Community to one to three in favor of the US, in 2004[155]). However, as much as the main economic-utilitarian argument supporting this peculiar *sui generis* right to non-original databases collapsed, under the weight of the Report by the right's own 'fathers', the European Community has hitherto shown no tendency whatsoever to repeal the Directive altogether, or at least to repeal this *sui generis* protection, whereas both proposals were cited, among others, in the Report as possible for the future.

This abstention reveals perhaps more that anything else that the real reason behind intellectual property rules promulgated by the European Commission towards harmonization and promotion of the European market for information products was in fact the legislative expression of the will of lobbying parties who stand to benefit from the rules, of the direct beneficiaries, such as the European database producers and big publishing houses. This is an expression neither related to any previous measurement of costs and benefits of the rules examined and proposed, nor even connected to a real intention that harmonization be a goal in itself.[156]

The way the European Union proceeded with enacting European copyright laws, and especially the Directives, followed a 'piecemeal' approach:[157] from the special protection of certain information works/products, such as software and databases, to an impressive body of specialized rules which however, lacks a measure of coherence.[158] Many crucial topics (authorship, moral rights, the relation of contracts with the exceptions and limitations of copyright, the safeguarding of the freedoms of users in relation to digital rights managements etc.) remain untouched by the harmonization process.[159] In total, the trend of the Directives represent an unmistakable shift from the traditional view of copyright as an author's personal right, a right stemming from her personality, to the economic-utilitarian approach, in short, to the common law copyright.[160] And from this aspect, the US legislator appears a thousand times more sincere, and loyal to the American copyright history and tradition, than his European counterpart.

In this shift towards common law copyright, the European legislator has also shown an impressive indifference to the results of academic studies and writings, sometimes commissioned by the European Commission itself. A remarkable example is the 'forward-looking package' on Intellectual Property, released by the European Commission on July 16, 2008. The package includes the proposal for a 45-year extension of the (50-year) copyrights of performing artists and phonogram producers. But the proposal completely ignores and fails even to mention one major study on EU copyright law and policy, drafted on the Commission's own tender,[161] in which the idea for a term extension was rejected after a thorough economic and legal analysis as harmful to consumers and society at large, while benefiting only a small handful of already famous recording artists and their record labels. This total indifference gave rise to the declaration that the Commission's policies are less the product of a rational decision-making process than of lobbying of stakeholders.[162]

It is true that, while the European legislator left important matters such as the author's moral rights to the discretion of the national legislators, this does not mean that the statutes of the Member States on copyright are not (also) founded on natural law rights of the author's natural rights. On the contrary, statutes such as the statutes of France and Greece contain analytical provisions protecting the moral rights of authors. In the legislative schemes of German and French law and their many derivatives, moral rights rank as a category at least the equal of economic rights.[163] For example, under the Greek statute, L. 2121/1993, Art. 4, the right to paternity, the right to integrity, the right to access one's work, the right to withdraw one's work from circulation are all protected in detail. Besides, even the UK statute[164] also provides for the protection of the author's right to be identified, his right to object to derogatory treatment, his rights against false attribution, his rights of privacy etc. In this respect, if we see the totality of the civil (Continental) copyright law, mainly European countries, the statutes remain founded upon both economic-utilitarian and natural law principles upholding the rights of authors. In this sense, the Member States 'look' at the author's rights as also resting on natural law. This is why we see in the copyright treatises of various European states statements such as 'the common law system of copyright is centered around the work, whereas the civil (Continental) law system is centered around the author' etc. But the trend, coming from upwards harmonization by the European Union, is definitely towards the strengthening of only the economic-utilitarian aspects of copyright laws. And we do not yet know, nor we can foresee the future with any real certainty, to what extent this trend and upwards harmonization, in connection with other lobbying forces and perceived market necessities, will, at some point, have an effect upon the national laws of the Members States, in opposition to the natural law rights of authors. As Directive by Directive is incorporated in the Member States' copyright statutes, they definitely alter the picture of the principles upon which the copyright system rests, with an unmistakable mark of the priority of economic considerations.

3. A NOTE ON TRADEMARKS

Trademarks have existed since antiquity. People who sold products were always interested in marking them with signs showing where those products came from. It was important in many cases, including when goods were recovered at sea; with the marks, the true owners could be identified.[165]

A word, a design, a product shape, a number, a slogan may be a trademark, if it identifies and distinguishes a company's products from another's. The key concept in trademark law is distinctiveness; the capacity to distinguish takes the places of novelty in patent law and originality in copyright law. The initial target of the law is to indicate the source of the product sold, so that the consumer may match her desires to a particular product. A trademark provides information to the consumer, to the public, which may not be deceived. Apart from this initial observation, the common and civil law trademark systems differ in their approaches to trademarks.

a. US Trademark Law

i. Basics

Trademarks in the US were never constitutionally protected like, for example, patents. They were never incorporated as products of the mind in the Patent and Copyright clause. The power of Congress to regulate trademarks was sharply limited in 1879, when the Supreme Court ruled that only trademarks involved in interstate commerce could be federally regulated, and only under the Commerce clause.[166] The reason was that, according to the Court, a trademark was neither an invention, a discovery, nor a writing within the meaning of the eighth clause of the eighth section of the first article of the Constitution.

In the US, the first function of a trademark is to identify source by giving information. The purpose of this identification is to help a consumer avoid confusion as to where a product comes from (McCarthy 2002). The public is the object of protection and must not be misled. Actual confusion about a mark and mere *likelihood* of confusion were both recognized as actionable infringements of trademarks. Trademarks in this sense are devices for communicating product quality information to the market, and the goal of trademark law is to prevent others from using similar marks to deceive or confuse consumers. In this sense, the core of trademark law is based on a model which could be called the 'information transmission model': trademarks are devices for communicating product quality information to the market (Bone 2005).

Apart from that, a vibrant dispute about the objectives of trademark law is evident (Miller and Davis 2000). Trademarks are also seen as property of the people who 'created' them and who have 'invested' in promoting a business, often by costly advertising. In this sense, trademark protection comes to safeguard the abstract notion of another's goodwill against free riding. Here the focus is on sellers, against unfair misappropriation of their marks. The misappropriation of another's goodwill by using another's trademark or a close imitation of the mark approached the idea of misappropriation of another's property and brought closer the related but different torts of trademark infringement and unfair competition.[167] Moreover, it is also supported[168] that the traditional view on trademark infringement was producer-centered (not consumer-centered) and rested on natural law principles for the protection of property.

ii. Dilution

Trademarks are also protected against dilution, which is, under the Lanham Act, par. 43c, the lessening of the capacity of a famous mark to identify and distinguish goods and services, regardless of the presence or absence of competition between the owner of the famous mark and other parties or likelihood of confusion, mistake or deception. Dilution is designed to protect the goodwill, the marketing value or selling power associated with famous marks, regardless of whether consumers are confused.

Dilution entered federal law as late as in 1995. Congress amended the Trademark Act (Lanham Act) to provide a remedy for dilution (blurring and/or tarnishment of famous marks). The Lanham Act was again amended in 2006 by the Trademark Dilution Revision Act of 2006.[169] The law overrules an important decision on trademark dilution, namely *Moseley v. Secret Catalogue*.[170]

In *Moseley*, the Supreme Court, interpreting the (amended) Lanham Act on dilution, held that proof of actual dilution is a condition of the remedy. In this case, owners of the famous mark VICTORIA'S SECRET, selling lingerie, sued a couple (the Moseleys) who operated a store in Boston selling sex toys, gag gifts and lingerie. The store was initially named VICTOR'S SECRET and then, after protests by the onwners of VICTORIA'S SECRET, was renamed VICTOR'S LITTLE SECRET. The Court declared that whatever difficulties of proof may be entailed, they are not an acceptable reason for dispensing with proof of an essential element of a statutory violation. The Lanham Act demanded actual dilution to be proven, and in this case actual dilution was not supported by the evidence. Concrete loss of sales because of actual dilution was not necessary to be proven, but the existence of harm by dilution (not its magnitude) had to be proven. The new rule on actual dilution, coming as a response to this judgment, is that now the plaintiff needs to prove a likelihood of dilution and not actual dilution.

The theoretical basis of trademark protection, therefore, is no longer the justice of protecting the public from confusion. People buying sex toys in the VICTOR'S LITTLE SECRET store know that they are not buying a product by VICTORIA'S SECRET. Nor can the Lanham Act be justified here upon a theory of misappropriation related to unfair competition. The turn is towards protection of a mark *qua* mark, a trademark valuable in itself, the use of which must always be condoned by its 'owner' in every case.

iii. Some final comments

The story of trademark protection in the US is a story of constant expansion of protection. 'Use' of a trademark, as a condition for registration of a trademark, became 'intent to use' sufficient for registration. Even when consumer confusion was almost a fact, early courts had denied relief when the plaintiff could not prove that this confusion resulted in diversion of *his* customers (and, hence, tie the illegal act with a concrete personal loss[171]). However, this demand for proof of consumer 'confusion' as a condition of a lawsuit soon became instead demand for proof of mere 'likelihood of confusion'.

The requirement of competition between the parties was also relaxed in time. In 1917, for example, in *Aunt Jemima Mills Co v. Rugney & Co*,[172] it was held that the mark 'Aunt Jemima's' for pancake batter could not be used for pancake syrup, even if the products were completely different and people could not be deemed to mistake flour for syrup. And in 1928, in *Yale Electric Corp. v. Robertson*,[173] the use of the nark YALE, known for locks, was disallowed for flashlights and batteries, even though these products were clearly dissimilar. What mattered, as we see in the judgments, was the producers' interests in their reputation as other sellers, even in wholly different markets, could offer products of lower quality but with the same marks.

Similarly and most importantly, (actual) dilution became 'likelihood of dilution'. And in the digital world, the 1999 Anti-Cybersquatting Consumer Protection Act is a new extension of trademark protection.

From the non-constitutionally founded protection of the public from misinformation as to products, trademark law turned to unfair competition models of protection against the usurpation of a competitor's goodwill. Then, it moved again, towards the protection of any unauthorized use, from non-competitors (simple users), and for non-commercial purposes (such as, for example, pure parody) – uses that, in copyright terminology would be declared fair uses of another's trademark.

Trademarks, it follows, have acquired an ever stronger power as owned intellectual objects: they are not only protected *erga omnes* and for unlimited time, but also for any non-commercial purpose and in no connection with any non-related product and actually with any product sold at all. Legilsation has been voted on without any previous evidence as to the harms and risks it purported to address: dilution is alleged to protect consumers against increased search costs, but 'whether this is significant risk in the real world is unknown and unproven' (McCarthy 2004).

At the same time, unlike patent and copyright, trademark law does not tie its prerequisites for protection to a need for additional incentives. We have no evidence to prove that society, or even an efficient market, needs more trademarks. It also does not define its protection to ensure an appropriate incentive level. As a result, it is supported (Lunney 1999) that trademark's expansion risks creating an incentive structure fundamentally at odds with social welfare: 'trademark monopolies' (Lunney 1999).

b. EU Trademark Law

Trademark law in the European Union was harmonized as early as in 1989 by the Trademark Directive 89/104/EEC. The Directive was supplemented later by Council Regulation 40/94 on the Community Trademark. Ever since, the European Court of Justice has heard many trademark cases, with the result that a number of trademark judgments, construed the Trademark Directive. Additionally, unlike patents, the EU has managed to enforce a procedure for Europe-wide trademark protection, with the registration of a 'Community' trademark with the Office of Harmonization in the Internal Market (Trade Marks and Designs), located in Alicante, Spain.

Likelihood of confusion is a steady foundation of European trademark protection. Two marks will be compared as to similarities of sight, sound and meaning. Similarity as to products and services is also a prerequisite. We must note that the products/services compared need not be in direct competition with each other. In this, the European law has followed the expansion of trademark protection we have also seen in the US laws. Clothes and perfumes, for example, have been found to be related products. Likelihood of confusion is mainly dependant upon the indication of origin of the mark. Both the Community Trademark Regulation and the Trademark Directive stress that trademarks are protected in particular to guarantee the trademarks as indications of origin.

Under the Trademark Directive, likelihood of affiliation (not only likelihood of confusion) is also considered. In particular, if the affiliation of one product with another may lead to likelihood of confusion, then this affiliation is actionable. Likelihood of affiliation cannot stand alone, as it does under US trademark law.

Apart from this, the European Directive on trademark protection does not refer explicitly to trademark 'dilution' or 'unfair resemblance', although these terms were developed in many European jurisdictions, as supplements to classic trademark protection. It does incorporate a form of anti-dilution trademark protection. Under Art. 4 para. 3 of the Directive, a (Community) trademark shall not be registered if it is identical with, or similar to, an earlier Community trademark and is to be registered for goods and services which are not similar to those for which the earlier Community trademark is registered, where the earlier Community trademark has a reputation in the Community and the use of the later trademark without due cause would take unfair advantage of or be detrimental to the distinctive character of the repute of the earlier Community trademark. Also, Art. 5 para. 2 provides that the proprietor of a mark shall be entitled to disallow third parties from using any sign which is identical or similar to the trademark in relation to goods and services which are not similar to those for which the trademark is registered, where the trademark has a reputation in the Member State and where use of the sign without due cause takes unfair advantage of, or is detrimental to, the distinctive character or the repute of the trademark. The Articles are, in one view, one example of the unfortunately usual bad drafting by the European legislator (Chrissanthis 2004).

It follows that trademarks which have a reputation (the Directive does not use the words 'famous marks', as it does not use the word 'dilution') and the use of which for dissimilar goods and services causes unfair advantage or is detrimental to the distinctive character or the repute of the trademarks are protected by EU trademark law. Therefore, it is fair to state that the US notion of dilution is wider than its European counterpart: in Europe, the 'owner' of the mark must also prove unfair advantage or detriment (=harm), before securing the exclusive use of the mark also for dissimilar goods and services.

Apart from the indication of origin, it is clear from the above that, as the European Court of Justice has accepted (Cornish & Llewelyn 2003), the system protects the advertising and 'investment' function of marks. In this sense, the focus has changed from consumers (protection of the public) to producers (protection of marks' owners), and therefore from an unfair competition model towards a property rights' model.

NOTES

1. Its history is described in some detail in the second chapter.
2. What is here omitted refers to copyrights.
3. 409 U.S. 63, 93 S.Ct. 253, 34 L.Ed.2d 273 (1972).
4. 437 U.S. 584 (1978).
5. 450 U.S. 175 (1981).
6. No. 92-1381, Fed. Cir. July 29, 1994 (en banc).
7. See letter by the representing firm of http://www.swiss.ai.mit.edu/6805/assorted-short-pieces/alappat-summary.html, last accessed April 30, 2009.
8. Id, per Judge Newman.
9. 149 Fed. 3rd 1368 (Fed.Cir. 1998).
10. See Hulse R. (2000).
11. *State Street & Trust Co. v. Signature Financial Group, Inc.*, 149 F.3d 1368 (Fed. Cir. 1998).
12. *Amazon.com. Inc v. barnesandnoble.com, Inc.*, 73 F. Supp. 2d (W.D.Wash. 1999), vacated and remanded, 239 F. 3d 1343 (Fed. Cir. 2001).
13. See http://igdmlgd.blogspot.com/2007/10/amazon-one-click-patent-rejected-by-us.html, last accessed April 30, 2009.
14. See Bednarz (2006).
15. Example by Hulse (2000), 7.
16. For an analysis of this debate see Noehrenberg (2006) pp. 170–86.

17. See for example AMA Council on Ethical and Judicial Affairs, 'Ethical Issues in the Patenting of Medical Procedures', 53 *Food & Drug LJ* 341 (1998). The AMA strongly disfavors medical and surgical procedure patents, stating that they compromise patient privacy rights, practitioners' freedom, access to information and affordable access to health care.
18. See also Melvin (2007). Melvin refers to the immunity from liability for infringing a medical procedure patent which has been codified in 35 U.S.C. section 287(c), leaving in fact, any medical procedure patent violation without any remedy.
19. 447 U.S. 303, 100 S.Ct 2204, 65 L.Ed.2d 144, 206 U.S.P.Q 193.
20. The most notable cases on this matter after *Diamond v. Chakrabarty*, 447 U.S. 303 (1980) were *Ex parte Hibbard*, 227 U.S.P.Q. (BNA) 443 (PTO Board of App. & Int. 1985), granting patent rights to new plant (corn) varieties and *Ex parte Allen*, 2 U.S.P.Q. (BNA) 1425 (PTO Board of App. & Int. 1987). There it was decided that patent rights could be granted to a kind of oysters, polypoid oysters, which were man-made life forms and, therefore, non-naturally occurring manufactures or compositions of matter and, hence, patentable. The particular application was in the end rejected, but not for unpatentability of subject-matter, but for obviousness under the teachings of prior art. In 1998, the Patent Office granted a patent right to a kind of man-made mouse, a transgenic non-human mammal all of whose germ cells and somatic cells contained a recombinant oncogene sequence introduced to this mammal (a mouse) under a genetic engineering procedure known as microinjection.
21. See Gene Patent Guidelines at http://frwebgate.access.gpo.gov/cgi-bin/getdoc.cgi?dbname=2001_register&docid=01-322-filed%20. See also Bjornstad & Dummer (2002).
22. See Kevles (2002).
23. *In re Allen*, 2 U.S.P.Q.2d 1425 (1987).
24. Research by Harvard University, Patent No 4,736,866 (DuPont company).
25. *J.E.M. AG Supply Inc. v. Pioneer Hi-Bred International*, Inc., 534 U.S. 124 Ct. 593, 151 L.Ed. 508, 60 U.S.P.Q2d 1865 (2001). The Court noted that after *Chakrabarty*, those seeking plant patents preferred the broader protection of a utility patent and did not claim their patents under the special Plant Variety Protection Act or the Plant Patent Act; therefore only 1,800 patents under the special acts were issued for plants and seeds.
26. 383 U.S. 519 (1966), at 536, S.Ct. 1033, 16 L.Ed.2d 69 (1966).
27. Justice Fortes continues: '[a patent] is not a reward for the search, but compensation for its successful conclusion ... a patent must be related to the world of commerce rather than the realm of philosophy': id, at 536.
28. *Brenner v. Manson*, 383 U.S. 519 (1996). In this Supreme Court case, the condition of utility was interpreted as 'substantial utility representing specific benefit': see also Roberts (1994) at 32.
29. Venter proposed the wholesale patenting of human gene fragments. His lab sequenced not whole genes but random fragments of cDNA (DNA complementary to the coding regions in genomic DNA): see Kevles (2002) at 81.
30. US Patent No 5817479, granted in 1998.
31. For an analysis of reasons see Llewelyn (1994).
32. 15 F. Cas. 1018, 1019 [C.C.D. Mass 1817].
33. Id. at 1019.
34. *Juicy Whip Inc. v. Orange Bang*, Inc., 185 F.3d 1364, 51 U.S.P.Q.2d 1700 (Fed.Cir. 1999).
35. In *Graham v. John Deree Co.*, 383 U.S. 1, 17, 86 S. Ct. 684, 693–4, 15 L. Ed.2d 545 (1966).
36. *Winner International Royalty Corp. v. Ching-Rong-Wang* 202 F.3d 1340, 53 USPQ2d 1580 (Fed. Cir. 2000).
37. *Gambro Lundia AB v. Baxter Healthcare Corp.*, 110 F. 3d 1573, 1579, 42 USPQ2d 1378, 1383 (Fed. Cir. 1997).
38. *In re Kahn*, Fed. Cir. 2006, 04-1616.
39. See more in Samuelson (date unavailable).
40. 127 S. Ct. 1727 (2007).
41. *Autogiro Co. of America v. US*, 384 F. 2d 391, 400 (Ct.Cl. 1967).
42. Per Learned Hand J, in *Royal Typewriter co. v. Remington Rand Inc.*, 168 F. 2d 691, 692 (end. Cir. 1948).

43. 377 U.S. 476, 84 S.Ct. 1526, 12 L.Ed. 457 (1964).
44. (2004) 1 S.C.R. 902, 2004 SCC 34, 239 D.L.R. (4th) 271, 31 C.P.R. (4th) 161.
45. See Albright (2004) pp. 51–2.
46. Note also, though, the view that the European Patent Organization is independent of the EU and therefore the European Patent Convention is not European Union law: Ann (2006).
47. European Commission Press Release, Proposal for a Directive on the patentability of computer-implemented inventions, see http://europa.eu/rapid/pressReleasesAction.do?reference=IP/02/277&format=HTML&aged=1&language=EN&guiLanguage=en, last accessed April 30, 2009.
48. See http://www.epo.org/about-us/office/annual-reports/2006/2006-in-review.html, last accessed September 30, 2007. A revised Convention, the European Patent Convention 2000, entered into force on December 13, 2007. Its changes are merely linguistic.
49. In 2006, in Case C–4/03, *Gesellschaft für Antriebstechnik v. Lamellen und Kupplungsbau Beteiligungs KG*, (2006) ECR I-6509 and Case C–539/03, *Roche Nederland BV v. Primus*, (2006) ECR I-6535.
50. Available at: www.european-patent-office.org/legal/guiex/e/c_iv_2_3_6.htm, last accessed April 30, 2009.
51. For a detailed account of patenting software under the Convention see Beresford (2000).
52. For a view supporting these patents as a giant step see Basinski (1999).
53. Computer Program Product II/IBM T 0935/97. For details see www.epo.org/topics/issues/computer-implemented-inventions.html, last accessed April 30, 2009.
54. For a list of these patents see http://www.iusmentis.com/patents/businessmethods/epoexamples/, last accessed April 30, 2009.
55. See Rogers (2007).
56. For an account of the state of the implementation of the Directive in Member States, see http://ec.europa.eu/internal_market/indprop/docs/invent/state-of-play_en.pdf, last accessed April 30, 2009.
57. See, as an example, 'No Patents to Seeds and Animals', at http://www.no-patents-on-seeds.org/index.php?option=com_content&task=view&id=45&Itemid=32, last accessed April 30, 2009.
58. European Patent Office, Decision of the Technical Board of Appeal, 3.3.2. of October 3, 1990.
59. For a detailed analysis of patents and morality see Sterckx S. (2004).
60. Plant cells/PLANT GENETIC SYSTEMS, 21 February 1995, T 356, Official Journal of the European Patent Office (1995) 545 paras. 5 and 6.
61. Id. para. 18.
62. Council Regulation 1768/92/EEC creates a supplementary protection certificate especially for medicinal products [1992] OJ L182/1. Also, a supplementary protection certificate for plant protection products.
63. COM(2001)96 final. The key purposes of the program for action are to increase affordability of essential medicines (with special attention to issues related to taxes and tariffs in developing countries, adopting tiered pricing for the least developed countries), to maximize the impact of measures to strengthen the national health care systems, to promote pharmaceutical research (building increased capacity for research in developing countries is a priority) and to reduce poverty. The Program was recently updated by two Commission Communications COM(2003)93 and COM(2004)726.
64. The central theme of inventiveness is present in both cases. However, the European Patent Office uses the 'problem and solution' approach to this analysis of inventive step, meaning that the inventive step is seen as a step from the technical problem to its solution (see Bently & Sherman 2001, at 440–41, who also note that in Europe, for an invention to be patentable the solution must not have been obvious to the person skilled in the art).
65. See Shava (2000) at 58. Shava is an Indian physicist and director of the Research Foundation for Science, Technology and Natural Resource. She was the one who initiated the challenging of the patent in 1995, in which she succeeded after a five-year campaign. See also Albright (2004) at 42–4.
66. See Norman (1986) at 308–09.

67. For example, Lehman, the US Commissioner of Patents, declared in 1997 that the Patent and Trademark Office would in general reject patents that were 'injurious to the well-being, good policy and good morals of society': see Kevles (2002) at 81.
68. See for example the patent of Hormone Relaxin 1995 OJ EPO 388 (Opp.Div.), patent of a DNA sequence encoding for a protein used during childbirth.
69. An amendment to the Copyright Act added an article on certain authors' rights to attribution and integrity (17 U.S.C. sec. 106A).
70. *Burrow-Giles Lithographic Co. v. Sarony*, 11 U.S. 54 (1884).
71. *Goldstein v. California*, 412 U.S. 546 (1973).
72. 17 U.S.C. sec. 101.
73. Copyright Act of 1790, full text available at: www.copyright.gov/history/1790act.pdf last accessed April 30, 2009.
74. *Feist Publications, Inc. v. Rural Tel. Services Co.*, Inc., 499 U.S. 340 (1991).
75. *Eldred v. Ashcroft*, 537 U.S. 186 (2003).
76. The statute, sec. 103, provides:

    (a) The subject matter of copyright as specified by section 102 includes compilations and derivative works, but protection for a work employing preexisting material in which copyright subsists does not extend to any part of the work in which such material has been used unlawfully. (b) The copyright in a compilation or derivative work extends only to the material contributed by the author of such work, as distinguished from the preexisting material employed in the work, and does not imply any exclusive right in the preexisting material. The copyright in such work is independent of, and does not affect or enlarge the scope, duration, ownership, or subsistence of, any copyright protection in the preexisting material.

77. The case is widely cited as the origin of the idea/expression doctrine: Samuelson (2005) alleges that the idea/expression distinction predated Baker. Definitely, in *Donaldson v. Beckett*, 2 Brown's Parl. Cases 129, 1 ER 837; 4 Burr. 2408, 98 ER 257 (1774), for example, we see speeches of the Lords exactly stressing this distinction very eloquently (see chapter 2 on intellectual property history).
78. 101 U.S. 99 (1879).
79. Ibid., at 104.
80. *Feist Publications v. Rural Telephone Services* 499 U.S. 340 (1991), citing *Harper & Row Publishers, Inc. v. Nation Enterprises*, 471 U.S. 539, 556 (1985).
81. *Miller v. Universal City Studios Inv.*, US Court of Appeals, 5th cir., 650 F. 2d 1365 (1981).
82. 17 U.S.C. sec. 101.
83. 347 U.S. 201 (1954).
84. Currently 37 C.F.R. sec. 202.10(a).
85. 17 U.S.C. sec. 101.
86. For an eloquent history of software copyright protection see Branscomb (1994).
87. 1980 Computer Service Copyright Act, enacted December 1980, P.L. 96-517, Sec. 10; 94 Statutes at large 3028, Title 17 U.S.C. Sec. 101, 117.
88. *Apple Computer, Inc. v. Franklin Computer Corp.*, US Court of Appeals, 3rd cir., 714 F.2d 1240 (1983).
89. *Whelan Assocs, Inc. v. Jaslow Dental Laboratory*, 797 F. 2d 1222 (3rd Cir. 1986).
90. *Lotus Development Corp. v. Paperback Software Int'l*, 740 F. Supp. 37 (D. Mass. 1990).
91. *Lotus Development Corp. v. Borland Int. Inc.*, 49 F. 3d 807 (1st cir) 1995, affirmed 516 US 233 (1996).
92. 1984, 17 U.S.C.A. 902 et seq.
93. 17 U.S.C. 101.
94. 'The copyright in a compilation ... extends only to the material contributed by the author of such work, as distinguished from the preexisting material employed in the work, and does not imply any existing material employed in the work and does not imply any exclusive right in the preexisting material': 17 U.S.C. 103 b.

95. For example, see *Webb v. Powers et al.*, 29 F. Cas. 511; 1847 US App. Lexis 595, 10 Law Rep. 12, concerning a dictionary of flowers also containing poems.
96. *Feist Publications v. Rural Telephone Services*, 499 U.S. 340 (1991).
97. *Matthew Bender & Co. v. West Publishing Co.* (1998), 158 F 3rd. 674 2nd Cir (1998) cert. denied, *West Publishing v. Hyperlaw Inc.* cert. denied, S. Ct, 526 US 1154 (1999).
98. US Congress, House of Representatives, HR 3531, 104th Congress, 2nd session, 23rd May 1996.
99. Such as the HR 354 Collections of Information Antipiracy Act of 2000, the HR 1858, Consumer and Investor Access to Information Act of 1999 (this one as a response of the opponents to draft bills favoring copyright protection for databases), the 2003 Database and Collection of Information Misappropriation Act etc.
100. First Evaluation of Directive 96/9/EC on the legal protection of databases, http://ec.europa.eu/internal_market/copyright/prot-databases/prot-databases_en.htm, last accessed April 30, 2009.
101. *Feist Publications Inc.v. Rural Services*, 499 US 340 (1991).
102. *Burrow-Giles Lithographic Co v. Sarony*, 111 US 53, 4 S. Ct. 279 (1884).
103. *Bleistein v. Donaldson Lithographing Co,* 188 U.S. 239, 23 S. Ct. 298 (1903), a famous decision by Justice Holmes who wrote: 'Personality always contains something unique. It expresses its singularity even in handwriting, and a very modest grade of art has in it something irreducible, which is one man's alone. That something he may copyright unless there is a restriction in the words of the act': id.
104. *Alfred Bell & Co. v. Catalda Fine Arts, Inc.*, 191 F.2d 99 (2d Cir. 1951). Alfred Bell had under contract sole access to various museums and it undertook the copying of many painting masterpieces for sale as reproductions. When another company, which had no access to the originals, copied the copies, the Court accepted the reproductions as copyright works (no novelty is necessary; only minimum originality).
105. 499 US 340 (1991).
106. Ibid.
107. 9 F. Cas. 342 [C.C.Mass. 1841]. In this case, the use was called 'justifiable'; fair use, as a term, comes from the subsequent *Lawrence v. Dana*, 15 F. Cas. 26 [C.C.D.Mass. 1869].
108. One of the most cited passage in copyright law books is the 'opening' of *Folsom v. Marsh*, 9 F. Cas. 342 [C.C.Mass. 1841]: 'Patents and copyrights approach, nearer than any other class of cases belonging to forensic discussions, to what may be called the metaphysics of the law, where the distinctions are, or at least may be, very subtile and refined, and, sometimes, almost evanescent'.
109. Section 107, 17 U.S.C. 1976.
110. *Campbell v. Acuff-Rose Music Inc.,* 510 U.S. 569 (1994).
111. The fair use examples here come from HR Rep. No 94-1476, 94th Congress, 2nd Sess. 53 (1976) pp.65–70 (the Copyright Act's House Report).
112. *Sony Corp. of America v. Universal City Studios, Inc.*, 464 U.S. 417 (1984).
113. *Harper v Row Publishers Inc. v. Nation Enterprises* 471 U.S. 539 (1985).
114. *Campbell v. Acuff-Rose Music Inc.,* 510 U.S. 569 (1994).
115. *Stewart v. Abend,* 495 U.S. 207 (1990).
116. See generally Nimmer & Nimmer (2002).
117. Such as, for example, the case of *Religious Tech. Ctr. v. Lerma* 908 F. Supp. 1231 (E.D. Va 1995), where the *Washington Post* was sued for publishing L.Ron Hubbard's writings (on the Church of Scientology), or *Belmore v. City Pages* Inc., 880 F. Supp. 673 (D. Minn. 1995), dealing with copying from a police newsletter to demonstrate racism. Fair use was recognized in these cases. For a full list of US Court of Appeals cases after 1994 see Nimmer (2003) at 269–77.
118. 112 Stat. 2860 (1998). For a history of the Act see Litman (2001).
119. See (among others) Tyrainen (2005) and Armstrong (2001).
120. 537 U.S. 186 (2003); 123 S. Ct. 769, 154 L. Ed. 2d 683, 71 U.S.L.W. 4052.
121. *Walt Disney Productions v. Filmation Associates*, 628 F. Supp. 871 (1986).
122. *Stowe v. Thomas*, 23 F.Cas.201 [C.C.D. 1853]. The defendant did not use the same language in which the conceptions of the author were clothed, so the Court dismissed the case.

123. *Playboy Enterprises, Inc. v. Hardenburgh*, Inc., 982 F. Supp. 503 (N.D. Ohio 1997).
124. *Folsom v. Marsh*, 9 F. Cas. 342, 344–5 (Cir. Ct. Mass. 1841).
125. *Nichols v. Universal Pictures Corp.*, 45 F.2d 119 (2nd Cir. 1930).
126. *Roth Greeting Cards v. United Card Co.*, 429 F.2d 1106 (9th Cir. 1970).
127. *Nichols v. Universal Pictures Corp.*, 45 F. 2d 119, 121 (2d Cir. 1930), per Learned Hand, J.
128. In *Walt Disney Productions v. Air Pirates*, 581 F 2d. 751 (9th Cir.) 1978, Disney's cartoon characters such as Mickey Mouse, Donald Duck, the Big Bad Wolf and others, were reproduced in a magazine as taking drugs. The characters were held protectable.
129. See Goldstein (2001) at 289–90.
130. A work of visual art for the purposes of application of VARA is not: any poster, map, globe, chart, technical drawing, diagram, model, applied art, motion picture or other audiovisual work, book, magazine, newspaper, periodical, data base, electronic information service, electronic publication or similar publication. Also, works made for hire are not covered, nor are any merchandizing items or advertising, promotional, descriptive, covering or packaging material or container.
131. On the protection of moral rights under the Lanham Act see *Krigsman* (1983).
132. H.R.Rep. No. 609, 100th Cong., 2d Sess. 32–4 (1988).
133. *Dastar Corp. v. Twentieth Century Fox Film Corp.*, 539 U.S. 23 (2003).
134. Copyright Office Report, '*Droit de Suite*: The Artist's Resale Royalty', 17 *Colum.-VLA J. L. & Arts* 381 (1992).
135. See, for example, *Kenrick & Co. v. Lawrence & Co* (1890) 25 QBD 99.
136. For an analysis here see Strowel (1993) at 144.
137. Hugenholtz et al. (2008).
138. The test is also included in the WIPO Copyright Treaty (Art. 10), in Directive 91/250/EEC on the protection of computer programs (Art. 6.3), in Directive 96/9/EC on the legal protection of databases. An application of the test is found in two WTO cases: see Ficsor (2002). For a general account of limitations see Guibault (2002).
139. Case C–53/05, *Commission v. Portugal*, 2006 ECR I-6215, and Case C-36/05 *Commission v. Spain*, 2006 ECR I-10313. The rule attacked was Portugal's provision under copyright law ruling that public, school or university libraries, museums, public archives, public foundations and private non-profit-making institutions were not subject to the remuneration obligation for public lending acts.
140. Case C–198/05, *Commission v. Italy*, ECJ 26 October 2006.
141. See www.ifla.org/III/clm/p1/PublicLendingRigh.htm, last accessed April 30, 2009.
142. Case C–293/98, *EGEDA v. Hosteleria Asturiana SA* [2000] ECR I-231.
143. For a detailed presentation of moral rights see Cornish & Llewelyn (2003) at 453.
144. Cour de Lyon, 17 July 1845, D.1845.2.128.
145. Cour de Cassation, 21 August 1867, D.1867.1.369.
146. Tribunal Civil de la Seine, 16 Decembre 1899, D.1900.2.152.
147. *Camoin et Syndicat de la Propriété artistique v. Francis Carco, Aubry, Belattre et Zborowski*, Trib.Civ.de la Seine, 15 Novembre 1927, DP.1928.2.89, confirmed in *Carco et autres v. Camoin et Syndicat de la propriété artistique*, Cour d'Appel de Paris, 6 March 1931, DP.1931.2.88.
148. Ibid., at 92.
149. A list of alleged negative consequences of the DMCA in relation to users can be found in EEF, 'Unintended Consequences: Seven Years under the DMCA', available at: www.eff.org, last accessed June 30, 2008. The list includes threats to free expression and scientific research, jeopardizing fair use, impeding competition and innovation and interfering with computer intrusion laws. Generally, there exists extensive commentary against the DMCA.
150. For a comparison between the DMCA and the EU Information Society Directive on fair use see Grodzinsky & Bottis (2007).
151. Cour de Cassation, 28 February 2006, *Studio Canal SA and Universal Pictures Video France SAS v. Mr Stephane X. and others.*
152. See Mikko Valimaki (2007).

153. In *Universal City Studios, Inc. v. Reimerdes*, 11 F. Sup.2d 294 (S.D.N.Y. 2000) and *321 Studios v. MGM*, 307 F. Supp. 2d 1085 (N.D. Cal. 2004), the argument was rejected.
154. Recital 3 states that 'the resale right is intended to ensure that authors of graphic and plastic art share in the economic success of their original works of art. It helps to redress the balance between the economic situation of authors of graphic works of art and that of other creators who benefit from successive exploitations of their works'. Recital 7 refers to the internationalization of the Community market in modern and contemporary art being speeded up by the effects of the new economy. Recital 9 refers to harmonization needs, as some Member States recognize the resale right and others do not. Recital 10 mentions the direct negative impact of these disparities on the proper functioning of the internal market in works of art. The same thoughts about market needs are repeated in Recital 11. Recitals 12, 13, 14, 15, 16 and 17 all analyze the resale right in 'market needs', 'distortion of competition', enabling economic operators' and similar terms. To put this simply, the enacting of a European resale right was not a matter of natural justice; it was a matter of a more efficient art market.
155. See First Evaluation of Directive 96/9/EC on the legal protection of databases, p. 22, available at: ec.europa.eu/internal_market/copyright/docs/databases/evaluation_report_en.pdf, last accessed June 30, 2009.
156. European Commissioner Bolkestein, who supervised the drafting of the Information Society Directive, lamented the existence of an 'unprecedented lobbying onslaught' over the Directive: see Statement of February 14, 2001, available at: http://europa.eu.int/comm/internal_market/en/intprop/news/01-210.htm last accessed April 30, 2009.
157. Hugenholtz B. et al. (2006) p. 16.
158. Id., p. 21.
159. Montagnani M. L. & Borghi M., 'Promises and Pitfalls of the European Copyright Harmonization Process', in Ward D. (ed.), *The European union & The Culture Industries: Regulations and the Public Interest*, Ashgate 2007. The chapter is available at SSRN: http://ssrn.com/abstract=1020992, p. 18, last accessed April 30, 2009.
160. On this point see Koelman (2004) pp. 603–638, *passim*. The author argues in the end, however, that the Copyright Directive (the Information Society Directive) 'fits well in the droit d'auteur view of copyright perception, which regards it to be a natural right for the author to harvest what he has shown and that it would be premature to speak of a paradigm shift for the European copyright law. We disagree with this conclusion and we believe that the whole analysis before it tends to prove that there is, indeed, a paradigm shift towards the common law economic-utilitarian copyright. A mere reading of the Recitals to the Directives on intellectual property, we think, prove exactly this point. This point is also more than obvious in texts such as the First Evaluation of the Directive 96/9/EC on the legal protection of databases, available at: ec.europa.eu/internal_market/copyright/docs/databases/evaluation_report_en.pdf, last accessed June 30, 2009. There is ample evidence in this text that economic considerations were the most important propellers for the promulgation of the Directive and also for its evaluation under EU law. Koelman does state, moreover, that 'the recitals in the Copyright Directive may be read to imply that economic considerations have played an important part in drafting the Directive': id. (Exactly).
161. A major study completed by the Institute for Information Law, in Amsterdam, The Recasting of Copyright and Related Rights for the Knowledge Economy, available at: http://www.ivir.nl/publications/other/IViR_Recast_Final_Report_2006.pdf, last accessed April 30, 2009.
162. In an 'Open Letter concerning European Commission's "Intellectual Property Package"', to the President of the European Commission, the Director of the Institute for Information Law Pr. Bernt Hugenholtz exposes these facts: see www.ivir.nl/news/Open_Letter_EC.pdf, last accessed April 30, 2009.
163. See generally Cornish & Llewelyn (2003) at 453.
164. Copyright, Design and Patents Act 1998, ss. 94–5.
165. On the history of trademarks see Schechter (1925).
166. 100 US 82 (1879). These cases are known as 'the Trade-Mark cases'.
167. For a detailed history of the concept of goodwill in trademark law see Bone (2006).
168. For an analytical description of this view see McKenna (2007).
169. Pub.L. 109–312, § 2, 120 Stat. 1730, 1730–32 (2006).

170. 537 U.S. 418 (2003).
171. See for example *New York & Rosendale Cement Co. v. Coplay Cement Co.*, 44 F. 277 (C.C.E.D. Pa 1890). The defendant, not located in Rosendale, used 'Rosendale' for his cement, but the plaintiff, being one of the 20 manufacturers of cement located in Rosendale, could not prove that he was the one that the defendant aimed at harming and not the other 19. The court noted that the plaintiff was not the only one entitled to use the word 'Rosendale' and that this was not his exclusive property.
172. 247 F. 407 (2d Cir. 1917).
173. 26 F. 2d 972 (2d Cir. 1928).

REFERENCES

Albright M. (2004), *Profits Pending: How Life Patents Represent the Biggest Swindle of the 21st Century*, Monroe, Maine: Common Courage Press.

AMA Council on Ethical and Judicial Affairs (1998), 'Ethical Issues in the Patenting of Medical Procedures', 53 *Food & Drug Law Journal* 341.

Ann C. (2006), 'Patents on Human Gene Sequences in Germany-on bad lawmaking and ways to deal with it', 7 *German Law Journal* 3, available at: http://www.germanlaw-journal.com/article.php?id=716.

Armstrong T.K. (2001), 'Digital Rights Management and the Process of Fair Use', 20 *Harvard Journal of Law and Technology* 49; available at: http://ssrn.com/abstract=885371.

Basinski E. (1999), 'Computer Program Product Claims Allowed by the EPO-Impact on Software Patent Claiming', available at: http://library.findlaw.com/1999/Mar/1/128760.html.

Bednarz A. (date unavailable), 'IBM sues Amazon for patent infringement, Network World', available at: http://www/netwrokworld.com/news/2006/102306-ibm-sues-amazon.html.

Bently L. and B. Sherman (2001), *Intellectual Property Law*, New York: Oxford University Press, 2nd ed.

Beresford K. (2000), *Patenting Software under the European Patent Convention*, London: Sweet & Maxwell.

Bjornstad D. and C. Dummer (2002), 'An Introduction to Issues Underlying Patent Policy for the Emerging Genetic Information and Medical Treatment Industry', available at: http://jiee.org/pdf/2002_05_patent.pdf.

Bone R. (2006), 'Hunting Goodwill: A History of the Concept of Goodwill in Trademark Law', *Boston University Law Review*, (forthcoming); available at: http://papers.ssrn.com/sol3/papers.cfm?abstract_id=874788.

Branscomb A. (1994), *Who Owns Information? From Privacy to Public Access*, New York: Basic Books.

Chrissanthis C. (2004), 'Legal Aspects of Trademarks Protection Before Civil Courts', 56 (4) *Međunarodni problemi* 370.

Copyright Office (1992), 'Droit de Suite: The Artist's Resale Royalty', 17 *Columbia VLA Journal of Law & Arts* 381.

Cornish W. and D. Llewelyn (2003), *Intellectual Property: Patents, Copyrights Trade Marks and Allied Rights*, London: Sweet & Maxwell, 5th ed.

Department of Commerce, Patent and Trademark Office (2001), 'Utility Examination Guidelines', 66 (4) *Federal Register* 1092.

EEF (2006), 'Unintended Consequences: Seven Years under the DMCA', available at:

http://www.eff.org/deeplinks/2006/04/unintended-consequences-seven-years-under-dmca.
Ficsor M. (2002), 'How much of what? The 'three-steps test' and its application in two recent WTO dispute settlement cases', 192 *Revue Internationale du Droit d'Auteur* 110.
Goldstein P. (2001), *International Copyright: Principles, Law and Practice*, New York: Oxford University Press.
Grodzinsky F. and M. Bottis (2007), 'Private Use as Fair Use: is it Fair?', 37 (2) *Computers and Society* 11.
Guibault L. (2002), *Copyright Limitations and Contracts, An Analysis of the Contractual Overridability of Limitations and Contract*, London/The Hague/Boston: Kluwer Law International.
Hugenholtz et al. (2006), 'The Recasting of Copyright and Related Rights for the Knowledge Economy', final report, available at: www.ivir.nl.
Hulse R. (2000), 'Patentability of Computer Software after State Street Bank & Trust Co v. Signature Group Inc.: Evisceration of the Subject-Matter Requirement', *U.C. Davis Law Review* 491.
Kevles D. (2002), 'A history of patenting life in the United States with comparative attention to Europe and Canada', Luxembourg: Office for Official Publications of the European Commission.
Koelman K. (2004), 'Copyright Law & Economics in the EU Copyright Directive: Is the Droit d'Auteur Passé?', 6 *International Review of Intellectual Property and Competition Law* (IIC), 603.
Krigsman F. (1983), 'Section 43(a) of the Lanham Act as a Defender of Artists' "Moral Rights"', 73 *Trade-Mark Report* 251.
Litman J. (2001), *Digital Copyright*, Buffalo: Prometheus Books.
Llewelyn M. (1994). 'Industrial Applicability/Utility in Genetic Engineering: Current Practices in Europe and the United States', 11 *EIPR* 475.
Lunney G. (1999), 'Trademark Monopolies', 48 *Emory Law Journal* 367.
McCarthy T. (2004), 'Proving a Trademark Has Been Diluted: Theories or Facts?', 41 *Houston Law Review* 713.
McKenna M.P. (2007), 'The Normative Foundations of Trademark Law', 82 *Notre Dame Law Review* 207, available at: SSRN: http://ssrn.com/abstract=889162.
Melvin E. (2007), 'An Unacceptable Exception: the Ramifications of Physical Immunity from Medical Procedure Patent Infringement Liability', 91 *Minnesota Law Review* 1088.
Mikko Valimaki (2007), 'Keep on Hacking: a Finnish Court says technological measures are no longer "effective" when circumventing applications are widely available on the Internet', 4:2 SCRIPT-ed.
Miller A. and M. Davis (2000), *Intellectual Property: Patents, Trademarks, and Copyright*, 3rd ed., New York: West Wadsworth.
Montagnani M. L. and M. Borghi (2007), 'Promises and Pitfalls of the European Copyright Harmonization Process', in D. Ward (ed.), *The European Union & the Culture Industries: Regulations and the Public Interest,* Aldershot: Ashgate; available at: SSRN: http://ssrn.com/abstract=1020992.
Nimmer D. (2003), '"Fairest of them all" and other Fairy Tales of Fair Use', 66 *Law and Contemporary Problems* 263.
Noehrenberg E. (2006), 'The Realities of TRIPS, Patents and Access to Medicines in Developing Countries', in Meier Perez Pugatch (ed.), *The Intellectual Property De-*

bate, Perspectives from Law, Economics and Political Economy, Cheltenham UK and Northampton MA USA: Edward Elgar.

Norman C. (1986), 'A New Twist in AIDS Patent Fight', *Science* 232 (4748) 308.

Roberts C. (1994), 'The Prospects of Success of the National Institute of Health's Human Genome Application', 1 *EIPR* 30.

Rogers D. (2007), 'EPO Decision of Exclusion of Methods of Business Research from Patentability, Requirement of Technical Character of an Invention', 2 *Journal of Intellectual Property Law & Practice* 640.

Samuelson P. (2005), 'The Story of *Baker v. Selden*', Berkeley Center for Law and Technology. Law and Technology Scholarship (Selected by the Berkeley Center for Law & Technology), Paper 10, available at: http://repositories.cdlib.org/bclt/lts/10.

Samuelson P. (date unavailable), 'Legally Speaking: Why Reform the U.S. Patent System', available at: www.people.ischool.berkeley.edu/~pam/papers/cacm%20patent%20 reform.pdf.

Schechter F.I. (1925), *The Historical Foundations of the Law Relating to Trademarks*, New York: Columbia University Press.

Shava Vandana (2000), 'North-South Conflicts', 12 (4) *Intellectual Property Peace Review* 58.

Sterckx S. (ed.) (2004), *Biotechnology Patents and Morality*, 2nd ed., Aldershot/Brookfield USA/Singapore/Sydney: Ashgate.

Strowel A. (1993), *Droit d'auteur and Copyright – Divergences and Convergences*, Paris: LGDJ.

Tyrainen P. (2005), 'Concepts and a Design for Fair Use and Privacy in DRM', 11 (2) *D-Lib Magazine*, available at: http:// www.dlib.org/dlib/february05/tyrvainen/ 02tyrvainen.html.

4. Protesting intellectual property rights

Many legal scholars, philosophers, and journalists now call into question the suitability of exclusive intellectual property rights embodied in a legal regime such as TRIPs. They regard the traditional conception of intellectual property as stifling and antiquated. They are unconvinced about the validity of some sort of 'natural' ownership right to the intellectual products of the mind. How can ideas and immaterial, abstract objects be 'owned' by someone? Why should the government restrict access to intangible goods which are meant to be shared? Why should we regard the source of these intellectual objects as creators and authors of their ideas, rather than as 'mere transmitters' of eternal verities (Hesse 2002, p. 32)?

The effort to extend property rights has often been referred to as the second 'enclosure' movement.[1] Enclosure occurs when a durable, proprietary right is assigned to an intellectual work or some other form of 'common' property so that it becomes unavailable to the public unless they are willing to pay something like a licensing fee. Thus, these expansive property rights encroach with impunity upon the public domain. Knowledge appropriated from the public domain is privatized and made virtually inaccessible for long periods of time. The extension of property rights to the human genome is often cited as an illustration of how common property, belonging to everyone, can become subject to 'enclosure'.[2] But what are the costs of gene patents or an ownership stake in one's genetic information? Normative analysis is rightly skeptical of these property claims. The antidote to this enclosure movement is readily apparent: fewer patents (or perhaps none at all), copyrights with a short duration, an abundance of open source software code, easily accessible digital content, and a robust, dynamic intellectual commons.

Numerous polemical tracts and articles underscore the need to overcome a 'property' theory of abstract objects and to promote the radical revision of intellectual property law. Some economists advocate business strategies based on nonexclusivity and free competition, rather than the assertion of property rights. These efforts have had little effect, but the endurance of this exclusive rights-based approach to information production and distribution has made the cries for reform even louder.

Moderate voices declaim the exaggerated focus on free riding and piracy as they protest the presumptive entitlement of intellectual property owners to appropriate the full value of their creation.[3] Scholars worry about the 'creeping propertization' that has happened in the sciences to the detriment of research and innovation (Merges 1996, p. 146). Intellectual property rights may be necessary, these critics say, but their scope should be severely limited.

Other voices paint a bleak picture. We are informed that 'the combination of intellectual property rights with free market ideology … is lethal for the less privileged sectors of society, especially the children' (Perelman 2002, p. 207). There are dire predictions about 'an ominous descent into a new Dark Age' unless we reverse the current trends (Shulman 1999). There is much hyperbole in this rhetoric even if it does remind us about the logical incoherence and excesses of recent copyright litigation.

More nuanced critiques express grave concerns about copyright's negative effects on free speech. Lemley and Volokh (1998, pp. 165–6), for example, explain how 'copyright law restricts speech: it restricts you from writing, painting, publicly performing, or otherwise communicating what you please'. One problem is that efficacious speech sometimes requires copying at length from copyright works. Those who support these claims also object to tight intellectual property controls as a means of controlling social meaning in popular culture. Property rights should be limited in order to 'open up more cultural space' so that new authors can reshape the culture (Aoki 1993, p. 836).

Detractors of intellectual property protection come in many stripes, but almost all of them complain about the broadening scope of intellectual property rights. One of the most outspoken critics is Lessig (2004) who laments the demise of 'free culture' where public works are shared, borrowed, and creatively transformed without the constraints of rigid copyright and trademark laws. In his seminal book on software 'code', Lessig (1999, pp. 30–42) had underscored the abrupt transition in the Internet's architecture from an idyllic 'innovation commons' to an 'architecture of control'. Thanks to the 'original Internet's' open protocols, individuals could use this resource to develop and deploy new applications without restrictions or permission (Lessig 2001, p. 44).

Lessig and many others favor openness and a 'commons model' as a viable alternative to tight proprietary controls. They argue that a significant level of innovation would occur in the absence of strong, broad, exclusive rights.[4] Proprietary standards, on the other hand, often raise the cost of innovation for new innovators who must often pay licensing fees for inputs. As Landes and Posner (1989, p. 328) argue, 'stronger appropriability will not yield more innovation in all contexts and, where it does, innovation may come at excessive cost'.

According to Lessig (2001), the swift transformation of the Internet into an architecture of proprietary control has had a negative impact on innovation and creativity. It has commercialized a space where creativity and liberty once flourished. The open commons so conducive to innovation has been designed away through opaque code that embeds tight property controls. This shift in

Internet architecture, orchestrated by media conglomerates and other commercial information producers, is but one example of the growing threat to innovation and the movement away from a free culture, which is far more conducive for the creative human spirit.

Some proponents of the current intellectual property entitlement system see it as symptomatic of a deeper problem: the deliberate perpetuation of social and economic inequities through information imperialism. Intellectual property rights are little more than state-granted corporate subsidies, which should only be granted when absolutely necessary.[5] According to this viewpoint, these exclusive entitlements are simply another tool of oppression, another form of monopolistic control. Along these lines, Aoki (1996) contends that intellectual property 'underwrites the private sovereignties of multinational companies' (p. 1307). As proof of these claims critics point to the concentrated hegemony of media conglomerates and pharmaceutical companies, which exert substantial power over the world's information resources.

Rebukes of current intellectual property law frequently cite the strengthening of exclusive intellectual property rights as a source of international discord. They argue that developing nations have been coerced to accept Western property rules to the detriment of the world's cultural vitality and scientific progress. The extension of copyright law around the world limits the ability of many countries to benefit from information technology. The economic benefits of intellectual property rights are appropriated by developed nations and major corporations. Some of these critical works are punctuated with activist language that sounds like a call to arms. Carla Hesse (2002), for example, advocates the urgent need 'to dismantle commercial monopolies on the circulation of thought and to spread knowledge freely among our citizens' (p. 45).

This antagonism toward thick intellectual property rights, especially in academic circles, has continued to intensify in the last several decades. Although there are many reasons behind this opposition, it will be instructive for us to focus on four main factors: the emergence of new technologies which facilitate democratic expression and naturally resist 'containment'; the expanding and pervasive influence of post-modern, deconstructionist theory, which has undermined the basic assumptions undergirding strong individual intellectual property rights; worries about excessive protection, as evidenced by the entertainment industry's tightening grip on its digital content; and valid concerns about the negative impact of substantive property rights on the economic health of developing economies.

This chapter will briefly address each of these concerns, beginning with the merits of information libertarianism. After reflecting upon the pointed deconstructionist critique of intellectual property rights, we turn to the excessive level of copyright, patent, and trademark protection which has emerged in countries like the United States. Overprotective litigation has stimulated anti-property rhetoric and led to the calls for sweeping reform. Given the need for balanced property rights, some of this criticism is perfectly valid, but it's important to avoid overreacting to this situation by calling for an evisceration of exclusive intellectual property rights. The chapter will conclude with a terse assessment of the claim that intellectual property rights engender social inequity by fostering a system of 'information feudalism' (Drahos and Braithwaite 2002). The problem of intellectual property rights and developing countries is a delicate one, but the answer is not the complete abolition of patents and copyrights as some have proposed.

1. THE LIBERTARIAN PERSPECTIVE

The emergence of the Internet and the digitization of information are changing the rules. At a minimum, digital technologies have triggered many questions about the ongoing relevance of intellectual property rights. Our networked information system is equipped finally to liberate information and cultural goods. Digital information, after all, is easy to store, reproduce and share with others, so why should there be artificial restrictions on this new form of data? According to Barlow (1994), once information is digitized, it is virtually impossible to contain or control: '[t]he enigma is this: if our property can be infinitely reproduced and instantaneously distributed all over the planet without cost, without its even leaving our possession, how can we protect it?' Barlow implies that it's no longer feasible to protect intangible objects that are not attached in some way to a tangible medium. At the same time, digital networks can help us reconceive conventional notions of authorship. According to Chon (1996, p. 265), 'The binary structure of copyright law, dependent as it is on a strict division between author and reader, or original artist and copyist, is being corroded by networked digital information'.

Information libertarians who subscribe to these beliefs also argue on moral grounds that cultural products such as movies and music should be freely available online to anyone who wants them, since culture is meant to be shared. Thus, we should allow these digital technologies to liberate people from the grip of authors and owners. Libertarians prefer anarchy to the oligarchic and stable structure represented by the current system (Vaidhyanathan 2004). Whatever enters the realm of cyberspace as a digital file should be fair game for all consumers of information. The emergence of peer-to-peer (P2P) networks has facilitated the exchange of such information. Unlike the traditional client/server model, data can be easily accessed and distributed from any node in a P2P network.[6] The founder of the radical peer-to-peer (P2P) network Freenet, for example, has described copyright as 'economic censorship', since it retards the free flow of information for purely economic reasons (Roblimo 2000). Thanks to digital information and the P2P architecture, there is growing support for an anti-copyright model which defies traditional copyright protection.

The rallying cry of the information liberationist is simple enough: 'information wants to be free', so let it flow freely across the Internet as it has been designed to do. According to Barlow (1994):

> ... all the goods of the Information Age – all of the expressions once contained in books or film strips or newsletters – will exist as thought or something very much like thought: voltage conditions darting around the Net at the speed of light, in conditions that one might behold in effect, as glowing pixels or transmitted sounds, but never touch or claim to 'own' in the old sense of the word.

Barlow would not be disturbed by the 'darting around' or free flow of copyrighted works on P2P networks, since these digital networks help the Net to realize its true potential as a highly efficient distributor of digital information. These technologies lower the costs of copying and distribution, and these low costs can ultimately provide benefits for copyright holders so long as they are willing to adapt their business models in the face of this new reality.

Grodzinsky and Tavani (2005, pp. 249–50) develop a variation of this general argument as they underscore the fundamental importance of information sharing. In their view, it is important to 'defend the principle "information wants to be shared", which presumes against the "fencing off" or enclosing of information in favor of a view of information that should be communicated and shared'. Of course, information has no 'wants' or 'aspirations', so the argument being proposed here must be the normative claim that the distribution of information as widely as possible should be promoted and encouraged (Spinello 2008).[7]

Not everyone agrees with Barlow's vision of information or the anti-copyright model. Nor does everyone accept the anarchistic ideology codified in P2P technologies such as Freenet. For those who recognize the value of the Internet and P2P networks for sharing digital content and also respect the beneficial dynamic effects of intellectual property rights, some important questions need consideration. What about the moral propriety of sharing copyrighted files without permission? According to some schools of thought, moral restrictions are not apposite in this context. While Lange (2003) does not argue that such file sharing is morally acceptable, he claims that there is considerable 'softness' on the side of those who make the opposite claim. He points out that many people do not accept that digital music is a valid form of property and, in Lange's view, there is some merit to this claim. Therefore, the issue of a legitimate property right in such intellectual objects 'is still very much unsettled ... [and] it may yet be that the idea of property and exclusivity will prove unable to withstand the popular will' (Lange 2003, p. 32).

The problem with this version of information libertarianism is twofold. First, contrary to Barlow's predictions, it is quite possible to control and regulate the flow of digital information just as we regulate the flow of information in the physical world. Architectures such as encryption and digital rights management (DRM) are not popular technologies among the liberationists, but they provide a measure of secure protection for digital works.[8] DRM can provide lawful access to media content, and it represents a trend of inscribing legal constraints into technology. The *responsible* deployment of DRM systems is a logical and morally acceptable response to the massive level of copyright infringement envisioned by Barlow. Second, contrary to Lange, a powerful ethical case can be made that property rights in intangible objects are valid and that 'sharing' without permission is a form of theft. Although it is costless to distribute digital information, there are still production and editing costs for on-line content, so intellectual property rights are not irrelevant in a digital environment. Creators deserve to be rewarded for their efforts even if the results of those efforts are vulnerable to copying. We cannot treat this issue here in any depth, but let it suffice to say that theft should be understood as an 'unfair taking', or a misappropriation of another's property contrary to the owner's reasonable will. In the case of intellectual property (such as digital movies and music), unless the copyright holder's consent can be reasonably presumed, using that copyright holder's creative expression in a way that exceeds her permission is using it contrary to her will (Spinello 2008).

What about the deeper, related argument that strong copyright protection, particularly in a digital environment, is incompatible with broad free speech rights required by the First Amendment? Is there such a conflict and should property rights be attenuated to promote self-expression by non-owners? Why should the author be given such an extended opportunity to fix the social meaning of his work in the mind of the public? We will address these questions more fully in Chapter 6, but it is worth noting that in the eyes of the US Supreme Court, both copyright and the First Amendment share the same goal of promoting free speech.[9] Courts have repeatedly ruled that copyright's internal 'safety valves' such as fair use and the idea/expression dichotomy do an adequate job of reconciling intellectual property and free speech rights.[10] In addition, what good is a right to free speech if the message one is communicating gets deliberately garbled or distorted by those seeking to recode that message in real space or cyberspace. According to Hughes (2006), who echoes the Supreme Court's opinion, copyright fortifies free speech rights: 'any system that emphasizes that the audience should receive the speaker's intended message must protect the speaker's expression from distortion' (p. 1057 n.295).

2. THE DECONSTRUCTIONIST CRITIQUE

Critics of intellectual property have found fault with many aspects of intellectual property law such as its tendency to deplete the intellectual commons. They also fault intellectual property rights, especially those controlled by large corporations, because they often lead to monopoly rents that do not enhance social welfare. Strong property rights typically promote rent-seeking activities which often dissipate resources as companies frantically search for the next big innovation. More radical critics demand free cultural goods, at least in the realm of cyberspace, and seek to undermine the foundation of copyright through anarchistic technologies such as Freenet or Darknet.

Other reformers challenge the foundations of copyrights and patents on philosophical grounds. Their aim is to deconstruct intellectual property doctrine through a critical examination of the commonplace assumptions underlying that doctrine. They are inspired by the pillars of post-modern philosophical thinking, those great 'masters of suspicion' such as Derrida and Foucault. These thinkers, who trace their roots back to the philosophies of Nietzsche and Heidegger, are skeptical of any objective truth or foundational principles, let alone ideologies that support hierarchical controls such as intellectual property rights. Can intellectual property rights survive under the conditions of post-modernity?

Postmodernism is notoriously difficult to define, but Lyotard (1984, p. xxiv) characterizes this movement as an 'incredulity toward metanarratives'. There is no norm or standard beyond anyone's individual, idiosyncratic narrative. This 'incredulity' would assuredly extend to the implicit metanarrative about the history and normative justification of intellectual property rights, which constitute a form of conceptual and economic 'tyranny'. On the other hand, post-modern philosophers seek to subvert our traditional notions of rights, intellectual property, and even human subjectivity. Exclusive property rights awarded to a single author or corporate producer are highly suspect because they generate market power and chills cultural dialogue. These rights silence 'the Other' who struggles against the integrity of authorial works (Craig 2007, p. 221 n.76). The justification of these 'moral rights' has a hidden subtext, for it may simply be a means of cloaking the aggrandizement of wealth or a means of 'imped[ing] the free circulation … and recomposition of fiction' (Foucault 1977, p. 159).

How precisely are these entrenched concepts deconstructed? To begin with, there is a high level of suspicion about the conventional notion of authorship, which has been a basic underlying principle of copyright law since the days of the European Enlightenment. As we discussed in Chapter 2, the human author or creator has long been entitled to control his or her creative objects through some form of exclusive property right. In recent years, however, a group of legal scholars, influenced by the post-modern tradition, claim that the conception of individualized authorship or some type of solitary 'creator' has been overly emphasized and romanticized. Copyright law exists, they argue, to reward the work of the creative author, the artistic 'genius', and to glorify the individual who has the ultimate power over a work's meaning. But this socially constructed notion of authorship which perpetuates a myth of the lone author entitled to exclusive rights in his creative efforts must be deconstructed.

Why is this conventional notion of authorship such a problem? The trouble comes about because copyright often overvalues the work of the individual author, while discounting the contribution of the author's diverse cultural sources or social inputs. Society sees this 'romantic maximizer' as an original creator or inventor who opens new horizons and crafts something novel and original (Benkler 2006, p. 33). By granting this work some protection we can justly reward its author and set that work apart from the public domain. And since this work is original, the presumption is that this exclusivity will not diminish the common stock of knowledge and ideas which remain in the commons. The problem, according to Boyle (1996, p. 114), is that the excessive weight attributed to authorship 'play[s] down the importance of external sources by emphasizing the unique genius of the author and the originality of the work'. This state of affairs can be counterproductive since strong authorial rights often interfere with the creative expression of new authors, who cannot get the necessary access to copyrighted materials.

Critics cite several legal cases that seem to demonstrate how authorial personality plays a big factor in the preservation and overextension of robust property rights. When authors have a discernible creative role, courts will give them the benefit of the doubt, while works of 'low authorship' such as a simple computer database are not eligible for strong protection (Ginsburg 1992, pp. 339–41). According to one influential court ruling which denied copyright to a compilation of data: '[f]acts do not owe their origin to an act of authorship; the distinction is one between creation and discovery … '.[11] Commentators argued that the court's reasoning (though not its decision) was flawed because it insisted on the inter-connected requirements of authorship and originality. The law often fails to recognize non-individualistic cultural productions, including the works of folklore, because these works cannot be conceived as coming from a discrete, identifiable author. Jaszi (1992) regards *Rogers v. Koons*[12] as an example of the Court giving precedence to the individual creative author over collaborative efforts to create art.[13]

But why should an individual be entitled to exclude others from use of their work provided by the copyright and patent statutes if they themselves have been so dependent upon pre-existing sources? Isn't the author more of a cultural transmitter than a creator? The creative author does little more than recombine the resources and ideas found in the commons. Thus, there appears to be a lack of sound logic in copyright doctrine which unjustly rewards people who copy and repackage the works of others with these lucrative exclusive rights. That doctrine has misconstrued the nature of authorship and the limited role of the author in the creative process. Moreover, the problem, suggested by Boyle and Jaszi, is that copyright debate or discourse is too frequently distorted in favor of this inflated view of authorship. Authors, as traditionally understood, are sympathetic figures and they tend to win copyright infringement cases.[14]

Many scholars make similar arguments aimed at dethroning the romantic author figure from its lofty pedestal. According to Halbert (1999), the autonomous 'proprietary author' is a 'myth' of the copyright system, a product of economics (pp. 124–35). She questions the author's 'coherent identity' (Halbert 1999, p. 122), and reaffirms Boyle's argument that the notion of individual authorship is socially constructed according to a Romantic ideal. According to this line of reasoning, we must be especially wary of associating a creative work exclusively with a discrete, individual 'author'. Despite the author's concerted efforts, his or her creative output is not a product of this one individual but of various social forces and multiple cultural inputs that make up the author's work.

There are two significant implications in this critical analysis of individuated authorship. First, what's being called into question is the traditional humanist conception of the author as the origin of meaning who deserves glorification along with an exclusive property right. We need to re-focus our attention *away from the individual*, broaden our conception of 'authorship', so that we consider more seriously the author's multiple sources, possible collaborators, and the input of his or her audience. This re-focusing should allow us to account for collective and collaborative forms of authorship, some of which are facilitated by new technologies. The second implication is that the author herself is not fully autonomous or in control since the author's work is shaped so heavily by his or her social experiences. As Ginsburg (2003, p. 1092) contends, the author 'succeeds in exercising minimal personal autonomy in her fashioning of the work'. Also, according to Moxey (1994, p. 146), 'the assertion of the autonomous power of the artist has increasingly been called into question as a legitimate ambition for artistic production … '. The author, therefore, is not a true creator, but more like a medium or a 'conduit' for the communication of ideas and themes that already exist in the intellectual commons. The author doesn't create *ex nihilo* but merely channels, sometimes unconsciously, certain elements of humanity's vast cultural resources (McGowan 2005). This sentiment is commonly found in contemporary art criticism. In her analysis of the 'multiple meanings' of several Rothko paintings, a distinguished art critic, Professor Ann Chave (1980, p. 30), writes: 'whether Rothko would have ratified the meanings set forth here or recognized his conscious intentions in them is not the crucial issue'.[15]

Similarly, just as there is no genius autonomous author, there is no such thing as a 'genius' inventor. The inventor too has been romanticized to some degree.

All inventors are nothing more than pedestrian producers, however clever they may seem to be. Perelman (2002, p. 81) cites the work of economists like Alfred Kahn to demonstrate the impossibility of claiming a proprietary right to an invention because the inventor merely amalgamates what already exists. According to Kahn (1940, p. 479):

> Strictly speaking, no individual makes an invention, in the usual connotation of the term. For the object, which, for linguistic convenience, we call an automobile, a telephone, as if it were an entity, is, as a matter of fact, the aggregate of an almost infinite number of individual units of invention, each of them the contribution of a separate person. It is a little short of absurdity to call any one of the interrelated units of the invention, and its 'creator' the inventor.

Kahn's bizarre argument, advanced by Perelman to support the case against strong property rights, seems to defy logic, since it denies that things have the property of unity or oneness. Unity is far more than a 'linguistic convention'. Unless we accept the principle that a real object such as an airplane or a telephone has extrinsic unity there is no objective basis for referring to it as *this* thing; there is no *something* which exists in the singular, just a plurality of parts. If we keep breaking down things into a multiplicity of parts we end up with a pure multiplicity, which is a logical impossibility.

Regrettably, say the property rights skeptics, the romantic idea of authorship has been calcified in the legal tradition, and until it is dislodged we will not be able properly to reconstruct intellectual property law. According to Jaszi (1992, p. 295), 'the persistence of the notion of 'authorship' in American copyright law makes it difficult for any new legal synthesis … to emerge'. Similarly, Halbert (1999, p. 126) argues that the 'author is so embedded in our thought processes that we look to the author as owner instead of looking behind the role of authorship to the production of discourses in society'. Correlative concepts such as autonomy, originality, genius, and creativity should also be reconfigured.

For example, copyright doctrine calls for awarding a copyright to an original expressive work, but is anything really original? As one judicial opinion sums up the problem: '[i]n literature, in science and in art, there are, and can be, few, if any, things, which, in an abstract sense, are strictly new and original …'.[16] In addition, according to Litman's (1990, p. 1019) trenchant analysis, 'originality is a conceit', since the author's work is shaped so definitively and thoroughly by her experiences and by the other works of authorship she has assimilated. As an example, she explains that 'composers recombine sounds they have heard before' (Litman 1990, p. 966). If this is true, then 'genius' too must be yet another socially constructed category (Moxey 1994). A great artist like Michelangelo only *appeared* to be a genius to his patrons and admirers in the sixteenth century, but his work was merely a product of the social and religious forces operative upon him at the time. According to Rose (1993, pp. 25–6), even the eminent William Shakespeare was unoriginal and so it is appropriate to characterize Shakespeare the playwright as a 'reteller of tales'.

Another problem stems from the traditional notion that the author creates a static work with a fixed meaning and therefore deserves to control the meaning of that work, at least for a limited amount of time. Post-modernists largely dismiss this claim. Authorship, says Foucault (1977, p. 123), was concocted to give each text an arbitrary boundary: 'the author remains at the contours of texts – separating one from the other, defining their form …'. These boundaries are artificial since all creative works are inter-connected, with their ideas merging and flowing together. Thus, the text or the artistic creation, supposedly created *ex nihilo* by a genius author, is unstable and variable, subject to many different interpretations. The meaning and continued existence of these creative works often depend on their audience. Derrida (1981) claims that a text lacks identity or literal meaning since any stable identity is imposed by different subjects who read and interpret the text within variable social and historical contexts. According to Barthes (1977, p. 146), 'a text is not a line of words releasing a single "theological" meaning (the "message" of the author-God) but a multidimensional space in which a variety of writings, none of them original, blend and clash'. A creative work, therefore, is open-ended and completely elastic – no interpretation is precluded and none is warranted. Many literary and legal scholars have assimilated this dogma as they reflect upon the origin of meaning. As Vaidhyanathan (2001) observes, 'audience members have such complete control over the construction of meaning that the text itself is everything and the intent of the author means nothing' (p. 31).

Following the lead of Derrida and Barthes, legal scholars like Rotstein (1992) argue that we must regard creative works as dynamic processes or 'texts' rather than as static or reified products with a fixed meaning. We must recognize the instability of meaning and avoid the temptation of reification. Each text has fluid boundaries and all interpretation must be intertextual. In order to guard against complete indeterminacy, these dynamic texts should be classified as 'speech activity', which occurs within 'interpretive communities' (Rotstein 1992, p. 741). The texts or speech activity would be regulated in the same way we regulate other forms of speech. Readers and listeners should be considered the *co-creators* of a text, which is open-ended and subject to a wide range of interpretations.

Thus, thanks to the work of the deconstructionists, the text-centered and author-centric approach, so dominant in Western jurisprudence since the Statute of Anne, has finally been subverted in favor of a more realistic and unromantic vision of the author and the work he transmits. In summary, the notion of autonomous authorship 'is theoretically suspect, texts are unstable and determined in large part by their readers, and originality is more often a pose or a pretense rather than a definable aspect of a work' (Vaidhyanathan 2001, p. 8). Without this foundation how can exclusive property rights stand?

It is also instructive briefly to consider what lies at the root of these radical claims about authorship and originality: the philosophical premises of post-modern thinkers such as Michel Foucault who question the notions of human subjectivity and the stability of meaning. For Foucault and other post-modern thinkers, the process of deconstruction or *différance* exposes the multiplicity of 'differences' or different elements of reality which cannot be organized into categories or classified according to metaphysical species. It is the reader of a text who puts different elements together in order to create his or her own meaning. This process of *différance* represents 'acategorial' thinking and has no center or author. And if a text is without an autonomous author it must be without a unitary subject: 'the subject is constituted only in being divided from itself, in becoming space, in temporizing, in deferral' (Derrida 1981, p. 29). Thus, this questioning of authorial identity is part of the larger post-modern project to raise doubts about the existence or continuity of the autonomous, stable self.

Nietzsche first conceived the human self as a *dividuum*, lacking unity and coherence, where one force temporarily dominates. Nietzsche (1962, p. 27) described the self as 'a plurality … a war and peace, a herd and a shepherd'. Inspired by the philosophy of Nietzsche, Foucault and Derrida also regarded the human self not as a unified being but as fissured and divided. The post-modern tradition, then, conceives the self neither as an immediate unity nor as the ultimate source of activity, but as decentered and fragmented. Thus, the author-self as a stable being and the autonomous origin of meaning is simply an illusion. At most, the author is a transitional focal point in a fluid process rather than the source or creator of a stable work. According to Craig (2007, p. 234), we must 're-imagine the author not as source, origin, or authority, but rather as participant and citizen'.

If this general line of reasoning has merit, it will depose the author's authority over the work and undermine otherwise viable rationales for authorial entitlement based on moral arguments such as Locke's labor-based theory of ownership. If the notion of authorship is so inchoate, if the autonomous, individual author is more illusory than real, and if a text has no authentic boundaries, it makes little sense for an author to assert an entitlement to his distinct creative work. It will also be impossible to justify a property right based on the author's labor. Moreover, if originality is a 'pretense' there would be no basis for a valid copyright, at least as the copyright statute is currently configured.

The major problem with the traditional author construct is the unwarranted focus on the individual author and a neglect of the social nature of authorship. According to this argument, summarized by Cornish (2004, p. 50), authors derive more from the culture than they contribute in their work and so deserve no entitlement. With this in mind, Craig (2002, p. 36) argues that due to the 'interdependent nature of human culture' intellectual works 'ought to be owned collectively'. Similarly, since meaning is unfixed and is determined by the audience, the audience deserves some rights. This is particularly true of iconic trademarks, and so Wilf (1999) regards such a trademark not as the property of the company, which created it but as a 'joint interpretive enterprise between author and public' (pp. 45–6).[17]

But is there any plausibility to these unconventional viewpoints that destabilize the theoretical foundation of intellectual property law? Can the traditional concepts of authorship and originality withstand this withering post-modern critique? If not, how can property rights advocates deal with the expanding claims for collective or joint ownership? Although we cannot expose all of the flaws in the post-modern critique, let us address some of the more salient difficulties.

First, we must consider whether the ideal of the romantic author or 'romantic maximizer' is a valid explanation of what has happened in the evolution of copyright doctrine. Has copyright jurisprudence been heavily influenced by the romantic author vision, or have the courts simply been trying to balance the competing interests of creators and authors and the general public? It is certainly difficult to prove that copyright doctrine, such as fair use and the idea/expression dichotomy, and other safety valves, has been shaped by some romantic author vision rather than a desire to find that balance between overprotection and underprotection of an author's rights (Lemley 1997). Many court opinions such as this one from *Sayre v. Moore*[18] capture this particular tension: '[w]e must take care to guard against two extremes equally prejudicial: the one, that men of ability, who have employed their time for the service of the community, may not be deprived of their just merits, and the reward of their ingenuity and labor; the other, that the world may not be deprived of improvements, nor the progress of the arts be retarded'. Courts have repeatedly proclaimed that copyright law exists to promote discourse and to stimulate creative expression, and so it permits certain 'fair' uses that promote the growth of knowledge and culture. According to one recent opinion,[19] '[a]lthough dissemination of creative works is a goal of the Copyright Act, the Act creates a balance between the artist's right to control the work during the term of the copyright protection and the public's need for access to creative works'. In addition, there is little attention paid to cases where copyright is acknowledged despite the absence of the author.[20] On the other hand where is the evidence that the courts have been so preoccupied exclusively with authorship that they have consistently ignored the need for this balance by overprotecting the author's works?

Second, what are we to make of the argument that a creative work is inherently unstable, or Barthes' radical claim that a text does not have a single 'theological' meaning but is open-ended and subject to a wide range of meanings. As one legal scholar sums up this viewpoint, 'interpretive freedom is absolute' (Fiss 1982, p. 234). There are two salient problems with this argument. The first one involves the nature of Barthe's own text. For the sake of argument let us formulate Barthes' assertion as a simple proposition: 'no text or statement has a stable or fixed meaning'. But what about the meaning of *this* proposition? If Barthes' proposition (or text) has a fixed or determinate meaning, then the proposition contradicts itself. In this case, Barthes' theory self-destructs and loses its force as a critique. On the other hand, if this proposition too lacks a fixed meaning, we can interpret it any way we like; as a result, Barthes' position on the instability of meaning becomes relativized and is hardly worth our attention because it doesn't convey an objective or determinate truth. It is incoherent to claim that works do not have a stable meaning intended by their author. One purpose of copyright is to allow authors to safeguard the social meaning and integrity of their work. According to Kwall (1985), an author's intellectual property rights can help guarantee that the public will be able to 'enjoy the fruits of a creator's labors in original form' (p. 4).

Another problem is the apparent presumption of Derrida and Barthes that a text does not have a determinate, literal meaning intended by the author. But have these deconstructionists proven this point or just asserted it? It is difficult to discern in their writings a logical proof that would persuade us about the inevitable variability of all textual meaning. Just because readers interpret a text in many different ways, it does not necessarily follow that there is no literal or primary meaning being consciously projected by the author.

Third, some of the arguments offered in opposition to traditional notions of authorship and originality defy sound philosophical reasoning. It may surely be true that our notion of authorship is overly romanticized, and that not enough attention is paid to an author's sources and influences. At the same time, it is not a sensible idea to reduce the author's role to that of an impassive conduit who merely channels what is already present in the commons. To some extent, authors re-construct and re-shape the ideas they have borrowed from others. But this fact does not deny the single author's irreducible role as a *creative catalyst*, the conscious origin and source of a fresh interpretation, a new work developed through hard labor that often entails considerable imaginative input and sometimes advances the frontiers of knowledge. In this creative process the author as human subject who acts with intentionality endows a work with a certain meaning and stamps his or her unique personality upon that particular work. According to Justice Holmes, the creative work 'is the personal reaction of an individual upon nature; personality always contains something unique … that something he may copyright'.[21]

It is counterintuitive to suppose that the author is a passive and impersonal force, 'a vessel through which many influences and experiences are poured' (Zemer 2006, p. 251). The more our notion of authorship is linked with passivity

shipping and billing data. Amazon's innovation is an extension of 'cookie' technology which remembers a prior customer's purchase data. Barnes & Noble, Amazon's main competitor in the online book business, quickly imitated Amazon's innovation with its own expedited ordering system known as 'Express Lane'. As in Amazon's model, only one single action (such as a mouse click) needs to be taken in order for the consumer to complete his or her order.

Amazon immediately filed a patent infringement law suit against Barnes & Noble, and obtained a preliminary injunction prohibiting Barnes & Noble from using Express Lane's one-click feature. Barnes & Noble appealed the injunction to the Third Federal Circuit Court, claiming that its Express Lane feature did not infringe Amazon's patent. In its defense, Barnes & Noble further argued that there were serious questions about the validity of the Amazon patent, and it argued that the injunction was not warranted since there was not a reasonable likelihood of Amazon's success based on the merits of its case. The Appeals Court concluded that Barnes & Noble had raised 'substantial questions as to the validity of the 411 patent'.[34] Accordingly, it vacated the preliminary injunction and remanded the case back to the Federal District Court in Washington state. The case was eventually settled out of court. The settlement terms remain confidential, but Barnes & Noble's 'Express Lane' takes two steps to complete a transaction.

In a similar case the auction site, eBay, was sued for infringement by MercExchange for its 'Buy It Now' feature, a button on the auction site that lets buyers purchase at a fixed price if they choose not to bid on an item. To its surprise, eBay lost the first round of this patent case and was ordered to pay MercExchange $29.5 million. But the case was appealed to the US Supreme Court and it has been remanded to a lower court for a re-hearing.[35]

The obvious question triggered by these cases is the validity of business method patents. Are these patents necessary to encourage innovation? Do the incentives created outweigh the cost of exclusivity such as higher prices, trade restraints, and increased transaction costs? Do companies like Amazon.com truly deserve a full 20-year patent for developing a new business method such as the 'one-click' system? It is unlikely that the development of these minor and rather obvious innovations would require a substantial investment of labor and money. Complicated software derives its quality and value from the many hours of labor expended on design, coding and testing. Hence, those who create this software deserve to be rewarded for their efforts. On the other hand, developing this 'one-click' innovation takes a fraction of the time required to build a full software application or an operating system for the PC (such as Windows). The Lockean rationale for a property right, therefore, is not compelling in this case. Second, market savvy companies like Amazon are probably inclined to make incremental improvements to their operations without the incentive of a patent. Most companies routinely strive to enhance service to their customers in a competitive marketplace by adding new features to a web site that make it easier for users to make a purchase. Consequently, it is implausible to argue that such patent protection is warranted on utilitarian grounds.

Thus, intellectual property theories strongly suggest the invalidity of most business method patents from a purely normative viewpoint. Business method patents, as currently understood, represent another form of overprotection, which is particularly hard to validate from a moral or economic standpoint. Perhaps if these patents were granted on stricter terms for innovations that were truly *novel and non-obvious* the patentability of a business methodology might be more acceptable.

Nonetheless, these examples of overprotection do not nullify the need for exclusive intellectual property rights in the form of a patent. Patents are essential if companies are to appropriate the returns from their investments in discovery and commercialization.[36] Expensive new pharmaceutical therapies are better than none at all. But patents should not be awarded casually. As Dam (1994, p. 266) points out, the patent system operates through time. Therefore, 'to be an efficient system it must optimize the flow of innovation over time – the patent system must thus balance innovation today against innovation tomorrow'. What's needed is a recalibration of patent policy and careful scrutiny of patent applications, not a sweeping overhaul that will dilute patent protection or a switch to the enforcement of a patent right through a liability rule instead of a property rule.[37]

Finally, no account of excessive property protection would be complete without treatment of the much maligned Digital Millennium Copyright Act (DMCA) of 1998. In the eyes of most legal scholars the DMCA represents another example of misguided policy. They regard this legislation and its European counterpart, the European Copyright Directive (2001), as another means of precluding or restricting access to digital information in order to consolidate corporate power.

At the core of the controversial DMCA is an anti-circumvention provision which criminalizes the use of technologies that circumvent technical protection measures such as an encryption program. Prior to the DMCA, individuals could only be held liable for the infringement of a valid copyright under the terms of the Copyright Act. There are two types of anti-circumvention rules in the DMCA. The first rule [1201 (a) (1) (A)] outlaws the act of circumventing 'a technical measure that effectively controls access to a [copyrighted] work'. For example, if a copyright owner uses a digital rights management system or some type of encryption code to protect a digital book from unauthorized users, it would be illegal for anyone to break the encryption and access the book without the copyright holder's permission.

The DMCA also makes it illegal to manufacture or distribute technologies that facilitate various forms of circumvention. As Section 1201 (a) (2) indicates,

technologies constitutes a violation of the anti-trafficking provision. At the same time, the DMCA may serve a salutary function ignored by its detractors. If we grant the premise that software or code-based regulation is here to stay, the DMCA has an important role to play. It encourages the use of access control technologies or DRMs, but those DRMs need not be particularly potent to be eligible for protection by the DMCA. It seems safe to assume, therefore, that without the DMCA there would most likely be hyper-strong DRM systems to combat piracy, and those DRM systems, which lock up content as tightly as possible, could well diminish social welfare. But thanks to the DMCA, the incentive to build such systems is reduced. When DRM code is protected by law the net effect is to diminish the need for intense DRM safeguards (Wagner 2005).

4. INTELLECTUAL PROPERTY RIGHTS AND DEVELOPING COUNTRIES

The problem of intellectual property and developing countries is complex, but Steidlmeier (1993, p. 161) captures the essence of the moral issues at hand: 'developing countries argue that individual claims on intellectual property are subordinated to more fundamental claims of social well-being'. He notes that these countries also reject the so-called 'trickle down theory', that is, the notion that technological developments will eventually be transferred to others despite a strong system of protections. Perleman (2002) argues that the strengthening of intellectual property rights only results in an expansion of impoverishment among the poor. Also, developing countries give little credence to the utilitarian arguments supporting robust intellectual property rights, due to the heavy costs imposed upon them.

Some journalists paint a stark picture of the disparity between the information 'haves' and 'have nots'. They see a clash of cultures and a global battle between producers of intellectual property in the developed world and IP pirates in developing countries. According to one report, '[t]he propertied class loudly asserts its ownership and control. The insurgents cry for openness and exploit technological loopholes with abandon' (Howe 2004, p. 146). Hyperbole aside, developing countries like Africa account for only a very small percentage of world research and development, and as a result they are heavily dependent on the transfer of technology from developed countries.[45] Exclusive intellectual property rights impede the transfer of technology and intellectual resources which is desperately needed in many nations in sub-Saharan Africa, Asia, and Latin America.

Strong intellectual property protection is also seen as the chief impediment to affordable health care. Broad pharmaceutical patents are blamed for many

a more egalitarian world knowledge system. For example, Altbach (1995, pp. 6–7) has called for the attenuation of copyright terms of scientific journals to help support the Soviet Union's depleted libraries. But why should copyright owners subsidize inefficient economies? A stronger case can be made, however, to support such measures for developing countries which lack the resources to build their library systems.

Most developing countries perceive the need for some type of patent system that suits their particular predicament. New models may be necessary to protect the cultural and biological resources that do not fit into traditional categories. Nonetheless, if configured fairly and managed properly, intellectual property rights can be an opportunity even for developing countries, since they will incentivize key domestic industries and preserve their heritage from the hands of Western entrepreneurs.

5. CLEARING THE IMPEDIMENTS

In this chapter we have sought to assess some of the more salient arguments against thick but limited intellectual property rights. As part of this effort we have confronted the major barriers standing in the way of a proper understanding of authorial entitlement. These roadblocks and intellectual impediments must be cleared so that a coherent normative justification of intellectual property values can be put forth. It is particularly important to deal with the radical deconstructionists who seek to undermine the most fundamental underpinnings of exclusive intellectual property rights. Once the commonly accepted assumptions of autonomous authorship, originality, and creativity are exposed by the deconstructionists as part of an unfounded metanarrative, they are quickly discredited. If individual authorship and originality are suspect, so too are exclusive intellectual property rights.

The post-modernists have declared their hostility toward all forms of interiority, which seems to include the author's self-awareness, autonomy, and even his or her very selfhood (Taylor 1984). In their view, the human subject lacks any self-identity and is no more than a bundle of variable social constructs. One such construct is the self as autonomous author or artistic 'genius'. In reality, the author is merely a 'shadow', at best, a clever but unoriginal collaborator who assembles pre-existing cultural resources. We must abandon the confidence placed by the legal system in 'individual agency and control over discourse that involves, inevitably, a belief in the possibility of creative originality' (Randall 2001, p. 28). The vision of the author as agent must yield to a vision of the author as passive 'conduit' or participant.

Similarly, the various 'texts' the author supposedly creates *ex nihilo* are also socially constructed and subject to open-ended interpretation by audiences that bestow their own meaning. Contrary to common opinion, these creative works are not autonomous entities with a fixed textual meaning. This abstraction merely makes possible the propertization of abstract works. We should begin to see these works not as objects but as a 'process of action and reaction' (Craig 2007, p. 222).

Of course, these post-modern arguments cut both ways. Those who argue so passionately against intellectual property rights also lack autonomy or independence from social forces that shape their own way of thinking. They too lack control and authority over their own discourse. If someone claims that a text is unstable with an indeterminate meaning, what about the meaning of his or her own text which makes these declarations? If it has a determinate and authoritative meaning the author contradicts himself; if not, we can attribute any meaning we like to the text which seems to defeat the purpose of his effort to inform us of some definite truth. The foes of conventional authorship cannot escape the fact that their own authorial work is as suspect, 'unstable', unauthoritative, and open to diverse meanings as the work of any author. Also, Foucault's assertion that the 'author function' is socially constructed cannot rise to the level of objective truth since such a claim smacks of a metanarrative. And since the post-modern philosophers cannot be claiming to tell us some objective truth that transcends the social forces impinging upon them, their own position is immediately relativized.

In order to preserve any credible notion of human activity and autonomy it is necessary to overcome the negative anthropology implicit in the deconstructionist critique. Such a task is beyond the scope of this modest book, but let it suffice to indicate that the human self cannot be reduced to a set of constructs or a sheer multiplicity as favored by post-modern philosophy. Rather, if human experience and accountability is to retain its intelligibility, the human self must have autonomy and self-identity. It must be a dynamic substance with an intrinsic orientation to self-expressive action (Clarke 1994). If we reduce the human subject to a multiplicity of social forces or an effect of *différance*, we empty it of anything valuable that is worth expressing to others or sharing with others.

We cannot dispense with the transhistorical identity of the author as origin and cause. Every composed being or being that begins to exist, including those that are intangible, requires an efficient cause. It is radically unintelligible to assert the contrary. The fact that authors borrow from the works of others in the creative process does not negate the truth of this proposition. Novels and symphonies do not just appear out of thin air. To produce such works requires labor and effort which should be rewarded with a limited property right, partly because the author incarnates his or her personality in these works. Also, it is incoherent to claim that the collective collaborates with an author. Only the human subject is capable of acting or collaborating. We may want to re-think the criteria for originality in awarding property rights to expressive works, but it makes little sense to see an author's cultural resources as his or her co-creators or as entitled to some sort of shared property right.

At the same time, we have tried to demonstrate that originality is far more than a romantic myth or a pretense, as scholars like Rose (1993) and Litman (1990) have proposed. The word 'genius' can be applied to some authors and artists. While the level of originality will vary among authors, who can credibly quarrel with the claim that Shakespeare's plays or the compositions of Mozart and Beethoven are original works of genius? Mozart did not just blindly recombine what he found pre-existing in the commons. In Nietzsche's words, authors and artists are 're-creators', inspired by the past, but they are still 'creators' and not impassive transmitters of cultural resources. The genius does not reproduce but creates something different, even if that something different is the shedding of a brilliant new light on past creations. The author-as-conduit argument suggests a passive fatalism and deterministic view of creativity that does not square with our understanding of the creative process and the existence of transcendent and sublime works of art. Each creative work reflects in some way the author's individual personality, his or her unique experiences, and his or her inner selfhood. This creativity requires intellectual labor which is the securest normative foundation for the limited intellectual property rights recognized in the law. According to one judicial opinion, '[a] work is original if it is the independent creation of its author. A work is creative if it embodies some modest amount of intellectual labor'.[46]

The other criticisms enumerated in this chapter contain some merit and we will address them to some extent in the chapters that follow. There have been excesses that need to be addressed. However, intellectual property rights are not intrinsically unjust as some have argued, but they must be measured and properly limited by other basic human rights. In the pages ahead we will consider a balanced approach to property rights grounded in the normative justification provided by Locke, who convincingly demonstrates that creators and inventors are entitled to appropriate most of the social value of their creations.

NOTES

1. The first enclosure movement was the need for private property rights exercised over land in order to encourage development and prevent under-use, and forestall a 'tragedy of the commons'. See Boyle (2003).
2. In the wake of *Diamond v. Diehr*, 450 U.S. 175 (1981), the US Patent Office issued guidelines for the patentability of genetic sequence data provided that this sequence was connected to a human utility.
3. Cohen (2002) refers to the proclivity of those who hold intellectual property rights to regard them as absolute: 'a property right [is]delineated as absolute sovereignty over the disposition and use' (p. 379).
4. See, for example, Barney (2001).
5. Nachbar (2004) says that these exclusive intellectual property rights 'are merely another form

of regulation that Congress may, and frequently does, use to confer economic rents on favored special interests' (p. 272).

6. In the client server model a text file, an MP3 music file, or a movie file can be 'served' (or distributed) from a central computer or server based on a request from a user's client system. On the other hand, a P2P network is defined as one in which 'two or more computers share [files] without requiring a separate server computer or server software' (Cope, 2002).
7. There are some libertarians and information theorists (such as John Perry Barlow) who maintain that information has the quality of being a life form. See Himma (2005) for a useful discussion of this topic.
8. Rights management systems can also be utilized to determine what rights a user has with regard to content. According to Ku (2002), used in conjunction with a protective encryption system, 'rights management is the ability of a publisher of a work to define what rights subsequent users of her work will have to use, copy, or edit the work'.
9. See Hughes (2006), especially pp. 1054–5. Also in *Eldred v. Ashcroft,* 537 U.S. 186 (2003) (Breyer, J. dissenting) the Court opined that since 'the Copyright Clause and First Amendment were adopted close in time … the proximity indicates that, in the Framers' view, copyright's limited monopolies are compatible with free speech principles; indeed, copyright's purpose is to promote the creation and publication of free expression' (p. 219).
10. See *Suntrust Bank v. Houghton Mifflin Co.* 268 F.3d 1257, 11th Cir. (2001): 'Because of the First Amendment principles built into copyright law through the idea/expression dichotomy and the doctrine of fair use, courts often need not entertain First Amendment arguments in a copyright case' (pp. 1264–5).
11. *Feist Publications v. Rural Tel. Services Co.*, 499 U.S. 340 (1991), 347. In that case the Court opined that copyright should only protect original works 'founded in the creative powers of the mind', at 347. Aoki (1993) points out that this adoption of 'author-reasoning' oveshadowed other policy bases on which the case may have been decided (pp. 812–13).
12. 960 F. 2d, 2d Cir., 1992.
13. In this case Rogers (a photographer) alleged that Koons infringed his copyright by using one of his postcards as the source of sculpture that was produced with other artisans. There are other factors at work in this case, however, and so it seems presumptuous to claim that the Court was biased in favor of the individual artist versus collaborators.
14. For example, in *Basic Books, Inc. v. Kinko's Graphic Corporation,* 758 F. Supp 1522, S.D.N.Y., (1991) the Court apparently refused to consider that creation of an anthology was a form of 'authorship' because it concentrated too heavily on the authors who wrote the original works. According to the Court, the copying did not 'transform the works in suit, that is, interpret them or add any value to the material copied' (p. 1530).
15. For a more detailed analysis of the effects of post-modernism on art history and criticism see Kimball (2004), especially pp. 3–32.
16. *Emerson v. Davies*, 8 F. Cas 615, CCD Mass, (1845) at pp. 618–19.
17. See also Palmer (1990) who argues that if we want to recognize a copyright in a work that right 'should be in the audience, and not in the artist, for it is on the audience that the art work depends for its continued existence, and not the artist' (p. 848).
18. *Sayre v. Moore* (1785) quoted in *Carey v. Longman* 102 ER 138 (1801).
19. *Stewart v. Abend*, 495 U.S. 207 (1990) at 228.
20. See, for example, *Ansehl v. Puritan Pharmaceutical Company,* 61 F. 2d 131, 8th Cir., (1932). See also Hughes (1998).
21. *Bleistein v. Donaldson Lithographing Co.*, (1903). 188 U.S. 239 at 299–300.
22. For a more in-depth discussion on human agency see Macmurray (1978).
23. *Feist Publications v. Rural Tel Services*, 345.
24. Id. at 345.
25. Arguably, this is the meaning of Nietzsche's (1977) famous doctrine of eternal return, the seeds of which are found in one of his early and more accessible works, *Vom Nutzen und Nachteil der Historie für das Leben.*
26. Sonny Bono Copyright Term Extension Act, Pub. L. No. 105–298, 112 Stat. 2827 (1998), codified as amended at 17 U.S.C. 108 203(a) (2).
27. *Eldred v. Ashcroft,* 537 U.S. 186 (2003) (Breyer, J. dissenting).

28. Id. at 224.
29. Id., our emphasis.
30. *Diamond v. Diehr* , 450 U.S. 175 (1981).
31. *Diamond v. Chakrabarty,* 447 U.S. 303 (1980), at 309.
32. *State Street Bank & Trust Co. v. Signature Financial Group* (1998). 149 F. 3d 1368 (Fed. Cir.) (1998).
33. Id. at 1375.
34. *Amazon.com, Inc. v. Barnesandnoble.com, Inc.*73 F. Supp. 2d (W.D. Wash. 1999) at 1360, *vacated and remanded,* 239 F. 3d 1343 (Fed. Cir. 2001).
35. *ebay v. MercExchange, L.L.C.* 547 U.S. 388 (2006).
36. Kieff (2000) argues that patents are incentives 'to commercialize nascent innovations' (p. 746) and are especially important in industries where commercialization costs are high (such as pharmaceuticals). See also *In re Alappat,* 33 F. 3d 1526, Fed Cir. (1994), Newman, J. concurring. (1994): 'what seems to be missing in our country is an understanding that, no matter how much money we spend on research and development, the findings are not going to benefit the public unless there are suitable incentives to invest in commercialization' (p. 1571).
37. Kieff (2000) makes the case that a liability rule will only 'frustrate the commercialization goals of the system' (p. 735).
38. See, for example, 'Unintended Consequences: Four Years under the DMCA' (2003) published by the Electronic Frontier Foundation.
39. In the *Elcom* case, however, the Court characterized Elcomsoft's argument that the DMCA 'effectively eliminates' fair use as an exaggeration: *United States v. Elcom Ltd.* 203 F. Supp. 2d 1111 N.D. Cal. (2002), pp. 1130–31.
40. *Universal City Studios v. Reimerdes,* 111 F. Supp. 294, S.D.N.Y., (2000), aff'd *Universal City Studios v. Corley,* 273 F. 3d 429, 2d Cir., (2001).
41. Id. at 341.
42. Trial Transcript, *Universal City Studios v. Reimerdes,* 111 F. Supp. 294, S.D.N.Y., (2000).
43. See *ACLU v. Reno,* 929 F. Supp. 824 (E.D. Pa.) (1996) aff'd *Reno v. ACLU* 521 U.S. 844 (1997): 'Links from one computer to another, from one document to another across the Internet, are what unify the Web into a single body of knowledge, and what makes the Web unique' (pp. 836–7).
44. *Universal City Studios v. Reimerdes,* 111 F. Supp. 294, S.D.N.Y. (2000) at 329.
45. According to one report, Africa controls only about 0.4% of the world's intellectual property. See Aoki (1998), pp. 24–7.
46. *Baltimore Orioles v. Major League Baseball Players Ass'n* (1986). 805 F. 2d 663 at 668 n6.

REFERENCES

Altbach, Philip (1995), *Copyright and Development: Inequality in the Information Age*, Chestnut Hill, MA: Bellagio Publishing Network.

Aoki, Keith (1993), 'Adrift in the Intertext: Authorship and Audience Recoding Rights', 68 *Chicago-Kent Law Review* 805.

Aoki, Keith (1998), 'Neocolonialism, Anticommons Property, and Biopiracy in the (Not-So-Brave) New World Order of Intellectual Property Protection', 6 *Indian Journal of Global Legal Studies* 11.

Aoki, Keith (1996), 'Property and Sovereignty: Notes Toward a Cultural Geography of Authorship', 48 *Stanford Law Review* 1293.

Barlow, John P. (1994), 'The Economy of Ideas', *Wired,* March, 84–6; available at: http://www.wired.com/wired /archive/2.03/economy.ideas.html.

Barney, Jay (2001), 'Competence Explanations of Economic Profits in Strategic Management', in Jerry Ellig (ed.), *Dynamic Competition and Public Policy*, Princeton, NJ: University of Princeton Press.

Barthes, Roland (1977), 'The Death of the Author', in Stephen Heath (ed.), *Image-Music-Text*, New York: Hill & Wang.

Becker, Lawrence (1977), *Property Rights,* London: Routledge and Kegan Paul.

Becker, Lawrence (1993), 'Deserving to Own Intellectual Property', 68 *Chicago-Kent Law Review* 609.

Benkler, Yochai (2006), *The Wealth of Networks: How Social Production Transforms Markets and Freedom*, New Haven, CN: Yale University Press.

Boyle, James (1996), *Shamans, Software, and Spleens: Law and the Construction of the Information Society,* Cambridge, MA: Harvard University Press.

Boyle, James (2003), 'The Second Enclosure Movement and the Construction of the Public Domain', 66 *Law and Contemporary Problems* 33.

Chave, Ann (1989), *Mark Rothko: Subjects in Abstraction*, New Haven, CN: Yale University Press.

Chon, Margaret (1996), 'New Wine Bursting from Old Bottles: Collaborative Internet Art, Joint Works, and Entrepreneurship', 75 *Oregon Law Review* 257.

Clarke, Norris (1994), *Explorations in Metaphysics*, South Bend, IN: University of Notre Dame Press.

Cohen, Julie (2002), 'Overcoming Property: Does Copyright Trump Privacy?', 22 *University of Illinois Journal of Technology & Policy* 375.

Cohen, Morris (1927), 'Property and Sovereignty', 13 *Cornell Law Quarterly* 8.

Cope, J. (2002), 'Peer-to-Peer Network', available at: http://www.computerworld.com/networkingtopics/networking/story.

Cornish, William (2004), *Intellectual Property: Omnipresent, Distracting, Irrelevant?*, Oxford: Oxford University Press.

Craig, Carys (2002), 'Locke, Labor and Limiting the Author's Right: A Warning against a Lockean Approach to Copyright Law', 28 *Queen's Law Journal* 1.

Craig, Carys (2007), 'Reconstructing the Author-Self: Some Feminist Lessons for Copyright Law', 15 *American University Journal of Gender, Social Policy, & the Law* 207.

Dam, Kenneth (1994), 'The Economic Underpinnings of Patent Law', *Journal of Legal Studies* vol. XXIII (January) 247.

Derrida, Jacques (1981), *Positions,* trans. A. Bass, Chicago: University of Chicago Press.

Digital Millennium Copyright Act (DMCA), (1998) U.S.C., § 103, Title 17, § 1201.

Drahos, Peter (1996), *A Philosophy of Intellectual Property*, Aldershot: Dartmouth Publishing.

Drahos, Peter and John Braithwaite (2002), *Information Feudalism: Who Owns the Knowledge Economy*, New York: The New Press.

Dratler, J. (2005), *Cyberlaw: Intellectual Property in the Digital Millennium*, New York: Law Journal Press.

Easterbrook, Frank. (1990), 'Intellectual Property is Still Property', 3 *Harvard Journal of Law and Public Policy* 110.

Electronic Frontier Foundation (2003) 'Unintended Consequences: Four Years under the DMCA', Washington, DC: Electronic Frontier Foundation.

Fiss, Owen (1982), 'Objectivity and Interpretation', 34 *Stanford Law Review* 739.

Foucault, Michel (1977), 'What is an Author?', in D.F. Bouchard and S. Simon (eds.), *Language, Counter-Memory, Practice: Selected Essays and Interviews*, Ithaca, NY: Cornell University Press.

Ginsburg, Jane (1992), '"No Sweat"? Copyright and Other Protection of Works of Information after Feist v. Rural Telephone', 92 *Columbia Law Review* 338.

Ginsburg, Jane (2003), 'The Concept of Authorship in Comparative Copyright Law', 52 *DePaul Law Review* 1063.
Grodzinsky, Fran and Herman Tavani (2005), 'P2P Networks and the Verizon v. RIAA case: Implications for Personal Privacy and Intellectual Property', 7 (4) *Ethics and Information Technology*, 243.
Halbert, Deborah (1999), *Intellectual Property in the Information Age*, Westport, CN: Quorum Books.
Heller, Michael (2008), *The Gridlock Economy*, New York: Basic Books.
Hesse, Carla (2002), 'The Rise of Intellectual Property, 700 B.C. – A.D. 2000: An Idea of Balance', *Daedalus* (Spring), 26.
Himma, Kenneth (2005), 'Information and Intellectual Property Protection: Evaluating the Claim that Information Should be Free', in Richard Spinello (ed.), The American Philosophical Association *Newsletter of Law and Philosophy* (Spring), 2.
Howe, Jeff (2004), 'The Free and the Unfree', *Wired,* June, 146.
Hughes, Justin (1998), 'The Personality Interest of Artists and Inventors Intellectual Property', 16 *Cardozo Arts and Entertainment Law Journal* 81.
Hughes, Justin (2006), 'Copyright and Incomplete Historiographies: Of Piracy, Propertization, and Thomas Jefferson', 79 *Southern California Law Review* 993.
Jaszi, Peter (1992), 'On the Author Effect: Contemporary Copyright and Collective Creativity', 10 *Cardozo Arts & Entertainment Law Journal* 293.
Kahn, Alfred (1940), 'Fundamental Deficiencies of the American Patent Law', 30 (3) *American Economic Review* 470.
Kieff, F. Scott (2000), 'Property Rights and Property Rules for Commercializing Inventions', 85 *Minnesota Law Review* 697.
Kimball, Roger (2004), *The Rape of the Masters*, San Francisco, CA: Encounter Books.
Ku, Raymond (2002), 'The Creative Destruction of Copyright', 69 *University of Chicago Law Review* 167.
Kwall, Roberta (1985), 'Copyright and the Moral Right: Is an American Marriage Possible', 38 *Vanderbilt Law Review* 1.
Landes, William and Richard Posner (1989), 'An Economic Analysis of Copyright Law', 18 *Journal of Legal Studies* 325.
Lange, David (2003), 'Students, Music and the Net: A Comment on Peer-to-Peer File Sharing', 23 *Duke Law and Technology Review* 21.
Lemley, Mark (1997), 'Romantic Authorship and the Rhetoric of Property', 75 *Texas Law Review* 873.
Lemley, Mark and Eugene Volokh (1998), 'Freedom of Speech and Injunctions in Intellectual Property Cases', 48 *Duke Law Journal* 147.
Lessig, Larry (1999), *Code and Other Laws of Cyberspace*, New York: Basic Books.
Lessig, Larry (2001), *The Future of Ideas*, New York: Random House.
Lessig, Larry (2004), *Free Culture,* New York: Random House.
Litman, Jessica (1990), 'The Public Domain', 39 *Emory Law Journal* 965.
Lyotard, Jean François (1984), *The Postmodern Critique: A Report on Knowledge,* Minneapolis, MN: University of Minnesota Press.
Macmurray, John (1978), *The Self as Agent*, Atlantic Highlands, NJ: Humanities Press (Original work published 1957).
Martin, Brian (1998), *Information Liberation*, London: Freedom Press.
McGowan, David (2005), 'Information Regulation and the Freedom of Expression', 74 *Fordham Law Review* 435.

Merges, Robert (1996), 'Property Rights Theory and the Commons: The Case of Scientific Research', 13 *Social Philosophy & Policy* 145.

Moxey, Keith (1994), *The Practice of Theory: Poststructuralism, Cultural Politics, and Art History*, Ithaca, NY: Cornell University Press.

Nachbar, Thomas (2004), 'Intellectual Property and Constitutional Norms', 104 *Columbia Law Review* 272.

Nietzsche, Friedrich (1962), *Also Sprach Zarathustra,* Stuttgart: Philipp Reclam (Original work published 1892).

Nietzsche, Friedrich (1977), *Vom Nutzen und Nachteil der Historie für das Leben,* in Karl Schlechta (ed.), *Werke in Drei Bänden*, Munich: Carl Hanser Verlag, vol. I: 209 (Original work published 1874).

Palmer, Tom (1990), 'Are Patents and Copyrights Morally Justified? The Philosophy of Property Rights and Ideal Objects', 13 *Harvard Journal of Law and Public Policy* 817.

'Patents and the Poor' (2001), *The Economist,* June 23, 21.

Perelman, Michael (2002), *Steal this Idea*, New York: Palgrave.

Randall, Marilyn (2001), *Pragmatic Plagiarism: Authorship, Profit, and Power*, New York: Basic Books.

Roblimo, L. (2000), Posting to Slashdot, April 10; available at: http://slashdot.org/article.pl.

Rose, Mark (1993), *Authors and Owners: The Invention of Copyright*, Cambridge, MA: Harvard University Press.

Rotstein, Robert (1992), 'Beyond Metaphor: Copyright Infringement and the Fiction of the Work', 68 *Chicago-Kent Law Review* 725.

Shulman, Seth (1999), *Owning the Future*, Boston, MA: Houghton Mifflin Company.

Spinello, Richard (2008), 'Intellectual Property: Legal and Moral Challenges of Online File Sharing', in Kenneth Himma and Herman Tavani (eds.), *The Handbook of Information and Computer Ethics,* Hoboken, NJ: Wiley, 553.

Steidlmeier, Paul (1993), 'The Moral Legitimacy of Intellectual Property Claims: American Business and Developing Country Perspectives', 4 (2) *Journal of Business Ethics*, 157.

Taylor, Mark (1984), *Erring: A Postmodern A/Theology*, Chicago, IL: University of Chicago Press.

Vaidhyanathan, Siva (2001), *Copyrights and Copywrongs: The Rise of Intellectual Property and How it Threatens Creativity*, New York: New York University Press.

Vaidhyanathan, Siva (2004), *The Anarchist in the Library*, New York: Basic Books.

VerSteeg, Russ (1996), 'Defining 'Author' for Purposes of Copyright', 45 *American University Law Review* 1323.

Wagner, Polk (2005), 'Reconsidering the DMCA', 6 *Houston Law Review* 22.

Wilf, Steven (1999), 'Who Authors Trademarks', 17 *Cardozo Arts & Entertainment Law Journal* 1.

Zemer, Lior (2006), 'The Copyright Moment', 43 *San Diego Law Review* 247.

5. Foundations of intellectual property rights

So far in this book, we have considered the various forms of legal protection for intellectual property rights along with the history of how those rights have evolved. We have also confronted the obstacles posed by post-modern philosophy and demonstrated the validity of the traditional conceptions of authorship, genius, and originality. An author-based entitlement remains valid, notwithstanding provocative questions about authorship raised by philosophers such as Michel Foucault. We now turn to the underlying philosophical and normative justification for intellectual property law. It is important to understand the secure normative foundation for the legal infrastructure supporting intellectual property rights.

A property right is defined by Landes and Posner (1988, p. 266) as any 'legally enforceable power to exclude others from using a resource, without the need to contract with them'. These rights offer both static and dynamic benefits: they prevent the overuse or misuse of a resource and they also provide an incentive to create new resources or enhance and improve existing ones. Most philosophers would agree with this definition of a right since they acknowledge that the essence of a property right is the 'right to exclude others' (Cohen 1928, p. 12).[1]

According to W. F. Hohfeld's (1919) framework, property would be considered a claim-right, such that one individual (the right holder) has a claim on another (the duty-bearer) not to interfere with the right holder's property or use it against his or her will. In Hohfeld's classic work on rights theory, he distinguishes between a 'claim right', or right in the 'strict sense', and a liberty right. The right to property falls into the former category. According to Hohfeld (1919), A has a claim right that B should do Ø if and only if B has a duty to A to do Ø. The key point is that when claim rights are at stake, the action in question is an action on the part of others and not on the part of the person who has the right. A claim right is either a right to be given something, to be assisted in some way, or a right not to be interfered with or dealt with in a certain way (Finnis 1980). A property right, therefore, is a right to control and use one's property without interference from others.

But how is an intellectual property right justified? It seems particularly difficult to justify a right to intellectual property given the non-rivalrous nature of information. As Hettinger (1989) aptly observes, 'Why should one person have the exclusive right to possess and use something which all people could possess and use concurrently? The burden of justification is very much on those who would restrict the maximal use of intellectual property' (p. 39). Hettinger is skeptical of the typical theories proposed to resolve this enigma.

In response to Hettinger's important challenge, we must consider the plausibility of normative rationales that restrict the availability of intellectual property. Certainly many theories of property have been put forth to justify these exclusive rights, but those with the greatest intellectual resonance can be found in the philosophical writings of John Locke and G.W. F. Hegel and in the philosophy of utilitarianism. Locke is credited with providing the philosophical underpinnings of the labor theory of ownership, while aspects of Hegel's elaborate philosophical system form the basis for the so-called 'personality theory'. Utilitarianism contains a more pragmatic philosophical approach that has been most appealing to economists and legal scholars. All three theories are applicable to intellectual as well as physical property. We will briefly review the main tenets of each of these theoretical frameworks beginning with the philosophy of Locke.

This chapter presents a comprehensive overview of these competing (but possibly complementary) justifications without extensive critical comment. In the next chapter we will seek to defend the Lockean natural rights paradigm, which, in our estimation, offers the most promising justification for intellectual property rights. Locke, like Hegel, defends exclusive property rights on non-economic grounds, and his justification avoids the need for empirical validation demanded by the utilitarian approach. Property rights are not on a stable enough footing if they are based solely on how they contribute to the enhancement of social welfare by spurring innovation. On the other hand, these rights are more secure when sanctioned by natural law, for 'however much conventional law may change, rules based on nature are beyond the power of man' (Paton 1951, p. 80).

1. LOCKE'S LABOR THEORY OF OWNERSHIP

John Locke's prominent and nuanced theory of property is presented in *Two Treatises of Government* (1988),[2] which is an elaborate attack on monarchical forms of government and the divine right of kings. In Chapter 5 of the *Second Treatise* Locke brought property rights directly to the center of political philosophy as he sought to demonstrate that these rights were not dependent on the arbitrary claims of the monarchy. Locke's focus is on how property is validly acquired. The issue is often referred to as the problem of original acquisition. Locke is not so concerned with the issue of property use as were his ancient and medieval predecessors such as Plato and St. Thomas Aquinas. Plato, for example, taught that human persons ought to possess whatever they could use properly. But Locke's work ushers in the modern notion of property: the real property issue is the question of legitimate ownership: *how* has one's particular property been acquired?

Unlike Hobbes, Locke forcefully argued that property is a God-given, natural right that *precedes* civil society. He enunciates this position in the first treatise: 'It is reasonable to think that God who bid Mankind increase and multiply should ... give them all a Right to make use of the Food and Rayment, and other Conveniences of life, the Materials whereof he had so plentifully provided for them' (I: § 41).[3] Thus, we can discern valid property claims prior to civil society, which exists in part to protect that natural right along with other rights such as the rights to life and liberty. With Locke, the Hobbesian desire for self-preservation is transformed into the desire for the acquisition of property. Locke renders a solution to the political problem by economic means, because the legitimacy of the state is grounded in the need to protect property and man's acquisitive aspirations.

Locke seeks to justify a property right by showing how common property can be privatized, albeit within certain bounds of ethical probity and fairness. Property rights are not a matter of social convention or positive law. Rather, property is a natural right validated by the natural law. What could possibly be at the origin of such a right? As we shall see, Locke makes a persuasive case that human labor is the ultimate ground of this natural right to private property.

But exactly how can we derive a private right to something, such as a parcel of land, when that something was originally held in common? How can someone appropriate what belongs to the commons without violating the rights of other commoners? As Locke puts the matter, how can anyone 'make ... distinct titles to several parcels of the world for their private uses' without consent? (II: § 39). Locke is claiming that private property in the state of nature is not contingent on the consent of others. According to Locke, the people in common received the earth and its vast resources from God. Locke writes that God the Creator has 'given the world ... to men in common ... for the Support and Comfort of their being' (II: § 26).

Although the world has been given to man by God for his use and self-preservation, this great common resource cannot be put to good use unless it is individuated in some way. Also, nature as God gave it to man is not worth very much unless it is transformed into something more useful and assimilated into man's sphere of being. By conquering and individuating nature man can provide for himself and assure self-preservation: the earth and its fruits are 'given for the use of men [but] there must of necessity be a means to appropriate them, some way or other before they can be of any use, or at all beneficial to any particular men' (II: § 26). Man must work to appropriate elements of nature and make them a part of himself, and so it is labor that engenders a *particular* property right. Labor is the ground of all property rights but we must examine the arguments Locke puts forth to substantiate this position.

Locke presents two basic arguments in support of his property doctrine based on labor. The first argument is predicated on human needs, especially self-preservation, and God's intentions. The essence of this argument is that God wills man's self-preservation through the accumulation of private property that occurs through the process of labor (Simmons 1992). The second argument appeals to our right of self-governance through labor (Simmons 1992; MacPherson 1962).[4] It is often referred to as the so-called 'mixing argument'. This second argument has greater normative appeal and has commanded far more attention by intellectual property scholars, so it will be the primary axis of our discussion.

Let us follow how Locke's deceptively simple 'mixing' argument unfolds in the *Second Treatise*. It begins with Locke's understanding of human personhood, because the foundation of a property right is within the person himself: 'Man (by being master of himself, and proprietor of his own person, and the actions or labor of it) had still in himself the great Foundation of Property' (II: § 44). Thus, the origin of private property is not found in society but in the individual who is 'prompted by self-interest' (Strauss 1950, p. 236).

Locke's proposition about the person is a variation of the Thomistic argument that each person is *dominus sui* or 'master of himself' and therefore possesses himself (Aquinas 1948, I–II: q. 6, a. 2). One of the most distinctive elements of personhood for Aquinas is that each person is a free, self-governing individual. Man belongs to himself and he is not subject to the interference of anyone else. In Locke's conceptual scheme, self-dominion means that each person has a property right in him or herself; included in this right is the unequivocal right to be free from the control of others, who cannot use our bodies or our minds without our consent or against our will.

Since every person has 'property in his own person', by extension he also has property in 'the labor of his body and the work of his hands' (II: § 27). Thus, each person has a property right in him or herself and in the labor he or she performs. Locke's reasoning may seem rather odd, but if we concede that a person's self-dominion can be described in terms of a property right, his arguments have plausibility. It logically follows that if a person has a property right, understood as the right to exclude others from use, in her mind and body she must also have a property right in the physical or mental labor she performs, since labor is an extension of the person's mind and body. This property right in our person is simply the right of self-governance or the right to be free from the control and domination of others; in this regard, it is a 'restatement of the rights to life and liberty' (Becker 1977, p. 39).

Furthermore, it follows that a property right should also extend to the final product of that labor. According to Locke, when a person takes something from the commons, 'he has mixed his labor with it and joined to it something that is his own and thereby makes it his property … . For this labor being the unquestionable property of the laborer, no man but he can have a right to what that is once joined to' (II: § 27). Thus, Locke derives a property right to the fruit of one's labor from the more primordial property right in our person and labor. This property right we have in ourselves is the right to self-determination, to pursue our projects without interference, and to bring necessary material goods within our sphere of influence for this purpose.[5]

It should now be evident that labor allows for the privatization or individuation of what is held in common. As Locke clearly explains: labor 'puts a distinction between [appropriated objects] and the common … the labor that was mine, removing them out of the common state they were in, hath fixed my property in them' (II: § 28). Consider the issue of coming to own land that is held in common in the pre-political state of nature. According to this Lockean paradigm, if someone takes this common, unusable land and through the sweat of the brow transforms it into valuable farm land that person deserves to own this land. According to Locke, 'As much land as a man tills, plants, improves, cultivates, and can use the product of, so much is his property. He, by his labor does, as it were, *enclose it from the common*' (II: § 27; my emphasis). Property is an amalgamation of private labor mingled with common, unowned land.

The explicit moral justification for awarding such an entitlement or claim right against others is that it's harmful to take the product of the laborer's efforts and all persons have a duty to avoid causing harm to others (II: § 6). According to Olivecrona (1974), 'when the object [appropriated] has been included within the sphere of the [laborer's personality], it will be an injury of the possessor to deprive him of it' (p. 223).

Along the same lines, Locke's analysis recognizes that it would be unjust not to let people possess the benefits of their industry which they take such pains to procure. Implicit in Locke is the notion that a property entitlement is deserved as a just return for the laborers' difficult and strenuous work, and taking the product of that labor would be an unjust enrichment. As Locke stipulates, one who takes the laborer's property 'desire[s] the benefit of another's pains, which he has no right to' (II: § 34). Desert is an aspect of Locke's general mixing argument, but it must be kept in mind that I deserve what I have worked on primarily because labor is mine and the 'great foundation of property' is in man himself (II: § 44). I am justly entitled to the fruits of my labor because my labor is attached to those 'fruits', and only secondarily because that labor is often difficult, 'painful', or onerous.[6]

Much ink has been spilled over Locke's use of the 'mixing' metaphor. Some critics claim that the idea is incomprehensible or radically incoherent (Waldron

1988, p. 184). What exactly does it mean to say that a person mixes his or her labor with an object of some sort? The only way to sort out this question is consider what Locke means by labor. Locke provides many examples of labor including gathering acorns, picking berries, hunting, tilling the land, and so forth. Labor always has an end of satisfying human needs or making life easier.

Accordingly, Gordon (1993) and Becker (1977) emphasize that the 'appropriative labor' described by Locke, which is the source of a valid property claim, must be *purposeful*, that is, it must transform what is held in common in some way so as to make it useful or valuable so that it satisfies human needs. We must regard labor not as something that is literally mixed with things but as a purposeful activity whose aim is to satisfy basic human requirements, often by transforming nature. Labor incorporates things within our sphere of influence so that we can successfully pursue our plans and projects. According to Simmons (1992, p. 273), 'we bring things within our purposive activities ("mixing our labor" with them) when we gather them, hunt them, enclose them, and use them in other productive ways'.

We can also say that this appropriative labor creates value. As Locke explains, 'labor makes the far greatest part of the value of things we enjoy in this world' (II: § 42). However, value creation should not be regarded as an independent argument supporting property rights but as part of the overall mixing argument. By emphasizing that some forms of labor create value Locke can defend the enclosure of unowned land which would be worthless and useless without transformative labor. Improved land, on the other hand, is to everyone's benefit and actually makes the commons better off.

In summary, then, Locke provides a formidable rationale for his normative claim that a person's labor entitles that person to the object appropriated by means of that labor: (i) the right is derived from a prior property right in one's personhood and the labor that comes forth from the person's body and mind; objects appropriated through labor are an extension of a person's natural property in himself; (ii) this labor mingled with the commons puts a distinction between the appropriated object and the commons and thereby engenders private property to which the laborer is justly entitled; (iii) appropriative labor is purposeful and it allows the person to fulfill his needs and properly govern his affairs; (iv) from an ethical, deontic perspective, a property right is deserved in part for the laborer's 'pains', and the taking of that property against the laborer's will causes injury which is forbidden by the no-harm principle of the natural law. That principle is the pre-eminent law of nature: 'no one ought to harm another in his life, health, liberty, or possessions' (II: § 6). Hence, for Locke, an unowned item appropriated through the activity of labor is 'just property' (II: § 28).

However, people should only appropriate property sufficient for their needs. For Locke, there are moral limits on what man can acquire through labor. This restriction is known as the Lockean proviso. Locke formulates this proviso as follows: 'Labor being the unquestionable Property of the Laborer, no man but he can have a right to what that is once joined to, *at least where there is enough and as good left in common for others*' (II: § 27). According to this moral principle, one can only appropriate an object from the commons through labor when there is enough and as good for others. This proviso includes the *sufficiency* limitation which implies that one should only appropriate what is sufficient for his or her needs. In addition, individuals should not be wasteful and take from the commons more than they can use 'to any advantage of life before it spoils' (II: § 31). According to Locke, 'whatever is beyond this, is more than his share, and belongs to others' (II: § 31). This restriction is referred to as the *spoilage* limitation. The bottom line is that one must have a need and a use for what one appropriates from the commons and leave 'enough and as good' for others.

Thus, individuals can appropriate property by laboring on the commons subject to these two conditions. So long as there is 'enough and as good' left for others after the laborer has appropriated his fair share, then the act of appropriation 'does as good as take nothing at all' (II: § 33). The proviso protects those without property from harm, that is, from the exhaustion of the commons before they can appropriate property. What we take for ourselves cannot constitute an 'encroachment on the right of others' (II: § 51). Appropriation without prior consent is just as long as no one is harmed by this appropriation.

Some Locke scholars point out the practical difficulties of determining precisely when 'enough and as good' has been left for others. This is a fair criticism of the proviso. Nonetheless, the general idea is that someone is entitled to their fair share so that others have ample opportunity for their own self-preservation and self-determination. The fair share criterion, despite its ambiguity, still represents a threshold for how much one can accumulate in a world of scarce material resources. When my appropriation of property begins to interfere with the self-preservation of my neighbor or prevents him from filling his basic needs, I have obviously not met the terms of the proviso.

2. LOCKE AND INTELLECTUAL PROPERTY

Although Locke had in mind physical property such as land, it would surely seem that this theory is naturally applicable to intellectual property as well. Intellectual property is surely as much the fruit of one's labor as is physical property. Mental labor is no different from physical labor: both are extensions of the person and belong to the person. As Easterbrook (1990) remarks, 'Intellectual property is intangible, but the right to exclude is not different in principle from General Motors' right to exclude Ford from using its assembly line ...' (p. 109). It's certainly logical that those who expend intellectual labor be rewarded by ownership of the fruits of their labor and be allowed to 'enclose it from the common' (II: § 27). Thus, except in unusual cases, intellectual property and physical property should be treated identically in the law (Easterbrook 1990).

But what is the intellectual commons from which this intangible property is enclosed? This commons includes ideas, concepts, theories, scientific or research methods, scientific principles, mathematical algorithms, laws of nature, words, names, symbols, which are not subject to intellectual property protection. It also encompasses the contents of the public domain: works of literature, music, or art, whose copyright protection has expired. Finally, it includes copyrighted works that cannot be fully appropriated by others without permission, but these works still provide inspiration and ideas for authors. Creators bring their skill and imagination to these vast resources and the end result is a new creative work, a marginal contribution to the world's knowledge resources. The logic of Locke's argument implies an entitlement, a natural property right, in this finished product such as a novel, a poem, a computer program, or a musical composition. Using Locke' mixing metaphor, writers and creators who mingle their labor with the language, ideas, and concepts of the intellectual commons have produced works that deserve authorial ownership. We have seen that Locke's use of the term 'mixing' is best construed as purposeful labor that brings an object into the sphere of one's influence. Even if this sort of intellectual labor is not toil, it should still result in a property right since that labor is a purposeful activity with the aim of satisfying basic human needs such as the need for knowledge and recreation. It seems only fair and just that whoever uses his labor to produce an intangible creative work from common intellectual materials should have every right to appropriate their expression.

We can conclude, therefore, that copyright and other forms of intellectual property protection have a strong ethical basis in the primordial property right each person has in himself and in his labor. That labor is 'perfectly his own' and does not belong 'in common to others' (II: § 44). Expressive ideas and thoughts come forth from the person according to his will and should be eligible for his immediate appropriation. As Spooner (1971) wrote, 'Nothing is, by its own essence and nature, more perfectly susceptible of exclusive appropriation than a thought' (p. 58).

But an intellectual property right is by no means absolute and cannot be compared with other natural rights such as the right to life or the right not to be tortured. This right is subject to several limitations implied by the proviso to appropriate property while leaving 'enough and as good' for others (II: § 27). As we have seen, the proviso stipulates that people may improve their lot so long as no one else is made worse off. As long as this proviso is satisfied, then the appropriation 'does as good as take nothing at all' (II: § 33).

Thus, a Lockean approach to property rights requires that those rights must be properly configured to ensure that others are not harmed by the acquisition of property. For example the appropriation of abstract ideas or even words would be harmful to others and worsen their prospects for expressive activity. Hence ideas or a common language cannot be become someone's property. As Judge Learned Hand explained, 'the right thus secured by the copyright act is not a right to the use of certain words, because they are common property of the human race, and are as little susceptible of private appropriation as air or sunlight'[7] (*Holmes v. Hurst* 1898; p. 86). It is imperative to balance the right to the fruits of one's labor and intellectual effort with the need to sustain the ability of other creators to work with those intangibles that constitute the commons. This balance is achieved by protecting expression instead of general ideas, since ideas are the basic building blocks of creative works. Fichte's distinction between form and content is particularly apposite in this regard. Fichte (1793) argues that once a book is published, the ideal (*geistig*) aspects of the book belong to everyone, but the unique form of those ideas, the author's individualized expression, belongs solely to the author. It is not the general ideas of the work that should be protected, but the concrete incarnation of those ideas in a format that expresses the subjectivity and personality of the author. Fichte's neglected writings on this topic offer important insights about the proper configuration of property rights and will be explored in the chapters ahead.

In accordance with Fichte's mandate there should be no legal protection for common intellectual matter, ideas, algorithms, concepts, and so forth, but only for their tangible expression. We can say that when a property right is bestowed for a person's individual expression and the conceptual raw material is left in the commons the act of authorial appropriation also 'does as good as take nothing at all' (II: § 33). On the other hand, ideas and general concepts must be kept strictly off limits. According to Nimmer (2001, 13.03[A][1]), 'To grant property status to a mere idea would permit withdrawing the ideas from the stock of materials that would otherwise be open to other authors, thereby narrowing the field of thought open for development and exploitation'.

In most cases, it is erroneous to regard the bestowal of a copyright on a *de novo* creation as some type of 'enclosure' of the commons, as if a piece of the commons has been individuated and removed from public view. If the creative work is a novel, for example, it is available for all to read and enjoy. Appropriation of this work by means of a proprietary property right does not violate the rights of other commoners so long as the common intellectual material (such as generic plot or characters) remains intact for them to use for their own projects. An author who simply borrows from the ideas and tangible content in the public domain in order to create something such as a novel or play does not deplete the commons in any way.

As long as these limitations or internal 'safety valves' (such as fair use and the idea–expression dichotomy) are in place, when society respects the creator's rights and rewards creativity properly, the end result will actually be an enhance-

to a copyrightable work extends only to the expression of an idea and never to the idea itself'.[11] Ownership of ideas or facts would harm future creators and thereby violate the proviso. No one should be allowed to own the idea of representing a beautiful watercolor landscape; but an artist like Cezanne who labors to paint a particular watercolor landscape should be entitled to an exclusive right to this unique form of expression. In the first scenario other artists are harmed because they are prevented from painting their own landscape, but in the second scenario it is quite difficult to see how anyone is harmed when the artist is given exclusive rights to her particular work, at least for a limited amount of time so that she can appropriate the value of her work.

Copyright jurisprudence, which supports this dichotomy, recognizes the difficulty of differentiating ideas from their expression. As Judge Learned Hand puts it, 'Nobody has ever been able to fix that boundary [between idea and expression], and nobody ever can'.[12] But this differentiation is not an empty one as some anti-copyright rhetoric suggests. Though challenged to make this distinction in some difficult cases, the courts have done a reasonably proficient job of awarding protection to creative expression, while leaving generic material unprotected. In so doing, they have sought to reward the deserving individual creator while fostering the preservation and augmentation of the public domain.

According to Yen (1990, p. 524), the English natural law of property, rooted in the Roman doctrines of possession along with the Lockean principle of labor, strongly suggests that property rights cannot be awarded unless the author creates things that are 'capable of possession under the law'. Tangible expression in the form of a novel or an invention, but not an abstract idea, can be possessed. English natural law, therefore, along with Locke's important proviso can be interpreted to support a robust public domain along with individual property rights in concrete intellectual objects. We can affirm that a creator's mental labor leads to the production of intellectual objects that deserve some sort of property right, as long as we also affirm that this right must be prudently limited in scope and duration so as to preserve and enlarge the commons through full accessibility.

The Lockean theory may seem archaic and woefully outdated, but its normative force and intellectual merits are beyond dispute.[13] Locke's viewpoint has helped to shape modern intellectual property doctrine and jurisprudence, as it echoes through many US court decisions that have resolutely affirmed valid intellectual property rights. According to one eloquent judicial opinion, 'Sacrificial days devoted to ... creative activities deserve rewards commensurate with the services rendered'.[14] Similarly, in the landmark copyright case, *Harper & Row*, the Court strongly suggests that authors are entitled to a 'fair return' for their labor.[15] In *Ruckelshaus v. Monsanto*[16] the Court, quoting from Locke's *Second Treatise*, concluded that the treatment of trade secrets as a type of property was consistent with a labor theory of ownership. Finally, in the *Whelan* case the Court referred to its deep concern for 'just merits' for the author when considering copyright cases.[17] In our view these court opinions express the right instincts about a natural law foundation for property rights. The challenge is to structure copyright and patent law so that it achieves the right balance: it must grant the author a right to control the fruits of his or her creative labor and at the same time ensure the ongoing vitality and rich plenitude of the public domain.

3. HEGEL ON PROPERTY AND PERSONALITY

Another normative framework suitable for defending exclusive property rights centers on the intimate relationship between property and personhood. The fact that private property, such as a home, enables people to express their personalities should be morally significant. As Radin (1982, p. 986) explains, 'the more closely connected with personhood, the stronger the entitlement' to an exclusive property right. According to this perspective, in order to achieve fulfillment as a person, one needs some control over the resources in one's environment. Each person realizes him- or herself in the things he or she owns. If this theory provides an adequate account for the granting of property rights in general, then it is reasonable to assume that the personality theory could be extended to justify intellectual property rights as well.

This theory has its philosophical roots in the extensive and somewhat impenetrable writings of the German philosopher, G.W.F. Hegel (1770–1831). We find the topic of property addressed throughout Hegel's works including those of the Frankfurt and Jena periods where he first elaborates upon the notion of the 'ethical life' (*Sittlichkeit*) of the state. His *Early Theological Writings* consist of a number of essays, many of them centered around his pungent critique of Kant's formal moral philosophy. In one of the better known essays entitled 'The Spirit of Christianity and its Fate', Hegel argues that the 'spirit' of Judaism consisted of a radical duality between master and servant, between God's commands and the people submissive to those commands. That same structure is replicated in Kant where there is also a duality between the moral law and those on whom it is imposed.

In this context, Hegel developed a sophisticated ontology of life and evaluated both Judaism and Christianity according to their fidelity to the spirit of life. Hegel criticized the teachings of Jesus because they appeared to renounce the bonds of political life, especially those forms of self-expression of the individual achieved through property and family. Jesus discusses 'how hard it is for a rich man to enter the Kingdom of Heaven' (Mt.19:23), but, for Hegel (1948), 'such a command is without truth for us' He goes on to explain that 'the fate of property has become too powerful for us to tolerate reflections on it, to find its abolition thinkable' (Hegel 1948, p. 221). The abolition of property is 'unthinkable', a denial of life, since life requires free self-expression, and so individuals must be able to invest themselves in things. Hegel opposes what he regards as the anti-property sentiment of the Jewish–Christian tradition. In these early writings we encounter the seeds of Hegel's mature private property doctrine: the individual needs private property as a vehicle of personal freedom and self-expression.

On the other hand, property must be restricted since excessive property and wealth are also opposed to life. The Greek πόλις under Solon, praised profusely by Hegel as a superior form of political community, represented the proper attitude, since it limited the acquisition of property among the Greeks. According to Hegel (1948, pp. 197–8), the virtue most appropriate to property is honesty – people must manifest enough integrity and restraint to develop (or acquire) property only when necessary for the sake of self-expression. But they should not acquire goods and wealth just for their own sake, since those things merely 'tacked on to life … cannot be its property' (Hegel 1948, p. 221). Despite his views on property's limitations, for the early Hegel, the 'whole' or 'complete life', that is, the life of the people (*Volk*) within the State, demands certain property rights for the individual.

Hegel continues to emphasize the importance of strong property rights in his later works of speculative philosophy such as the *Philosophy of Right*.[18] In this book we encounter Hegel's mature and fully articulated political philosophy. Here he develops the notion of the State as an inherently rational system, such that the person can confidently rely on its laws as a firm basis of ethical action. The state's 'rational' institutions enable the person to achieve fulfillment as a person and enjoy freedom, which Hegel understands as rational self-determination. The pivotal notion in *The Philosophy of Right* is freedom. Hegel says that freedom is the 'absolute end' or goal of world history, which is the manifestation of the rational Idea (§129). According to Hegel, 'freedom is both the substance of right and its goal, while the system of right is the realm of freedom made actual' (§ 4).

One of the institutions that constitutes 'ethical life' is property. In the *Philosophy of Right* Hegel explains that a person must be able to control objects in his environment, otherwise the world will remain external and alien to him. 'Personality', writes Hegel, 'is that which struggles to lift itself above this [subjective] restriction and to give itself reality, or in other words to claim that external world as its own' (§ 39). In order to overcome this restriction the human subject requires 'the right of putting his will into any and every being and making it his property' (§ 44). Hegel argued with some insistence that a person must be allowed to 'translate his freedom into an external sphere' and that 'property is the first embodiment of freedom and so is in itself a substantive end' (§ 45).

When external things such as a house embody the person's will and express his personality, they must belong to him. For Hegel, the person cannot be free without property, since property allows one to overcome the opposition between self and world and freely to put one's personality into external objects that exist beyond the inner self. Property, therefore, is a 'substantive end' because it is essential for human freedom. This property must be privately owned because common property 'violates the right of personality' (§ 46).

Hegel goes on to say that the person must 'occupy' his or her property: 'occupancy makes the matter of the thing my property' (§ 52). Once the thing is so 'occupied', others will recognize the occupier as its rightful owner. Hegel explains that we take possession of a thing 'by directly grasping it physically, by forming it, and by marking it as ours' (§ 54). Hegel recognizes the importance of exclusive property laws to protect a person's property and his self-identity by ensuring universal recognition of what belongs to that person.

In elaborating his views on property Hegel is clearly developing themes announced in his earlier works of the Frankfurt and Jena periods: selfhood is enhanced by self-expression, by objectifying or embodying one's will in external objects and thereby appropriating those objects into the sphere of one's influence. Acting upon things is necessary for self-actualization (or self-expression). Without property there can be no authentic self-expression and without self-expression there can be no genuine freedom. According to Stillman (1991, p. 207), 'in owning property, men act in the external world; property is freedom because it gives the individual a scope for action and makes possible his extending and expanding his personality'.

The core insight of Hegel is this notion of 'embodied will', a reminder that we have intimate relationships with objects, which give our lives meaning and value. And these relationships justify ownership, since without ownership there will be no continuity in the way we relate to these valuable objects. According to Merges, Mennell, and Lemley (2000, p. 9), a person's expectations 'crystallize' around certain objects, and the loss of those objects causes 'disruption and disorientation'.

Hegel has consistently maintained, then, that property is an expression of personality, a mechanism for self-actualization, and a way for the person's self-identity to be recognized by others. This theory seems particularly suitable for intellectual objects as well as physical ones, since the connection between 'property' and 'personality' seems especially evident in literary works or works of art. If physical property is the 'embodiment of personality' (Hegel § 51), then the same can surely be said for intellectual property. As human beings freely externalize their will in various intellectual objects such as novels, works of art, or poetry, they create 'property' to which they are entitled because those intellectual products are a manifestation or embodiment of their personality. Each of these creative works is an extension of their being and as such belongs to

personality of their respective inventors, are developed simultaneously? Under what circumstances does imitative art work or music manifest enough unique personality in order to qualify for a copyright? What should be done about pedestrian intellectual objects such as computer software programs which rarely manifest the personality traits of their authors? On the other hand, what about works that are highly expressive and infused with personality, and yet are deemed to be derivative according to current US copyright law? Nevertheless, despite certain ambiguities, the Hegelian model remains a fruitful avenue for addressing intellectual property rights.

In summary, then, Hegel espouses the principle that property is a natural right with intrinsic value because it provides freedom for the self, which, through the exercise of that freedom, objectifies itself in the external world, that is, gives its personality a reality outside itself. Although these private property rights are subordinate to the rational state, Hegel has little use for socialized or common property. Finally, Hegel's notion that property is an expression of personality is well suited for intellectual property, since abstract objects are quite often invested with the creator's unique personality. Hence an ownership entitlement becomes an important vehicle of self-realization.

Hughes (1997) has suggested that the theories of Locke and Hegel are complementary and more theoretically cogent when synthesized in some way. He comes to this conclusion by focusing on the biggest weakness of each model: Locke's theory cannot account for 'the idea whose inception does not seem to have involved labor', and the Hegelian personality theory is hard to apply to 'valuable innovations that do not contain elements of what society might recognize as personal expression' (Hughes 1997, pp. 164–5). Thus, an intellectual property right is justified as a right to the fruit of one's labor *and* the expression of one's inner personality. This synthetic approach may find a more sympathetic audience even among some of those who find these theories to be morally unpersuasive when considered independently of each other.

4. CONSEQUENTIALIST ARGUMENTS

Intellectual property rights are also commonly defended from a purely consequentialist or utilitarian perspective. As we have seen, natural rights theories are deontological protection-based theories, focused on the need to safeguard natural property rights. Utilitarian theories, on the other hand, are more 'promotion-based', focused on the need for statutory rights in order to promote or induce creative expression and inventive activity (Kieff 2000, p. 698 n.2). Dukeminer and Krier (1993) have recognized that utilitarian property theory represents a sharp break from the Lockean natural rights perspective. Intellectual property is conceived as a 'social institution' whose purpose is primarily to enhance social welfare. They claim that 'this view is without a doubt the dominant view of property today ...' (p. 14).

Classic utilitarianism was developed by two British philosophers, Jeremy Bentham (1748–1832) and John Stuart Mill (1806–1873). According to this theory the right course of action is to promote the general good. This general good can also be described in terms of 'utility', and this principle of utility is the foundation of morality and the ultimate criterion of right and wrong. The term 'utility' simply refers to the net benefits (or good) created by an action. According to Frankena (1963, p. 29), utilitarianism is the view that 'the sole ultimate standard of right, wrong and obligation is the *principle of utility* or *beneficence,* which says quite strictly that the moral end to be sought in all that we do is *the greatest possible balance of good over evil* (or the least possible balance of evil over good)'.

In order to apply this theory to intellectual property rights it is necessary to convert this abstract moral ideal into a more practical standard. This standard is usually expressed in economic terms of 'wealth-maximization'. Thus, intellectual property rights, according to this paradigm, are justified on the basis of the fact that they enhance overall social welfare by providing an incentive for new innovation, where social welfare is understood as the maximization of aggregate wealth society gets from its scarce resources.

The utilitarian or instrumental argument for intellectual property proceeds as follows: those rights are necessary in order to maximize social welfare by providing authors, inventors, and other creators with the reward of an exclusive property right for their work. Without such a reward, which in the Anglo-American system take the form of strongly protected, limited monopolies of a reasonable duration, there will be fewer such creations or inventions. As a result, science, technology, and commerce will suffer. The reason is that ideas are public goods that are easily copied. Without intellectual property protection people will be more inclined to copy what has already been created rather than create new ideas. Also, free riders will force the price of the easily copied intangible creation down to its marginal cost of production. As a result, the creator or inventor will be unable to recoup the up-front development investment, which is usually quite high.

This version of utilitarianism known as 'incentive theory' represents a classic *ex ante* justification of property rights. It has been articulated in many works including those of Nordhaus (1969), who sought to demonstrate that an increase in the longevity or robustness of patents would stimulate more innovations. Moreover the disclosure of an invention once it becomes patented offers great benefits for society, since others will be able to develop incremental innovations based on the original invention.[25] The utilitarian justification, often referred to in economic terms as a 'reward theory', claims that exclusive rights are a necessary reward for the risks involved in developing intellectual products.

Following Moore (2001) and others who have explicated the broad lines of this theory, it can be concisely summarized as follows:

(i) Society should adopt legal regimes or institutions if and only if they are expected to yield the optimization of aggregate social welfare.
(ii) A legal regime that provides authors, creators, and inventors limited rights or control over their productions is expected to act as a strong incentive for the creation of intellectual works.
(iii) Stimulating the production and creation of intellectual works contributes to the maximization of aggregate welfare.
(iv) Therefore a legal regime for intellectual property protection should be adopted.

The presumption, of course, is that the development of scientific, literary and artistic works will promote general utility or social welfare. This seems to be reasonable, since it is hard to quarrel with any culture's need for a steady stream of such intellectual works and industry's need for technological innovation. And it was precisely this need that was recognized in the US Constitution that confers upon Congress the power 'to promote the Progress of Science and the useful Arts' by awarding exclusive property rights.[26] As this critical Article of the Constitution implies, society wants to maximize utility by the promotion of science and culture, and it does so through awarding generous incentives to create these goods.

Those who embrace a social utility foundation of property rights argue that legal protections that sharply curtail copying and free-riding will have a positive effect on the development of new forms of intellectual property. Consider the case of patents. Kieff (2000, pp. 705–10) makes a convincing case that a property right in the form of a patent is essential for facilitating investment in the invention *and* commercialization of new products. Popular alternatives such as cash rewards offered by the government to inventors do not address the commercialization activities that take place after an invention is developed but before it can be profitably exploited in the marketplace. On the other hand, an exclusive patent right provides an incentive to incur the costs necessary to commercialize this new product.

Some critics of the current patent law regime object to patents on the grounds that they yield monopoly power. Why not find other means besides the patent system to promote innovation? These critics, however, fail to realize that patents do not necessarily entail market power. There is no guarantee that a patented product will generate demand. As Dam (1994) observes, 'the right to exclude another from "manufacture, use, and sale" may give no significant market power', even when the patented product is sold in the market (pp. 249–50).

Of course, the utilitarian viewpoint acknowledges the need for limits on these rights such as limited duration, fair use, and so forth. According to Landes and Posner (1989, p. 335), while some copyright protection is essential to create incentives to incur the costs of creating a work that is easily copied by others, 'too much protection can raise the costs of creation for subsequent authors to the point those authors cannot cover them even though they have complete protection for their own originality'. Hence the need for balance is essential.

In contrast to Locke and Hegel, utilitarian philosophers argue that intellectual property rights are not a natural entitlement or a matter of natural justice. Rather, they should be awarded purely for pragmatic purposes as a means of inducing creative or inventive activity and thereby appreciably increase aggregate utility. Awarding these rights as a *quid pro quo*, as a mutual benefit for the author and society, ensures the optimal level of intellectual goods production.[27] This line of reasoning is evident in several influential cases such as *Wheaton v. Peters*,[28] which denies that an author's intellectual property rights in published works are a matter of common law. Such a right is based purely on statute and is contingent on the consensus of lawmakers. In many cases the courts have acknowledged the economic basis of intellectual property law while not necessarily repudiating other rationales. According to the US Supreme Court, 'The economic philosophy behind the clause empowering Congress to grant patents and copyrights is the conviction that encouragement of individual effort by personal gain is the best way to advance public welfare…'.[29] Similarly, in another case the Court validated copyright law according to a utilitarian standard: 'by establishing a marketable right to the use of one's expression, copyright supplies the economic incentive to create and disseminate ideas'.[30] In other words, the law exists primarily as an economic inducement to promote more expression in the form of novels, literary works, or other information goods.

Western societies, of course, have typically provided thick intellectual property rights with the hope of fostering a culture of innovation. They have tended to presume that without such protection creators would not always be able to recover their initial investment, and thus would refrain from creative activity. If society wants expensive pharmaceutical therapies, high-quality movies and a steady stream of technological innovation, it will have to protect those items from the hands of free riders. Precisely how that level of protection is calibrated in order to maximize productivity, however, is a matter of debate.

This incentive or 'reward' justification for thick, exclusive property rights continues to take precedence over other normative justifications such as the Lockean approach. As O'Rourke (2000, p. 170) observes, 'at least in American law, the leading theory probably still continues to be a utilitarian one … [which] emphasizes the need to provide incentives to the first comer to create while maintaining a viable public domain from which second comers may draw in improving and building upon the original work'. The persistence of this incen-

that utilitarian arguments resist empirical affirmation. A utilitarian or instrumental approach to these rights relies on empirical data that may fluctuate depending upon the economic context (Shiffrin 1991). As a result, some scholars argue that wealth maximization 'cannot serve as an acceptable foundation for the initial assignment of an entitlement' (Gordon 1989, p. 1350).[3]

On the other hand, it seems intuitively obvious that at least some public goods require that creators receive a substantial reward from their creation or there will be no incentive to innovate. As Gordon (1992) herself maintains, a market will remain underdeveloped where the initial investment is high and imitation of the product is trivial so that the price is forced down to marginal cost, thereby preventing the producer from recovering his investment. Nonetheless, given conflicting evidence and disputes about how to design and calibrate investment incentives, it is necessary to find a more secure footing for intellectual property entitlements.

Given these unresolved questions and also the imperative to consider issues of justice and fairness apart from economic factors, there is a compelling need to support intellectual property rights on non-economic grounds. While the economic or utilitarian side of the argument does not deserve to be dismissed, we believe that an even stronger case rests on non-economic terms. Thus, the foundation of property rights should be based on both economic and non-economic grounds.

As we discussed in the previous chapter, the Lockean model, basing limited property rights in the author's right to his or her labor, is the most morally persuasive non-utilitarian rationale. Also, thanks to its sufficiency proviso, Lockean theory does a reasonably good job of reconciling exclusive intellectual property rights with the common good as expressed in a robust intellectual commons. Paretian theory proposed in the last chapter supports a deontological justification for rights instead of a purely utilitarian one (Moore 2001). Recall that an action is Pareto superior if it leaves one person better off and no one else worse off than they were before the action is performed. In our view, this is the case with the creation of new content under most circumstances.

In this chapter we intend to substantiate these claims and to supplement Locke's analysis with some scrutiny of the labor theme that has recently appeared in the work of personalist philosophers and Christian social doctrine, where the link between labor and property rights has been given significant attention. Pope John Paul II, for example, clearly supported a labor theory of ownership, despite the fact that he disagreed with liberalism's premise of atomic individualism. The chapter concludes with a brief discussion of the myths about the so-called 'enclosure movement' and the tight controls imposed by intellectual property laws that harm the free flow of information. We begin all this with a vindication of Locke's basic theory.

1. DEFENDING LOCKE

As we have seen, Locke was the first philosopher seriously to thematize the problematic of property. For many property scholars, Locke's prolonged meditation on labor in the *Second Treatise* is the key to comprehending the meaning of personal property and the normative justification for a right to own property. The laborer, who has the foundation of a property right in his own person, mingles his labor with an object, endowing it with value, and, as a result, the laborer is entitled to a property right in that object. The worker has a right to what he has labored upon (under the conditions stipulated by Locke) because if it is misappropriated he is harmed. Locke (1988) is clear that to take the product of the laborer's effort without his consent is to cause injury to the laborer (II: § 27).

Locke has also argued that private property is necessary to help us meet our most basic human needs, and this argument supports his view that property is a legitimate entitlement. According to Hart (1971, pp. 200–201), 'the core of the notion of rights is neither individual choice nor individual benefit, but basic or fundamental individual needs'.[4] Since physical property is of vital importance for our human welfare, we *need* property not only for our survival but for our self-governance, the proper exercise of our self-dominion. Thanks to our intellectual nature, proclaims Locke, we are 'capable of Dominion' over ourselves (I: § 56), which is a God-given prerogative. Exercising that dominion, however, requires control of objects assimilated (by labor) into our sphere of influence. Thus, private property is rightly considered an entitlement or a claim right (in Hohfeld's terms). For both Locke and Hegel, property rights are natural entitlements, required as a just reward for the laborer's pains or as a means to achieve free self-expression.

Locke's theory, which continues to enjoy strong normative appeal, demands that rights be limited by concern for the public domain and the common good. As we have seen, Lockeans may insist on the need for a property right to the fruits of one's labors, but the bestowal of such a right cannot cause harm to others through a wasteful depletion of the commons.

The Lockean inspired argument for an intellectual property right is that one's *intellectual labor*, which borrows from the ideas, algorithms, generic plots, and other material in the intellectual commons, should entitle one to have a natural property right in the finished product of that work such as a novel or a musical composition. The ideas or building blocks remain accessible to the other commoners and only the final expression is protected. Hence, the common domain is undiminished and the proviso is fully satisfied. In the case of intellectual property, it is particularly hard to see how my entitlement would constitute 'an encroachment on the right of others' (Locke 1988, II: § 51). As Hughes (1997, p. 117) points out, people labor to express new ideas and produce intellectual content whose value undeniably 'depends solely upon the individual's mental "work"'. This approach contrasts sharply with utilitarian reasoning where proprietary rights are regarded as useful social instruments with a rationale grounded in the need for incentives to spur the steady production of intellectual objects.

What about the plausibility of Locke's core argument and its applicability to intellectual property? While it is unusual to speak about the body as 'property' the person surely has a right to exclude others from his or her body and its dynamic exertions through physical or mental labor. Day (1966) and others have questioned this notion of 'owning' one's labor. He explains that labor is an activity that a person performs, but can't really 'own'. In his view, it's unintelligible to speak of ownership rights when it comes to labor. However, if we understand the right of ownership in terms of the right to exclude, the declaration that a person has a right to his labor, that is, a right to exclude other people from appropriating his labor through coercion, is perfectly intelligible. If a person does not have a right to exclude others from his or her body and labor, the door is open for forced labor, slavery, or even rape.

If I have such a right to exclude others from my body and my labor, why not the products it makes? After all, the person's labor has been attached to that product which becomes integrated into that particular person's environment. Labor is a way of extending oneself into the natural or intellectual world. The essence of a property right is the right to exclude and determine how something will be used. This right should apply to my body, my labor, and the creative products in which I have invested that labor.[5]

By default, therefore, the laborer has a strong presumptive entitlement to the product of his labor, and that entitlement becomes a durable claim right when the terms of the proviso are satisfied. The person who carves a table from logs left to rot in the forest or who writes a poem about the harvest moon deserves ownership of these things in the name of justice. Like the labor that is theirs, these things cannot be separated from the person who makes them. For Locke, the person's purposeful activities are inseparable from him (Simmons 1992). Moreover, labor is the basis for a property right instead of a mere use right, because without that right to control and exclude others, self-governance becomes impossible (Locke 1988: I: § 41; Simmons 1992, pp. 274–5).

On the other hand, the claims of free riders for unlimited access to content or the demands for collective ownership lack the same moral force. Palmer (1990), for example, has argued that property rights for intellectual works 'should be in the audience and not in the artist, for it is on the audience that the work depends for its continued existence' (p. 848). A Lockean view, however, would recognize an essential disparity of normative significance between the interests of the playwright who invests his labors for many years to write a Broadway musical and the fleeting interests of the different audience members who show up each night to be entertained. Just because an audience responds positively to a creative work, there is no ethical or logical necessity for it to have an ownership right to that work. In some cases there may be a tiny minority of the audience who want to 'recode' or redefine a cultural object, but their interests are far outweighed by the vast majority who benefit from the stability of the author's message (Hughes 1999, pp. 341–2).

Himma (2007b) frames the Lockean thesis according to a slightly different line of argumentation, albeit one that is equally convincing. He maintains that each person has a 'morally significant interest' in his body and corporeal activities, including labor. This morally significant interest extends to the products of that labor unless it is outweighed by other, more compelling interests. Similarly, information producers have a prudential interest in controlling and distributing their creative works. That interest is based on the time, energy, money, and labor invested in one's creative project. These authors and inventors have created something of value, and justice considerations 'suggest that what people deserve is determined by the value or disvalue they introduce into the world by their free acts …' (Himma 2007, p. 58). This line of reasoning, focused on the value-creating aspect of Locke's vision, echoes Nozick (1974, p. 175), who claimed that 'laboring on something improves it and makes it more valuable, and anyone is entitled to own a thing whose value he has created'.

It seems quite tenable to regard this prudential interest as a presumptive right to exclude others based on the need for limited control over one's content. Unless a person's justified interest in his or her content is construed as a claim right demanding the respect of others, that content is at the disposal of others and the author may well be prevented from earning a livelihood or preserving the meaning and integrity of her creative works. Also, these creations do not diminish the commons but enhance it. If Joe writes a magnificent novel about the French Revolution, he has introduced something of value into the literary world. Moreover, this work will dynamically stimulate other thoughts and ideas, and it will not prevent other authors from writing their own novel about the French Revolution.

There is an unmistakable asymmetry between the physical commons and the intellectual commons. If a large portion of the rain forest is cut down and consumed, the earth's 'commons' is in fact depleted. But when Joe writes his novel borrowing from common ideas there is a new piece of intellectual content while those ideas remain available for others to use. Despite the copyright others can learn from this book, savor its ideas, and even borrow from its content in a limited way. If we assume that the copyright applies only to the expression of his work (and not the underlying ideas, generic plotlines, etc.) there is no impairment of the commons of intellectual goods.[6]

But how does the Lockean theory applied to intellectual objects stand up against its many detractors who believe that it has little persuasive applicability or that it is riddled with incongruities. Let us isolate some of the principal criticisms and then attempt to fashion as cogent a defense as possible. One major criticism is that Locke's arguments may have some merit for physical objects, but they do not work for intellectual property rights.[7] Drahos (1996, p. 47) alludes to this problem, pointing out that when Locke spoke about property 'it was the ownership of physical rather than abstract objects that occupied his attention'. Kimppa (2005) builds on this observation and contends that Locke's philosophy cannot ground intellectual property rights. Kimppa reluctantly concedes that Locke's arguments probably apply to material things, especially in a world characterized by scarcity. Ownership may be necessary, he argues, because material resources are scarce and not available for common use. Food, for example, can be hard to come by and its consumption requires exclusivity.

Immaterial property, however, does not suffer from the scarcity problem since it can be owned and used by countless individuals given its non-rivalrous nature. In Kimppa's view, the difference between a material and immaterial object is that someone can be deprived of the former, but not the latter. He explains that 'one can't have material that another has', but such is not the case regarding an intangible (Kimppa 2005, p. 80). There is no need, therefore, to erect artificial barriers around intellectual objects. Every person needs to appropriate some physical property for survival through such activities as tilling the land or picking wild strawberries. Accordingly, Locke argues for property ownership based on necessity, but this argument hardly applies to the immaterial. The scenario completely changes, however, when we transition to the world of the immaterial, where values like 'cooperation should be promoted' (Kimppa 2005, p. 80). The principle articulated by Kimppa is that scare material goods cannot be used simultaneously, since their consumption is rivalrous, so some sort of property right is necessary. On the other hand, non-rivalrous intangible goods are not scarce. They can be easily shared, so the values of sharing and cooperation should take precedence over an ownership value.

Shiffrin (2001, p. 156), who argues that Locke endorsed a common ownership thesis, also contends that Locke's theory only supports limited property rights for material goods. Private appropriation is legitimate when 'it is necessary for full and proper use to be made' of the object in order to fulfill the right of self-preservation. Intellectual property rights, concludes Shiffrin, do not meet this criterion. On the contrary, intellectual objects are put to their best use 'when contemplated by many, when their truths are commonly appreciated and implemented' (Shiffrin 2001, p. 156). These objects are better suited than their physical counterparts for common consumption and common ownership. All property should be presumptively common property unless the nature of the property demands otherwise.

Thus, Shiffrin also seems to assume a fundamental asymmetry in the need for physical property rights as opposed to intellectual property rights. She does not question a right to physical property (ownership of a house or a stereo), but intellectual property rights are far more ambiguous, given the peculiar characteristics of that property. Unlike its physical counterpart, an intellectual object is non-rivalrous and non-excludable: its consumption doesn't reduce the supply available to others, and it's difficult to 'exclude' or fence out those who haven't paid.[8]

We can offer two modest arguments in response to this line of criticism. First, both Shiffrin and Kimppa downplay the importance of labor in Locke's justification for property rights. Shiffrin (2001, p. 143) admits that labor plays only a 'subsidiary role' in her analysis, while she gives great prominence to the 'common ownership thesis'. However, at the core of Locke's analysis is not the nature of the property to be appropriated, but man's labor, and Locke's grand premise that man has 'still in himself the great Foundation of property' (II: § 44). As a result, one is harmed if one's labor, attached to unowned objects, is misappropriated. Just as forced labor is wrong so it is morally unjust to take the product of a person's labor against the laborer's will. The laborer himself has the principal claim on the results of his labor since that labor is his and justifies the integration of objects into the laborer's sphere of influence. Moreover, that labor has added new value and created social wealth, for labor 'puts the difference of value on every thing' (II: § 40). This moral principle is the centerpiece of the Lockean argument, which does not depend for its moral force on the kind of property to be appropriated or the nature of the work performed (mental or physical). Locke's argument is about a worker's just appropriation, framed in terms of an ability to exclude others from the fruits of one's labor. Scarcity is a secondary concern that is factored into the limits imposed by the proviso. The abundance of intellectual resources and their non-rivalrous nature would be irrelevant for Locke, who is concerned that 'as you sow, so shall you reap'.[9]

Second, Shiffrin dismisses the need for control of these objects to preserve their integrity, though she admits that sometimes intellectual objects will demand a certain level of control for their effective usage. How are we to differentiate which works need controls and which do not? A case can be made that most intellectual objects require such control in order to protect the interests of both producers and consumers of information. For example, the exploitation or misappropriation of a trademark could certainly hurt consumers who benefit from stability of meaning. Copyright and trademark protection makes intellectual objects commonly available while protecting the integrity of the author's meaning and message. Authors need the opportunity afforded by limited property rights to convey their message and stabilize its meaning in the mind of the public. Thus, just as control is required for the efficacious use of physical property, so is it required for the proper and effective use of most forms of intellectual property.[10]

Above all, the Lockean vision is most deeply concerned about the interests of laborers. What matters to Locke is primarily a just return for the 'laborer's pains' (II: § 33). Thus, a faithful application of Locke's theory would not focus on the nature and qualities of the product (tangible or intangible, excludable or non-excludable), but on labor and the value created by that labor. What is of primary importance is the creator's interests and her justified claim to the product of her labor which is a result of the time and energy expended in the creative process.

A second major criticism of Locke concentrates on the ambiguity of the meaning of the original community of goods left to man in common. Is it possible that, as Shiffrin (2001) argues, Locke himself believed in common ownership and that his commentators have given too much attention to the themes of labor and self-ownership? To unravel this issue we must consider what Locke meant by the 'original community of all things' (I § 40). Did Locke mean a negative community where nobody owns anything? This has been the prevailing interpretation proposed by most Locke scholars (Ryan 1984, pp. 29–30). Or did Locke understand the original commons as an initial positive community whereby everyone jointly owns the world? There is surely support for the standard interpretation since Locke never explicitly equates the commons with 'property'; rather, property is based upon the common right of use (I § 92). However, this notion of negative community does not square well with limits on private appropriation which were obviously important to Locke (Simmons 1992, pp. 238–9)

Perhaps Locke did have in mind some sort of initial positive community. According to Buckle (1991), 'in positive community, all men are joint owners, and so their explicit consent is needed before any part can be removed from the common' (p. 164). Thomson's (1976) interpretation of Locke suggests that he supported this idea of a 'joint positive community'. Tully, among others, argues that Locke understood the commons as an inclusive positive community, and he concluded that Locke supported an inclusive property right, that is, a protected right not to be excluded from the use of the commons. Each person has a right *to* property instead of a right *of* property. According to Tully (1980), 'Locke's property is … a right to one's due rather than one's own' (p. 61). If Tully is correct it would be necessary to redefine our understanding of the Lockean property model. In his view each person is entitled to his or her share of the commons, but that share is not to be considered as a person's individual property. Tully (1980) explains that 'since each man has a right to his due share and no more, acquisition cannot be robbery' (p. 127).

There is little evidence for Tully's position, however, and Locke seems to go out of his way to juxtapose other common rights with the right to property, implying that there is no property right *prior to* one's individual appropriation (I: § 86; Simmons 1992, pp. 239–40). Locke has been careful not to predicate 'property' of the commons itself. In addition, Locke's obvious eagerness to sanction the taking of private property without the consent of the other commoners seems to invalidate Tully's interpretation.

Despite this ambiguity, Simmons (1992, pp. 240–241) has credibly argued that Locke may have had in mind a 'divisible positive community' whereby humanity's common right is a power to take property or the right to be permitted to create property (through labor). Our right to the commons is not a property right *per se*, but the right of opportunity to appropriate property through labor (so long as we leave good and adequate opportunities of appropriation for our neighbor). Even if we accept the standard interpretation that the commons was originally a 'negative community', what is of critical importance is not so much the meaning of the original community, but the proviso which stipulates that appropriation is morally permissible if and only if no other person is harmed by that appropriation (II: § 33). The debate and disagreement about Locke's vision of the original commons raises many provocative questions. However, the nature of the commons is really a moot point, since most of the different interpretations put forth do not invalidate the essentials of Locke's position, which gives the person a right to acquire property independent of the permission or the will of other commoners.

A third major critique of Locke faults his underlying philosophical assumption of 'possessive individualism', which conceives the individual as 'the proprietor of his own person or capacities, owing nothing to society for them' (Macpherson 1962, p. 3). According to this line of reasoning, Locke's philosophy gives too much attention to the rights of the individual and not enough to the needs of community and the common good.[11] In Locke's philosophy, it appears that man owes everything to his own efforts and diligence. This critique of Locke's doctrine of individualism has been radicalized by some who now claim that this philosophy has led to the excesses of capitalism. It is no surprise, therefore, that communitarians who object to Locke's atomistic individualism would find fault with an orthodox Lockean interpretation of exclusive intellectual property rights. They argue that intellectual or abstract objects, whose inputs come from diverse intellectual sources, should be construed as collectively owned rather than the private property of one individual. Chon (1996), for example, argues against exclusivity, pointing out that when an intellectual work is produced it represents a joint activity 'undertaken by both author and audience' (p. 264). Likewise, Craig (2002) maintains that the 'interdependent nature of human culture' means that intellectual works 'ought to be owned collectively' (p. 36). As we discussed in Chapter 4, some argue that because of the author's social and cultural dependence on the collective (such as the public domain), we need a 'public authorship' model which gives the public unrestricted access to created works, thereby recognizing its role as collaborator (Zemer 2006, p. 252).

as one sees fit. The loss of exclusive ownership at the hands of a collective entity, managed by a bureaucratic apparatus, is tantamount to the coercive alienation of the worker from his work. Conversely, property rights ensure that the creative activities of the entrepreneur have protection and an opportunity to be successful.

These remarkable statements on work, economic initiative, and the entrepreneurial spirit represent an important contribution to the organic development of Catholic social doctrine. They emphasize the right of the individual to act independently or in collaborative groups of his choosing. The right of economic initiative, secured by a property entitlement, is essential for a stable and dynamic economic system. This right also allows people freely to realize themselves as acting persons through their work.

The bottom line is that Catholic social doctrine, which is deeply committed to the aim of social justice, has a significant contribution to make to the intellectual property rights debate. As we have seen, this doctrine on property, especially as it has evolved in the work of John Paul II, is surprisingly sympathetic to certain aspects of the Lockean point of view. It strongly resists a socialized approach to intellectual property protection with its insistence on the priority of the commons or its demand for collective or joint ownership. According to Pius XI's Lockean-inspired argument, the person's occupation of unowned land *or* labor on unowned objects creates personal property, so long as the appropriation of that property is consistent with the requirements of fairness. Papal teaching has consistently enunciated this position, following the spirit of Aquinas' thought, because it recognizes that the moral welfare of persons demands private property.[22]

John Paul II has gone one step farther and affirmed the moral right to the new forms of property ownership under normal circumstances because he recognizes that people rely for their security and well-being on proprietary knowledge, 'ownership' of certain skills, and the ability to control and dispose of abstract works of the mind. For this Pope, an intellectual property right, like all natural rights, serves the integrity of the human person. As we have seen, Locke is often assailed for his individualism, and there is little affinity between John Paul II's personalism and Lockean individualism. John Paul II rejected liberalism's assumption of the human self as an atomized or isolated individual. He embraced a relational anthropology which sees the human person as intrinsically relational, always existing in a network of inter-dependent relationships.

This anti-Lockean view, however, does not sound the death knell for individual rights like intellectual property as Craig (2007) and others have suggested.[23] On the contrary, self-determination remains an essential attribute of the relational self. As Aquinas (1948) said, 'man is naturally free and exists for himself' (II–II, q. 66, a.2). The exercise of freedom demands that a person's legitimate interests should not be subordinated to the utilitarian interests of other individuals or the State. Certain rights are essential for the free, self-governing person who is ordered to live in solidarity with others. Juridical rights provide the space for the person's freedom of choice and enable that person to shape his or her life, without unjust interference by others. Rights also provide a way for us to consider what is just from the viewpoint of the other to whom something is owed and who would be harmed if denied that something (Finnis 1980, pp. 220–22). In the case of intellectual property, we cannot overlook the creator's substantial stake in what he or she has created. Hughes (1999, p. 960 n168) explains that cultural objects are major events in the lives of their original creators, and hence the involuntary alienation of these objects would 'significantly disrupt the trajectory of that life'.

Locke's philosophy is a reminder that private property is a means to human well-being and that the person as laborer or entrepreneur has a right to exclude others from what he has worked upon as an expression of his self-governance. Of course, as a relational being he also has a duty to be prudent in what he appropriates and to respect the needs of others. On these points John Paul II and Locke would undoubtedly concur.

3. THE ILLUSION OF TOTAL CONTROL

In lieu of exclusive intellectual property rights, some have proposed various 'commons' models as a way of advancing the free flow of open information. These models tend to support 'access values' instead of 'property values' (Vaidhyanathan 2004, p. 23). Recall Rifkin's (2000) description of the information age as an 'age of access' which is probably best served by an information commons model. One version of the more anarchic commons model is embodied in open source software which enables the creation of neutral platforms that promote innovation (Lessig 2001). Under an open source model for software development users would have free and unrestricted access to the source code. The commons model is predicated on the idea that 'proprietary control is not necessary or desirable to encourage innovation' (Weiser 2003, p. 570).

This model has many virtues, and certainly open source software deserves its place among methods for software creation. The collective programming wisdom available on the Internet helps create software that is of better quality than any single individual or group of individuals in a company could construct. Whether this approach adequately resolves the public goods problem is another question. What the commons model and its adherents downplay is the dynamic incentive effects of intellectual property rights. As the Supreme Court has observed, the 'ultimate aim' of copyright and similar protections is 'to stimulate [the creation of useful works] for the general public good'.[24] As we have noted earlier, the problem with open source software is its failure to solve this vexing incentive problem. If patent and copyright protection were completely removed from software products it's highly likely that there would be underinvestment.

Critics of proprietary software and other forms of exclusive intellectual property rights, often referred to as 'control critics', also exaggerate the level of control that intellectual property rights enables. It is simply impossible to achieve 'complete exclusion' (Hughes 1997, p. 130). Hence these control critics ignore or fail to appreciate the concept of 'incomplete capture', that is, 'an intellectual property owner cannot possibly appropriate all of the information (and thus social value) generated by her creation' (Wagner 2003; p. 1002).[25] When an intellectual object becomes protected through a copyright, there can never be complete or perfect control of that object. Even architectural constraints, which are more restrictive than legal ones, cannot fully contain information embodied in the protected good or service.[26]

Following the general reasoning of the control critics, Craig (2007, p. 223) has argued that the commodification of abstract works obscures the 'communicative' nature of the work. Communication and broad dissemination is sacrificed on the altar of property interests. But this claim is surely exaggerated. These works can still effectively communicate their ideas despite their copyright protection. Many people can read or examine these works, which are usually priced modestly to attract a broad audience. People can share their ideas about these creative texts, write reviews, and even build on the ideas which they contain within the parameters of copyright law.

A copyrighted or patented intellectual object is not hermetically sealed off from public access. Fencing off non-physical objects proves to be exceedingly difficult because of the porosity of all forms of information. Control of information is imperfect and incomplete, and hence it's not equivalent to the control of land or other physical possessions. Not only is information naturally 'leaky', even the most comprehensive enforcement system cannot deter all forms of piracy, especially given the high costs of enforcement. The content industry, while lobbying for strong intellectual property protections, surely recognizes this reality.[27]

Thus, copyrighted intellectual creations or patented inventions make an ongoing contribution to the intellectual commons once they are disclosed to the public. There is usually a positive spillover effect as this information is assimilated by consumers, disseminated throughout society, and absorbed into the culture. While some information directly derived from the intellectual product is protected, other derivative forms of information fall outside the scope of intellectual property law.[28] For example when the reality show 'Survivor' first appeared it provided inspiration for many variations on this format (Wagner 2003).

As a result, intellectual objects subject to intellectual property controls have a positive impact on the diffusion of knowledge and the development of culture.

In fact, intellectual property rights, such as a copyright, will most likely enhance the intellectual commons, given the dynamic incentive effects of those rights and the cumulative nature of human knowledge and creativity. Despite the fact that these information products may be proprietary objects, 'owned' by their creators, they can still stimulate new creative ideas and in most cases serve as inputs in the creative process.

Consider copyrighted literary works. Once they are disclosed and disseminated, they convey information, ideas, and suggestions to many others who can utilize those ideas or follow up on these suggestions without violating that copyright. Some of the information stimulated may be only indirectly or obliquely affiliated with the new creation. For example, a successful novel (and subsequent movie) like *Cold Mountain* might engender new historical projects or additional fictional works on the Civil War. Thus, even fully protected intellectual goods can contribute to the spiraling growth of information resources and thereby enhance in some limited way the information commons (Wagner 2003).

The principal reason for this is simple enough: the information commons is quite dissimilar to the physical commons. There are no real limits to the information commons, given the fertility of the human mind. When physical objects are made into private property or destroyed, the commons undergoes depletion. But when a newly created intangible object is given proprietary protection, that object never existed before, so it is not removed from the commons. At the same time, it is still accessible for many valuable purposes despite the controls exercised by its owner. When protected information is revealed, it begets more information and dynamically generates additional creativity. Patents, for example, once they are disclosed to the public, invite others to develop incremental innovations on the original invention.[29]

It is difficult to measure the full impact of this positive spillover effect that ensues from incomplete control of information. Wagner (2003) cites the ample research of Grilliches (1992, p. 43) whose studies on corporate research and patents confirm that 'R&D spillovers are present, their magnitude may be quite large, and social rates of return remain significantly above private rates'.

This phenomenon of 'incomplete capture', the basic inability of authors to appropriate all of the economic and social value of their creations, supports the validity of the Lockean paradigm, particularly the proviso's applicability to intellectual property. When an information product is given a copyright or a patent, that appropriation does not deplete the commons, but rather enhances it: a new creative work is made available and the information embodied in this work will generate positive externalities as it flows to others and stimulates the creation of new information products. Hence this appropriation of one's intellectual product, such as a novel or an invention, surely meets even the most stringent interpretation of the Lockean proviso, so long as safety valves such as fair use and respect for the idea/expression dichotomy are in effect. The appropriation causes no harm, and in Locke's own words it 'does as good as take nothing at all' (1988: II § 33).

Unfortunately little attention has been given to this idea since the issue of property protection is usually seen in polarized terms as open code versus closed code or common property versus proprietary property. Control criticism concentrates on the negative effects of property rights such as the 'anticommons' effect of patents in the field of biotechnology (Heller and Eisenberg, 1998).[30] While the anticommons phenomenon should not be discounted in some circumstances, what's lacking in the literature is an understanding of the inherent constraints on controlling information and how those constraints contribute to social welfare. As Cohen (2000, p. 1818) points out, 'What is missing from the conventional economic wisdom about property rights in general and intellectual property rights in particular is a vocabulary for apprehending the link between "leaky" entitlements and public welfare, between chaos and creative ferment'.

One might object to this analysis by underscoring society's need for more complete forms of capture. What about the need to copy a cultural object in its totality, to use a song or an essay for various creative purposes? In these cases copyright's prohibition appears to be an obstacle for future creators and even a suppression of speech. Authors, however, have their own speech interests and their own autonomy rights, which demand that they be allowed to control the meaning and stability of their works for at least a limited time. Cast in the light of Hegel's theory, an author's personhood interests cannot be casually dismissed just because an audience member is interested in recoding a work. It might be nice to re-make a beloved cartoon character like Donald Duck to make a point, but there are many other avenues available to express the same ideas. The inability to copy at length without permission may be a problem in some circumstances, but there are relatively few cases in which such copying is absolutely essential (McGowan 2005).[31] Speech interests of author and audience must be balanced so that some copying and recoding is allowable, but this does not mean that the rights holder's interests in appropriating a work's value or controlling its meaning should be superseded by an audience's desires to copy works indiscriminately.

4. CONCLUDING REFLECTIONS

In the face of powerful advocates of collective ownership and open information, Locke's nuanced theory continues to have salience and strong normative appeal for information producers. It represents a plausible conception of intellectual property rights, able to withstand critical scrutiny and repeated challenges. Human labor is an intelligible ground for intellectual property rights so long as appropriation occurs within the bounds of fairness and ethical probity as delineated by Locke. Arguments that intellectual objects should be collectively owned or jointly possessed by the audience lack the same moral persuasiveness. Is an author's investment of time, financial resources, and energy equivalent to the audience's slight investment of energy when it reads a novel or listens to a piece of music? As we have argued, the audience's 'investment' is obviously disproportionate to the investment of the author and far less personal. Those who support the presumption of common ownership argue that authors can be compensated through other schemes such as compulsory licensing (Shiffrin 2001). But such schemes usually do not allow authors to control the integrity of their work and do not adequately safeguard their speech interests against those who want to distort or radically recode their expression. Copyright schemes that limit such recoding have at least two salutary effects. First, the public benefits from cultural objects with a stable meaning, including trademarks and iconic children's cartoon characters. Second, by allowing new creators to borrow limited amounts of intellectual property, the law forces them to express themselves 'by differentiating themselves from what has come before' (Hughes 1999, p. 981).

Locke's basic thesis has received support from Catholic social doctrine, which has steadfastly resisted collective ownership because it threatens personal freedom and its long held principle of subsidiarity.[32] This support is remarkable in some respects, given the Church's deep and abiding concern for social justice issues. Nonetheless, popes from Leo XIII to John Paul II have consistently recognized a natural private property right and have argued that labor provides the basis for such a right. John Paul II extended this teaching to intellectual objects, the new social wealth, which is also deserving of a certain form of ownership. While John Paul II rejected liberal assumptions about the human self in favor of a personalist perspective, he still affirmed the person's right to the fruit of his or her labor. Thus, we need not buy into the premises of atomic liberalism associated with Locke in order to accept the need for reasonable intellectual property rights which are closely tied to the right of economic initiative.

Finally, the appropriation of intellectual property typically does not injure other information commoners, as some have supposed, unless one interprets 'injury' in the broadest possible way. The over-wrought metaphor of 'enclosure' is inappropriate, given the permeability of information. For intangible objects, perfect control is virtually impossible. Thus, the information commons is not depleted or impaired by the granting of intellectual property rights so long as proper safeguards are in place. On the contrary, the information commons can actually expand when proprietary information is sanctioned with a property right, given the cumulative nature of human creativity along with the dynamic incentive of those rights.

NOTES

1. 347 U.S. 201 (1954) at 209, reh'g denied 347 U.S. 949 (1954).
2. See also *Sony Corp of America v. Universal City Studios, Inc.* 464 U.S. 417 (1984) ('the limited grant [of a copyright] is a means by which an important public purpose may be achieved … intended to motivate the creative activity of authors and inventors by the provision of a special reward'; at 465).
3. See also Yen (1990).
4. See Finnis' (1980) insightful account of natural rights, especially pp. 202–10.
5. According to Nozick (1974, p. 112), 'The central core of the notion of a property right in X, relative to which other parts of the notion are to be explained, is the right to determine what shall be done with X; the right to choose which of the constrained set of options concerning X shall be realized or attempted'.
6. See Himma (2007a) and Spinello (2008) for some additional commentary on these ideas.
7. Some scholars have argued that Locke's treatment of tangible property is inapplicable to intangible entities, but they take a different approach from Kimppa. See Reese (1995) who argued that Locke's discussion of tangible property 'might not simply apply *mutatis mutandis* to intangible intellectual property' (p. 708).
8. According to Romer (1990, p. 75), 'A purely rival good has the property that its use by one firm or person precludes its use by another; a purely nonrival good has the property that its use by one firm or person in no way limits use by another'.
9. *Harper & Row Publishers, Inc. v. Nation Enterprises* 471 U.S. 539 (1985) at 546.
10. According to McGowan (2004, p. 47), 'intellectual property is in fact the sort of thing that may have to be managed to be used effectively'.
11. In Locke's philosophy, 'the individual, the ego, had become the center and origin of the moral world, since man – as distinguished from man's end – had become that center or origin' (Strauss, 1952, p. 248).
12. Waldron (1993) goes even farther and contends that once a cultural good such as Mickey Mouse impinges on our world it has become a part of us and so it should now belong to the public domain.
13. The Eleventh Circuit Court eventually vacated the injunction against Randall's parodic work on grounds that it violated the First Amendment. The Court also opined that there was a strong fair use defense for this book. See *Suntrust Bank v. Houghton Mifflin,* 252 F.3d 1165, 11th Cir., (2001).
14. For more background on the criteria for fair use see *Campbell v. Acuff-Rose Music, Inc.*, 510 U.S. 569 (1994) along with the extensive discussion of fair use in Chapter 3 of this book. See also McGowan (2004).
15. See Aquinas' (1948) *Summa Theologiae*, I–II, q. 105 and II–II, q. 66 and q. 87. In q. 66 Aquinas affirms that the person may possess things *quasi proprium* ('as his own'), cf. II–II, q. 66, a.2.
16. See Hittinger (2006) for additional background, especially pp 9–12. Hittinger points out that Leo XIII certainly laid the foundations for the social doctrine of the Catholic Church referred to by Pius XI. See also Pope Pius XI, *Quadragesimo Anno* (1931).
17. Chenu (1979), for example, sharply criticized Catholic social teaching as a 19th century 'ideological relic' (p. 90), claiming that Pope Leo only told middle class Catholics what they wanted to hear about private property rights. For Chenu this doctrine simply confuses faith and ideology, especially when it comes to teachings about the need for private property.
18. For a summary of the Catholic Church's teaching on the moral foundation of property issues see Grisez (1993), especially pp. 792–5.
19. All references to John Paul II's encyclicals are to paragraph numbers in the English edition.
20. Other Vatican documents also support the validity of intellectual property rights. See, for example, Bishop Martino's (2001) discussion on TRIPs for a detailed exposition of the Church's views on the issue of essential intellectual goods such as pharmaceutical products. Martino explains that 'IP protection is necessary for progress and for the just compensation of researchers and producers'. At the same time, he criticizes the high price of drugs that keep

them out of the hands of those suffering from AIDS in impoverished countries like South Africa. See also Carey (2007) where this document is extensively quoted.

21. Quoted in Hughes (2006), pp. 1059–60.
22. Habiger (1990) illustrates the extraordinary consistency of papal teaching on property from Leo XIII to John Paul II.
23. Craig (2007, p. 257) writes that 'the notion of the relational self challenges the liberal conception of the autonomous individual as an independent bearer of rights'.
24. *Harper & Row Publishers, Inc. v. Nation Enterprises,* 471 U.S. 539 (1986), p. 546.
25. For examples of this control criticism criticized by Wagner, see Boyle (1996), Lessig (2001), and Benkler (2001, 2002).
26. But see Burk and Cohen (2001): 'New technological ... protections confer a degree of control over access to and use of copyrighted content that goes well beyond the rights afforded by copyright law' (p. 48).
27. See Wagner (2003) and Black (2001).
28. The US Copyright Act protects a direct derivative work defined as 'a work based upon one or more preexisting works, such as a translation, musical arrangement, dramatization, fictionalization, motion picture version ... or any other form in which a work may be recast, transformed, or adapted': 17 U.S.C. 101 (1976).
29. Sometimes there is a fine line between infringement and building upon an invention. See, for example, *London v. Carson Pirie Scott & Co.* 946 F.2d 1534, Fed. Cir. (1991): 'Although inventing around patents to make new inventions is encouraged, piracy is not'.
30. An anti-commons effect is produced when a plethora of property rights preclude the use of a certain public good. The problem is that too few resources are held in common and researchers are blocked from using source material (such as genes or genetic data) that have become privatized unless they negotiate with a multiplicity of owners. The rights of usage become so fragmented that it is virtually impossible to conduct productive research. For the relevance of this concept in the area of genetic research see Spinello (2004).
31. As McGowan (2005) indicates, even biographies can be composed without extensive quotations from the subject's works. See also *Salinger v. Random House, Inc.*, 811 F.2d. 90, 2d Cir., (1987) *cert. denied* 484 U.S. 890. (1987): 'when dealing with copyrighted expression, a biographer (or any other copier) may frequently have to content himself with reporting only the fact of what his subject did' (pp. 96–7).
32. According to the principle of subsidiarity, higher-order communities (e.g. local government) should not interfere in the internal affairs of lower-order communities (e.g. the family).

REFERENCES

Aquinas, St. Thomas (1948), *Summa Theologiae* in *Opera Omnia Sancti Thomae Aquinatis Doctoris Angelici*, Volumes IV–XI, Commission of Dominican Scholars (eds), Rome: Leonine.

Benkler, Yochai (2001), 'Siren Songs and Amish Children: Autonomy, Information and Law', 76 *New York University Law Review* 23.

Benkler, Yochai (2002), 'Coase's Penguin, or Linux and the Nature of the Firm', 112 *Yale Law Journal* 369.

Black, Jane (2001), 'Brass-Knuckle Marketing vs. the Pirates', *Business Week,* August 13, 48.

Boyle, James (1996), *Shamans, Software, and Spleens: Law and the Construction of the Information Society,* Cambridge, MA: Harvard University Press.

Buckle, Stephen (1991), *Natural Law and the Theory of Property*, Oxford: Oxford University Press.

Burk, Dan and Julie Cohen (2001), 'Fair Use Infrastructure for Rights Management Systems', 15 *Harvard Journal of Law and Technology* 41.

free-standing work or can it be understood only by its fluid merger with other inter-related texts? If her work lacks a clear boundary and a stable meaning how could the reader intelligibly appropriate her own *discrete* message about the dangerous politics of expanding ownership rights? Also, why can't the audience recode her message so that it conveys something completely different from what she is advocating?

As we have seen, those critics who argue for the historical contingency of authorship contend that the creative process is being radically transformed thanks to the wonders of digital networked technology. The hypertext novel, for example, was supposed to emancipate us from the repressive 'linear narrative'. But years after these claims have been made there is little evidence that the creative process is much different than it was in earlier centuries when authorship was presumably individualized. Granted that it's easier to collaborate, but many books are still written by single authors and many artists still produce their works with little or no collaboration.

Nonetheless, as we have argued throughout this book, intellectual property excesses must be curtailed. In some case this calls for drastic action. We have cited an abundance of sources that suggest to policy makers how they might proceed with these necessary policy adjustments. We can limit copyright terms which are far too long by even the most generous normative standards. In addition, we can clarify and simplify the confusing US copyright law. Enforcement of the law and protection of intellectual property rights have become exceedingly difficult, and part of the problem is that the law is so convoluted and opaque. Thus, any discussion on reform of the present system must take into account the complex issue of enforcement, especially in light of the recent resistance to this law which some regard as oppressive.

Reform should also consider the need for flexible compulsory licensing in developing countries, especially when it comes to life-saving drugs or similar patented inventions. We can curtail and limit patenting of life forms and genetic materials. We can eradicate most business method patents, or at least ensure that they are not granted for methods that are obvious or lacking any genuine novelty. We can insist upon reasonable amendments to the Digital Millennium Copyright Act of 1998 to include a provision for the protection of fair use. We can lobby corporations to design digital rights management code responsibly so that it incorporates the internal safety valves mandated by law. We can encourage the adoption and creation of more open source software. We can even encourage scientists and researchers to publish in open source journals, so long as they are not harmed professionally.

All this we can do to change the legal and social picture in search of the right balance that avoids excess and defects in the law and 'hits the mark' properly between over- and under-protection. What we cannot do, however, is to negate the unimpeachable natural law foundations of a person's right to both physical and intellectual property. We cannot force individuals to relinquish their limited natural rights in favour of collective ownership because of the mistaken idea that all creative works are collectively produced.[5] We cannot eliminate or hollow out copyright protection and thereby deprive the author of the ability to control the meaning of his or her work and appropriate that work's social value. Nor can we abolish patents and expect ground-breaking innovation in industries like pharmaceuticals. Intellectual property rights not only support the autonomy of authors and inventors, they also harness the energy of private self-interest to bring forth an endless succession of innovations and creative works that fuel the economy and enhance human welfare.

NOTES

1. See Lemley (2005, pp. 1041–4) for more details and case citations.
2. Cohen (2002) describes the growing tendency of intellectual property rights holders to regard their rights as virtually absolute. According to her analysis, these days 'a property right [is] delineated as absolute sovereignty over the disposition and use' (p. 379).
3. See Hughes (2003), who also notes that Congresswoman Mary Bono has advocated that the copyright term should 'last forever' (p. 784 n34)
4. US Constitution art. I, 8, cl. 1.
5. We have cited Zemer (2006) and Wilf (1999) in previous chapters, but see also Underkuffler (2003): the notion that intellectual property rights 'are presumptively free from collective claims has been decisively abandoned ...' (p. 2). Wilf has argued that the public participates in 'authoring' a popular trademark and therefore deserves a property right as co-author (pp. 1–6).

REFERENCES

Aristotle (1941), *Nicomachean Ethics,* R. McKeon (ed.), New York: Random House.

Cohen, Julie (2002), 'Overcoming Property: Does Copyright Trump Privacy', 2002 *University of Illinois Journal of Law, Technology and Policy* 375.

Craig, Carys (2007), 'Reconstructing the Author-Self: Some Feminist Lessons for Copyright Law', 15 *American University Journal of Gender, Social Policy, & the Law* 207.

Gordon, Wendy (1992), 'On Owning Information: Intellectual Property and the Restitutionary Impulse', 78 *Virginia Law Review* 149.

Halbert, Deborah (1999), *Intellectual Property in the Information Age*, Westport, CN: Quorum Books.

Hughes, Justin (2003), 'Fair Use Across Time', 50 *UCLA Law Review* 775.

Hughes, Justin (1999), '"Recoding" Intellectual Property and Overlooked Audience Interests', 77 *Texas Law Review* 923.

Lemley, Mark (2005), 'Property, Intellectual Property, and Free Riding', 83 *Texas Law Review* 1031.

Swift, Jonathan (1975). 'The Battle of the Books', in K. Williams (ed.), *A Tale of a Tub and other Satires*, London: Everyman's Library (Original work published 1704), p. 137.

Underkuffler, Laura (2003), *The Idea of Property: Its Meaning and Power*, Oxford: Oxford University Press.
Wilf, Steven (1999), 'Who Authors Trademarks', 17 *Cardozo Arts & Entertainment Law Journal* 1.
Zemer, Lior (2006), 'The Copyright Moment', 43 *San Diego Law Review* 247.

Appendix: Table of cases

321 Studios v. MGM, 307 F. Supp. 2d 1085 (N.D. Cal. 2004)
ACLU v. Reno, 929 F. Supp. 824 (E.D. Pa.) (1996) aff'd *Reno v. ACLU*, 521 U.S. 844 (1997)
Agnes Dit A. Sorel v. Fayard Frères, Tribunal Civil de la Seine, 16 Decembre 1899, D.1900.2.152
Alfred Bell & Co. v. Catalda Fine Arts, Inc., 191 F.2d 99 (2d Cir. 1951)
Amazon.com. Inc v. barnesandnoble.com, Inc., 73 F. Supp. 2d (W.D.Wash. 1999), vacated and remanded, 239 F. 3d 1343 (Fed. Cir. 2001)
Ansehl v. Puritan Pharmaceutical Company, 61 F. 2d 131 (8th Cir.) (1932).
Appellant's Brief (2001), *Universal City Studios v. Corley*, 273 F. 3d 429 (2d Cir) (2001)
Apple Computer, Inc. v. Franklin Computer Corp., US Court of Appeals, 3rd Cir., 714 F.2d 1240 (1983)
Aro Manufacturing Co. v. Convertible Top Replacement Co, 377 U.S. 476, 84 S.Ct. 1526, 12 L.Ed. 457 (1964)
Atari Games Corp. v. Nintendo of America, Inc., 975 F.2d 832, 24 USPQ2d 1015 (1992)
Aunt Jemima Mills Co v. Rugney & Co, 247 F. 407 (2d Cir. 1917)
Austin v. Michigan Chamber of Commerce, 494 U.S. 652 (1990)
Autogiro Co. of America v. US, 384 F. 2d 391, 400 (Ct.Cl. 1967)
Baker v. Shelden, 101 US 99 (1879)
Baltimore Orioles v. Major League Baseball Players Ass'n, 805 F.2d 663 (1986)
Basic Books, Inc. v. Kinko's Graphic Corporation, 758 F. Supp 1522 (S.D.N. Y.) (1991)
Belmore v. City Pages Inc., 880 F. Supp. 673 (D. Minn. 1995)
Bleistein v. Donaldson Lithographing Co., 188 U.S. 239, 23 S. Ct. 298 (1903)
Bonito Boats v. Thunder Craft Boats, Inc., 489 U.S. 141 (1988)
Brenner v. Manson, 383 U.S. 519, S.Ct. 1033, 16 L.Ed.2d 69 (1966)
Buckley v. Valeo, 424 U.S. 1 (1976)
Buffon v. Behemer, Judgment of 29 therm. an 11, Cass. civ., [1791] 1 Dev. & Car. 1.851
Burrow-Giles Lithographic Co v. Sarony, 111 US 53, 4 S.Ct. 279 (1884)

Camoin et Syndicat de la Propriete artistique v. Francis Carco, Aubry, Belattre et Zborowski, Trib. Civ.de la Seine, 15 Novembre 1927, DP.1928.2.89
Campbell v. Acuff-Rose Music Inc., 510 U.S. 569 (1994)
Carco et autres v. Camoin et Syndicat de la propriete artistique, Cour d'Appel de Paris, 6 March 1931, DP.1931.2.88
Case C–198/05, *Commission v. Italy*, ECJ 26 October 2006
Case C–293/98, *EGEDA v. Hosteleria Asturiana SA* [2000] ECR 231
Case C–36/05, *Commission v. Spain*, 2006 ECR I-10313
Case C–4/03, *Gesellschaft für Antriebsteschnik v. Lamellen und Kupplungsbau Beteiligungs KG*, 2006 ECR I-6509
Case C–53/05, *Commission v. Portugal*, 2006 ECR I-6215
Case C–539/03, *Roche Nederland BV v. Primus*, 2006 ECR I-6535
Coll Savings Bank v. Florida Prepaid Postsecondary Education, 527 U.S. 666 (1999)
Darcy v. Allein, 77 ER 1260 (King's Bench, 1603)
Daroll v. Brown, 7 F. Cas. 197 (C.C.D. Mass.) 1845
Dastar Corp. v. Twentieth Century Fox Film Corp., 539 U.S. 23 (2003)
Delprut v. Charpentier, Cour de Cassation, 21 August 1867, D.1867.1.369
Diamond v. Chakrabarty, 447 US 303, 100 S.Ct. 2204, 65 L. Ed.3d 144, 206 U.S.P.Q.193 (1980)
Diamond v. Diehr, 450 U.S. 175 (1981)
Donaldson v. Beckett, 2 Brown's Parl. Cases 129, 1 ER 837; 4 Burr. 2408, 98 ER 257 (1774)
eBay v. MercExchange, L.L.C., 547 U.S. 388 (2006)
Eldred v. Ashcroft, 537 U.S. 186 (2003)
Emerson v. Davis, 3 St. Rep. 780 (1845)
Ex Parte Hibbard, 227 U.S.P.Q. (BNA) 443 (PTO Board of App. & Int. 1985)
Ex Parte Allen, 2 U.S.P.Q. (BNA) 1425 (PTO Board of App. & Int. 1987)
Feist Publications, Inc. v. Rural Telephone Service Co. Inc., 499 US 340 (1991)
Fogerty v. Fantasy, Inc. 510 U.S. 517 (1994)
Folson v. Marsh, 9 F. Cas. 342 (C.C.Mass. 1841)
Gambro Lundia AB v. Baxter Healthcare Corp., 110 F. 3d 1573, 1579, 42 USPQ2d 1378 (Fed. Cir. 1997)
Gershwin Publishing v. Columbia Artists Mgmt, 443 F 2d. 1159 (1971)
Goldstein v. California, 412 U.S. 546 (1973)
Gottschalk v. Benson, 409 US 63, 93 S.Ct. 253, 34 L. Ed. 2d 273 (1972)
Graham v. John Deree Co., 383 U.S. 1, 17, 86 S. Ct. 684, 15 L. Ed.2d 545 (1966)
Harper & Row Publishers, Inc. v. Nation Enterprises, 471 US 539 (1985)
Holmes v. Hurst, 174 U.S. 82 (1898)
In re Alappat, No 92–1381, Fed. Cir. July 29, 1994 (en banc)

In re Allen, 2 U.S.P.Q.2d 1425 (1987)
In re Kahn, Fed. Cir. 2006, 04–1616
J.E.M. AG Supply Inc. v. Pioneer Hi-Bred International, Inc., 534 U.S. 124 Ct. 593, 151 L.Ed. 508, 60 U.S.P.Q2d 1865 (2001)
Juicy Whip Inc. v. Orange Bang, Inc., 185 F. 3d 1364, 51 U.S.P.Q.2d 1700 (Fed. Cir. 1999)
KSR v. Teleflex, 127 S. Ct. 1727 (2007)
Lawrence v. Dana, 15 F. Cas. 26 (C.C.D.Mass. 1869)
Lotus Development Corp. v. Borland Int. Inc., 49 F. 3d 807 (1st cir) 1995, affirmed 516 US 233 (1996)
Lotus Development Corp. v. Paperback Software Int'l, 740 F. Supp. 37 (D. Mass. 1990)
London v. Carson Pirie Scott & Co., 946 F.2d 1534, 20 USPQ2d 1456 (Fed. Cir. 1991)
Lowell v. Levis, 15 F. Cas. 1018 (C.C.Mass 1817)
Marle v. Lacordaire, Cour de Lyon, 17 July 1845, D.1845.2.128
Matthew Bender & Co. v. West Publishing Co., 158 F.3d 674 2nd Cir. (1998), cert. denied
Matthews v. Wozencraft, 15 F.3d 432 (Fed. Cir.) (1994)
Mazer v. Stein, 347 U.S. 201 (1954), reh'g denied 347 U.S. 949 (1954)
Millar v. Taylor, 4 Burrow 2303, 98 ER. 201 (K.B., 1769)
Miller v. Universal City Studios, Inc., US Court of Appeals, 5th Cir., 640 F.2d 1365 (1981)
Mitchell v. Tilgham, 86 U.S. (19 Wall.) 287 (1873)
Moseley v. Secret Catalogue, 537 US 418 (2003)
New York & Rosendale Cement Co. v. Coplay Cement Co., 44 F. 277 (C.C.E.D. Pa 1890)
Nichols v. Universal Pictures, 45 F. 2d 119 (2nd Cir.) (1930)
Papercutter Inc. v. Fay's Drug Co, 900 F. 2d 558 (2d Cir) (1990)
Parker v. Flook, 437 US 584 (1978)
Percy Schmeiser and Schmeiser Enterprises Ltd. v. Monsanto Canada Inc. and Monsanto Company, 1 S.C.R. 902, 2004 SCC 34, 239 D.L.R. (4th) 271, 31 C.P.R. (4th) 161 (2004)
Playboy Enterprises, Inc. v. Hardenburgh, Inc., 982 F. Supp. 503 (N.D. Ohio 1997)
Religious Tech. Ctr. v. Lerma, 908 F. Supp. 1231 (E.D. Va 1995)
Reyher v. Children's Television Network, 533 F. 2d 87 (2nd Cir.) (1976), cert. denied 429 US 980
Rickelshaus v. Monsanto, Co., 467 US 986 (1984)
Rogers v. Koons, 960 F. 2d (2d Cir.) (1992)
Roth Greeting Cards v. United Card Co., 429 F.2d 1106 (9th Cir. 1970)
Royal Typewriter Co. v. Remington Rand Inc., 168 F. 2d 691 (end. Cir. 1948)

Salinger v. Random House, 811 F. 2d 90 (2nd Cir. 1987)
Sayre v. Moore (1785) quoted in *Carey v. Longman* (1801) 102 ER 138
Seshadri v. Kasraian 130 F. 3d 798 (7th Cir.) (1997)
Sony Corp. of America v. Universal City Studios, Inc., 464 U.S. 417 (1984)
State Street Bank & Trust Co. v. Signature Financial Group, Inc., 149 Fed. 3d 1368 (Fed. Cir. 1998)
Steward v. Abend 495 US 207 (1990)
Stowe v. Thomas, 23 F.Cas.201 (C.C.D. 1853)
Studio Canal SA and Universal Pictures Video France SAS v. Mr Stephane X. and others, Cour de Cassation. 28 February 2006
Suntrust Bank v. Houghton Mifflin, 252 F.3d 1165 (11th Cir.) (2001)
Trade-Mark Cases, 100 US 82 (1879)
Twentieth Century Music Corp. v. Aiken, 422 U.S. 151 (1975)
United Christian Scientists v. Christian Science Board of Directors, First Church of Christ 829 F.2d 1152, 4 USPQ2d 1177 (D.C. Cir. 1987)
United States v. Elcom Ltd., 203 F. Supp 2d 1111 (N.D. Cal.) (2002)
Universal City Studios v. Corley, 273 F. 3d 429 (2d Cir) (2001)
Universal City Studios v. Reimerdes, 111 F. Supp.2d 294 (S.D.N.Y. 2000)
Universal Oil Products v. Globe Oil Co., 322 U.S. 471 (1944)
Walt Disney Productions v. Air Pirates, 581 F 2d. 751 (9th Cir. 1978)
Walt Disney Productions v. Filmation Associates, 628 F. Supp. 871 (1986)
Webb v. Powers et al., 29 F. Cas. 511; 1847 US App. Lexis 595, 10 Law Rep. 12 (1847)
West Publishing v. Hyperlaw Inc., cert. denied, S. Ct, 526 U.S. 1154 (1999)
Whealan Associates v. Jaslow Dental Lab, 797 F. 2d 1222 (3rd Cir.) (1986)
Wheaton v. Peters, 33 U.S. (8 Pet.) 591 (1834)
Winner International Royalty Corp. v. Ching-Rong-Wang, 202 F.3d 1340, 53 USPQ2d 1580 (Fed. Cir. 2000)
Yale Electric Corp. v. Robertson, 26 F. 2d 972 (2nd Cir. 1928)

Index